A-Z TORBAY

| Key to Map Pages | 2-3 |
| Map Pages | 4-39 |

Index t
Village
and sele

REFERENCE

A Road	A380	Car Park (selected)	P
B Road	B3195	Church or Chapel	†
Dual Carriageway		Cycleway (selected)	
One-way Street Traffic flow on A Roads is also indicated by a heavy line on the driver's left.		Fire Station	■
		Hospital	H
Road Under Construction Opening dates are correct at the time of publication.		House Numbers (A & B Roads only)	15 / 8
Proposed Road		Information Centre	i
Restricted Access		National Grid Reference	290
Pedestrianized Road		Park and Ride	Brixham P+R
Track / Footpath		Police Station	▲
Residential Walkway		Post Office	★
Railway	Level Crossing / Heritage Station / Tunnel / Station	Toilet	▽
		Viewpoint	
Built-up Area	MILL RD.	Educational Establishment	
		Hospital or Healthcare Building	
Beach		Industrial Building	
		Leisure or Recreational Facility	
Local Authority Boundary		Place of Interest	
Postcode Boundary		Public Building	
		Shopping Centre or Market	
Map Continuation	14	Other Selected Buildings	

SCALE

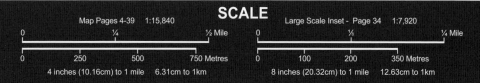

Map Pages 4-39 1:15,840

0   ¼   ½ Mile
0   250   500   750 Metres
4 inches (10.16cm) to 1 mile   6.31cm to 1km

Large Scale Inset - Page 34   1:7,920

0   ⅛   ¼ Mile
0   100   200   350 Metres
8 inches (20.32cm) to 1 mile   12.63cm to 1km

EDITION 7   2023

KEY TO MAP PAGES

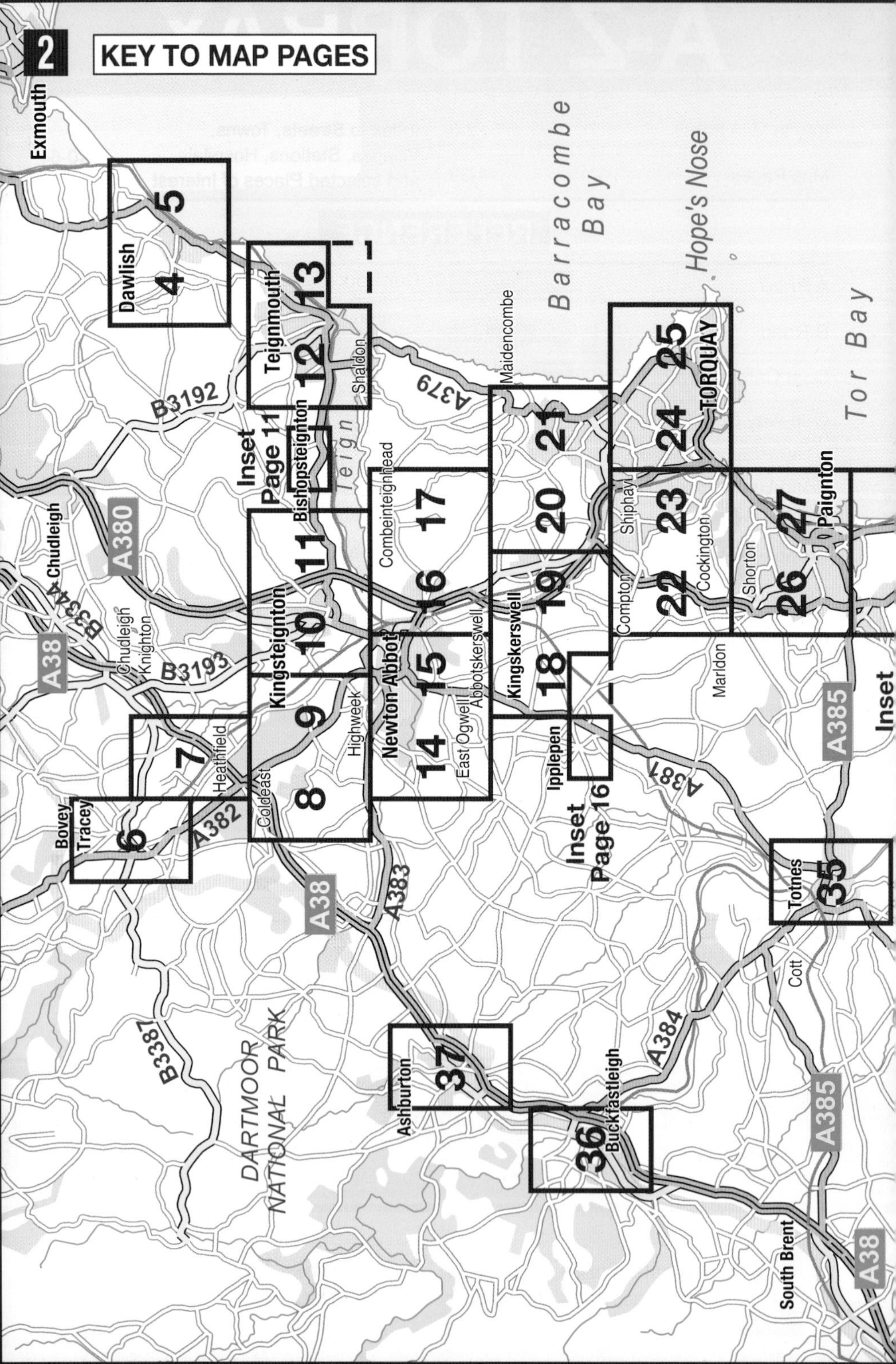

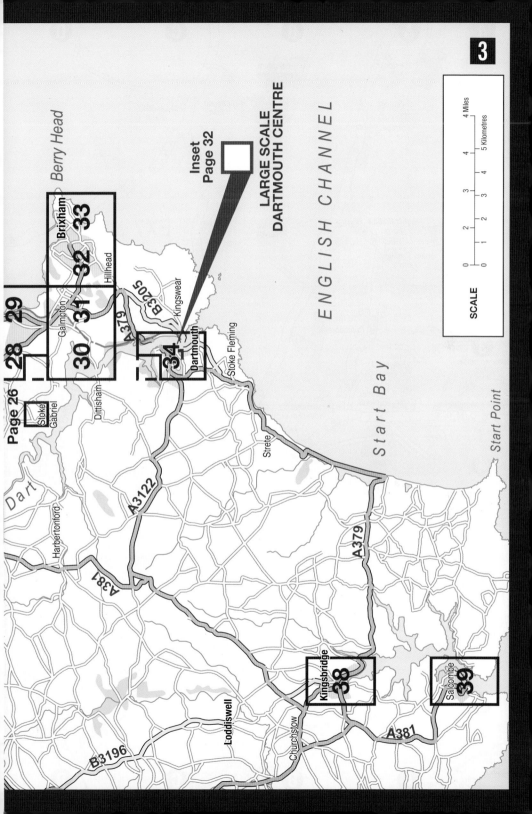

3

LARGE SCALE
DARTMOUTH CENTRE

Inset
Page 32

Berry Head

Brixham **33**

Hillhead **32 31**

Galmpton **30**

28 29

Page 26

Stoke
Gabriel

Dittisham

Dart

Harbertonford

A3122

A381

Kingswear
B3205

A379

Stoke Fleming **34** Dartmouth

ENGLISH CHANNEL

Start Bay

Strete

A379

B3196

Loddiswell

Churchstow

Kingsbridge **38**

A381

Salcombe **39**

Start Point

SCALE

| 0 | 1 | 2 | 3 | 4 Miles |
| 0 | 1 | 2 | 3 | 4 | 5 Kilometres |

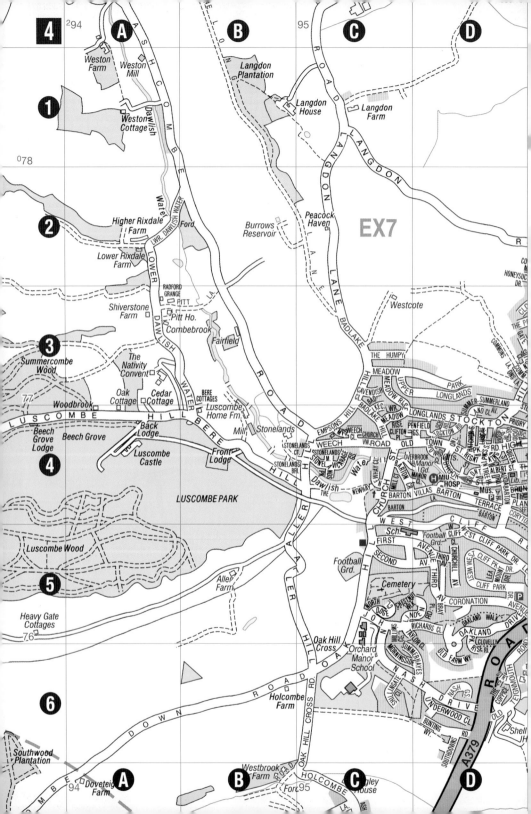

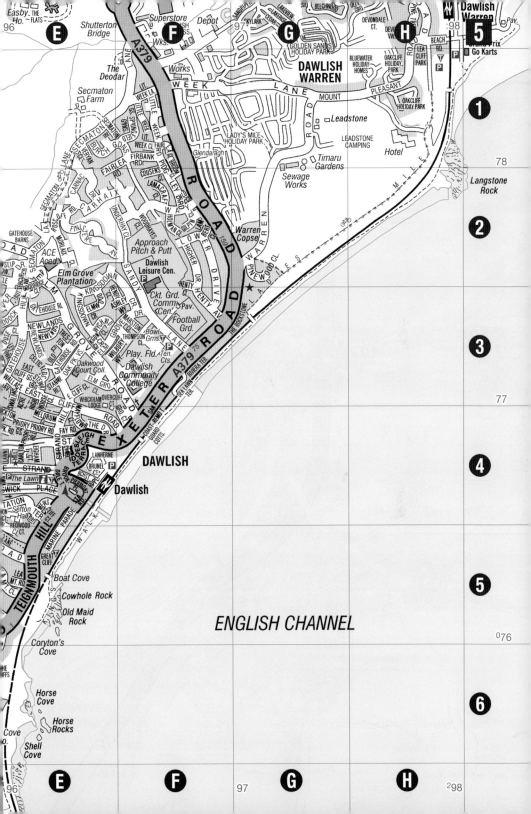

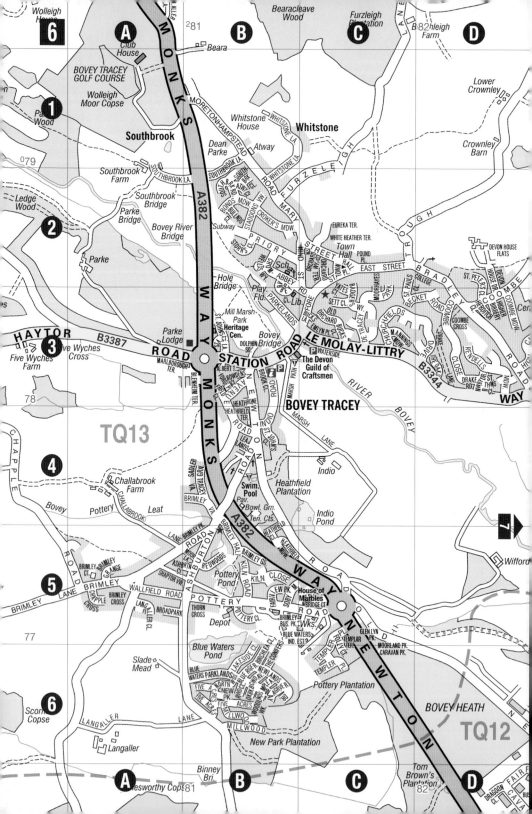

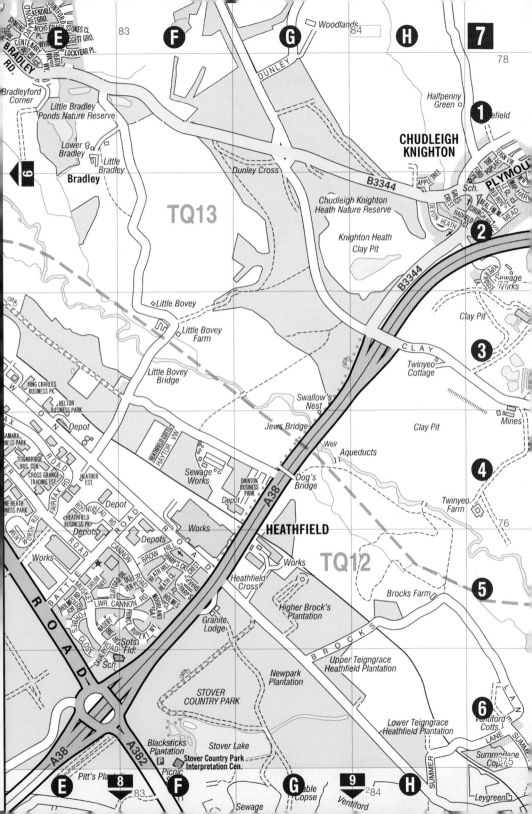

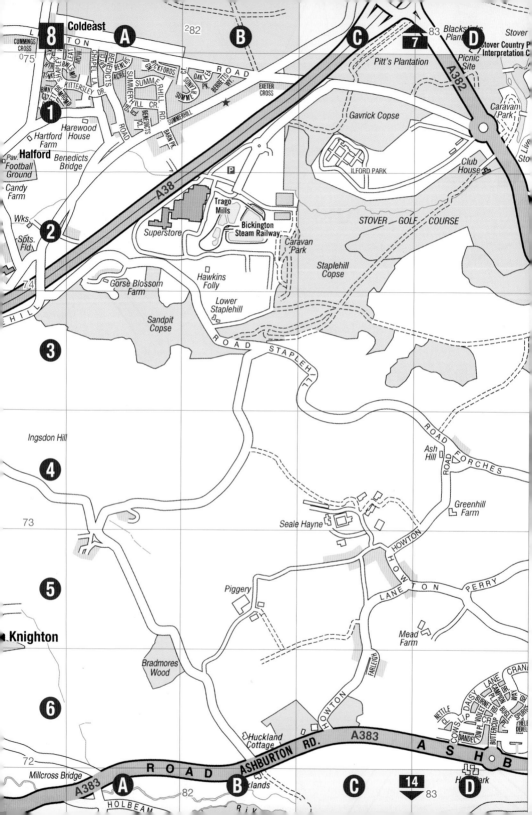

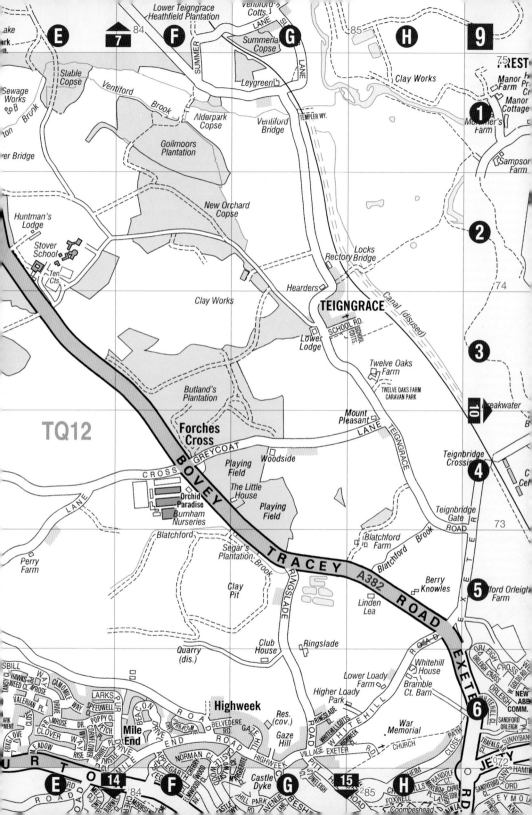

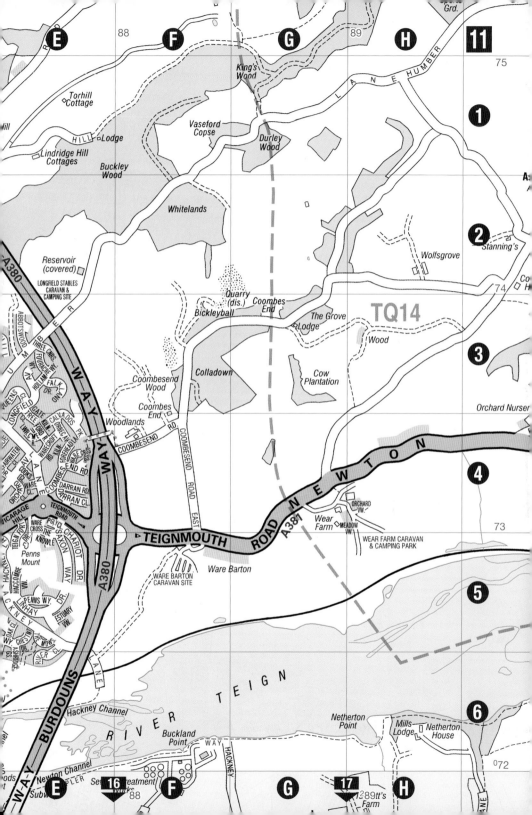

E F G 89 H 75

Grd.

King's
Wood

1

Torhill
Cottage

Vaseford
Copse

HILL Lodge

Durley
Wood

LANE HUMBER

Lindridge Hill
Cottages

Buckley
Wood

Whitelands

2

Stanning's

Wolfsgrove

Reservoir
(covered)

LONGFIELD STABLES
CARAVAN &
CAMPING SITE

Quarry
(dis.)

Bickleyball

Coombes
End

The Grove
Lodge

TQ14

Co
H

74

3

ABBOTSWOOD

THREE CRS.

FOUR ACRE WY.

HOLLAM

FALK DR.

Coombesend
Wood

Colladown

Wood

Cow
Plantation

Orchard Nurser

Coombes
End

Woodlands

COOMBESEND

COOMBESEND ROAD

EAST

NEWTON

4

ORCHARD
VW.

73

Wear
Farm

MEADOW
VW.

WEAR FARM CARAVAN
& CAMPING PARK

VICARAGE
HILL

TEIGNMOUTH
Road

CHARIOT DR.

SAXON WAY

A380

WAY

DARRAN RD.
DARRAN CL.

COOMBES END RD.

WARE CL.

TEIGNMOUTH ROAD

A381

Penns
Mount

THE KNOWLE

CROSS

PENNS WY.

HACCOMBE

ESTUARY VW.

Ware Barton

WARE BARTON
CARAVAN SITE

5

HACKNEY

LINHAY

RIVER CL.

CHES

MDWS.

ASHRIDGE

BURDOUNS

WAY

LANE

Hackney Channel

RIVER TEIGN

Netherton
Point

6

Mills
Lodge

Netherton
House

072

Newton Channel

Subw

Buckland
Point

WAY

HACKNEY

Sew Treatment Works 88

289tt's
Farm

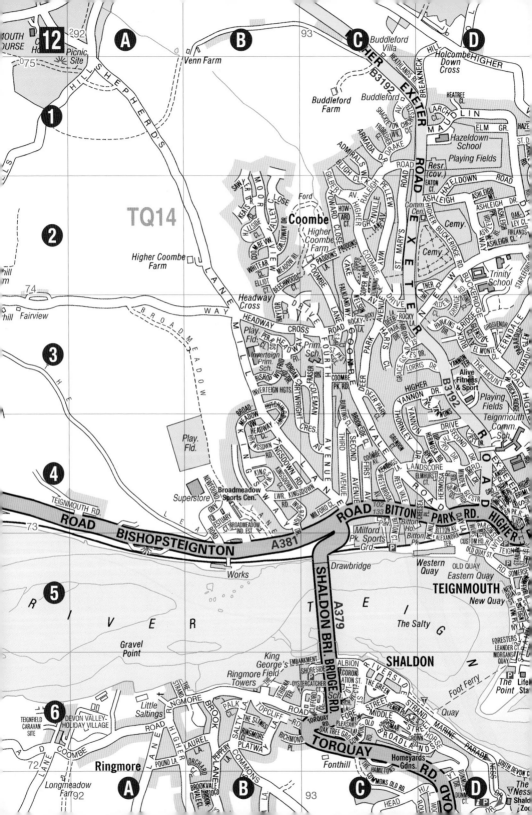

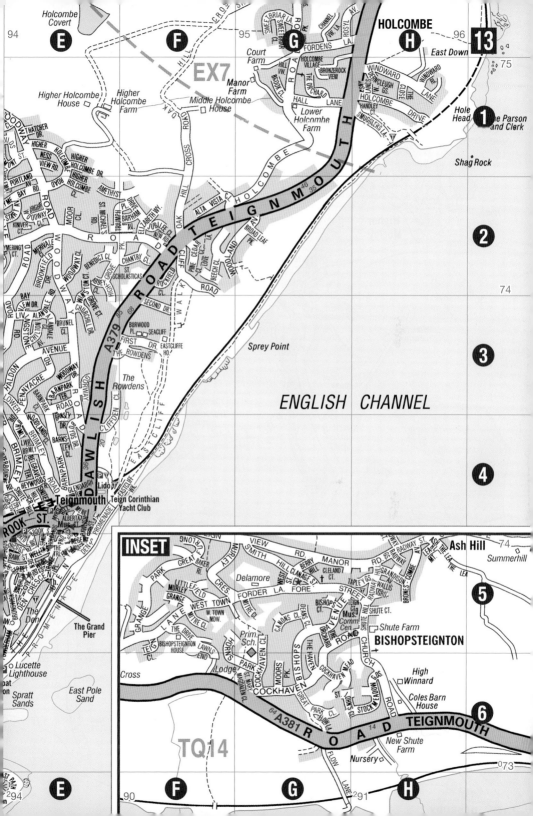

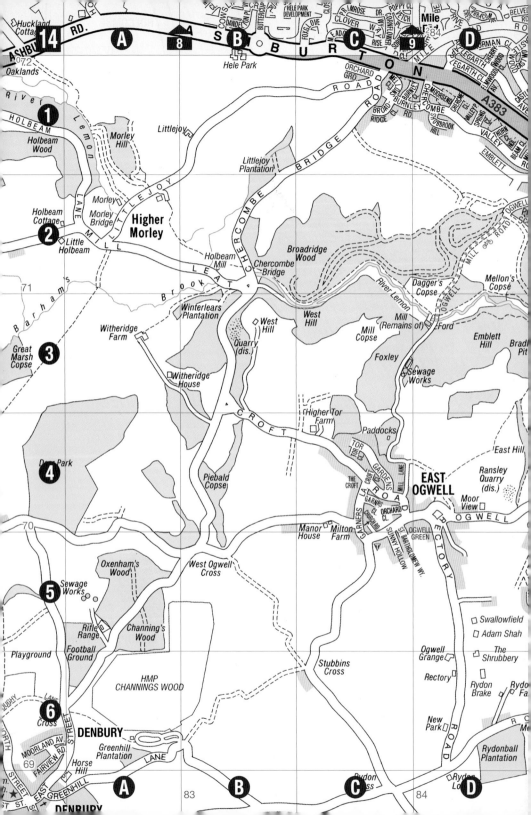

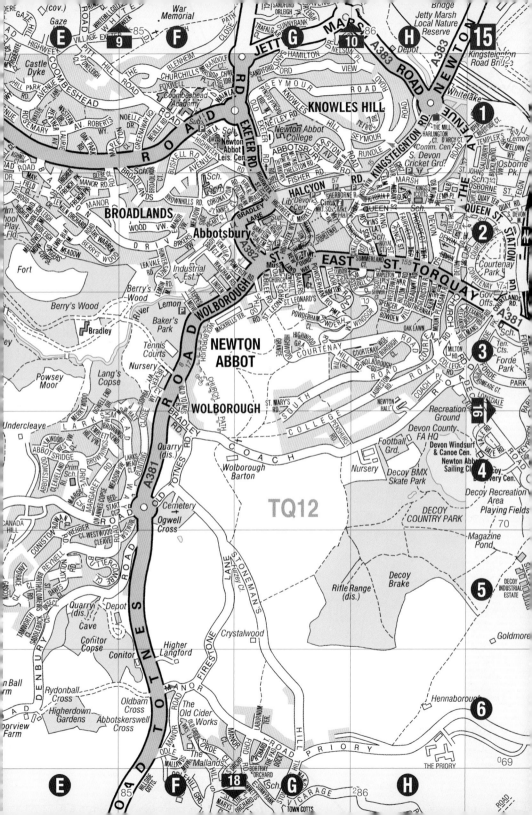

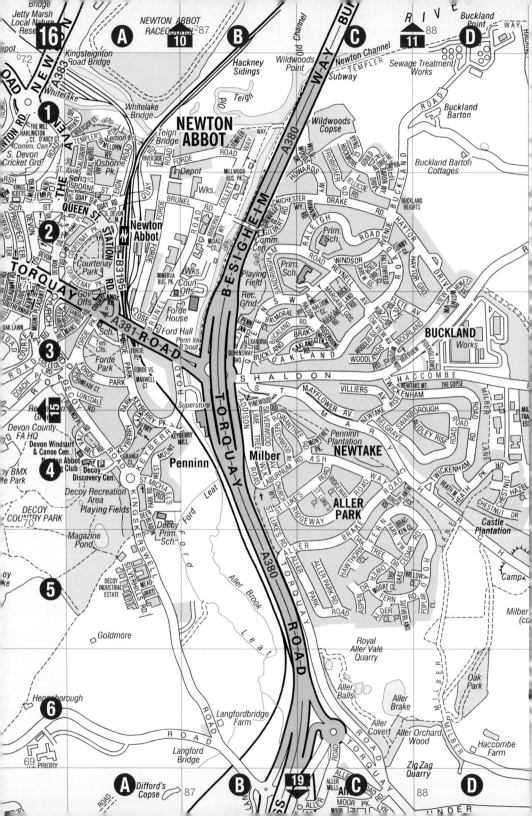

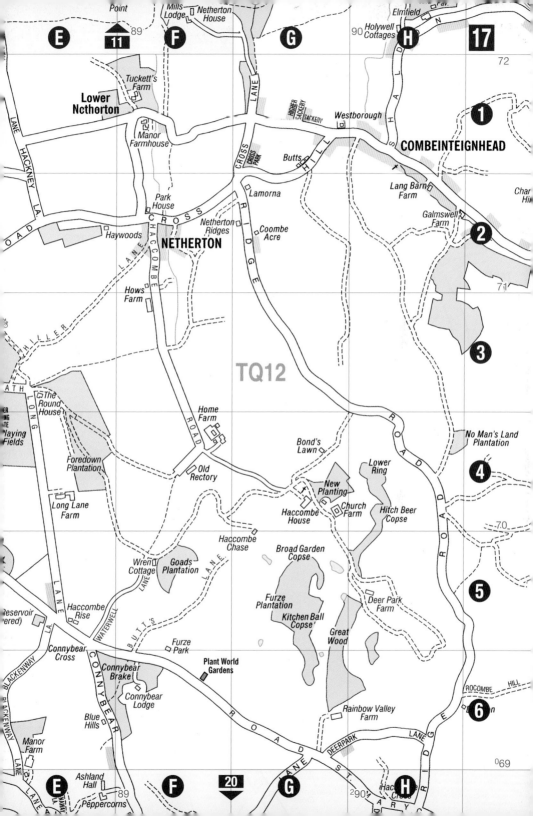

Point
Mills Lodge
Netherton House
Elmfield
Holywell Cottages

1

Tuckett's Farm

Lower Netherton

HIGHER SACKERY

Westborough

COMBEINTEIGNHEAD

Manor Farmhouse

HACKNEY LANE

LANE

ROAD

CROSS LANE

HILL

CROSS PARK

Butts

Lang Barn Farm

Char Hill

Park House

Lamorna

Galmswell Farm

2

Haywoods

CHACCOMBE LANE

CROSS

Netherton Ridges

Coombe Acre

NETHERTON

RIDGE

71

Hows Farm

3

HILLER

TQ12

ROAD

The Round House

Home Farm

No Man's Land Plantation

PATH

LONG

Playing Fields

Bond's Lawn

Lower Ring

4

Foredown Plantation

Old Rectory

New Planting

Haccombe House

Church Farm

Hitch Beer Copse

70

Long Lane Farm

ROAD

Haccombe Chase

Broad Garden Copse

Wren Cottage

Goads Plantation

LANE

Furze Plantation

Deer Park Farm

5

Reservoir (covered)

Haccombe Rise

WATERWELL LANE

BUTTS

Kitchen Ball Copse

Great Wood

LANE

Connybear Cross

Furze Park

Plant World Gardens

ROCOMBE HILL

BLACKENWAY

CONNYBEAR

Connybear Brake

Connybear Lodge

6

Blue Hills

Rainbow Valley Farm

LANE

DEERPARK LANE

RIDGE

Manor Farm

Ashland Hall

ST MARY

Haccombe Cross

Peppercorns

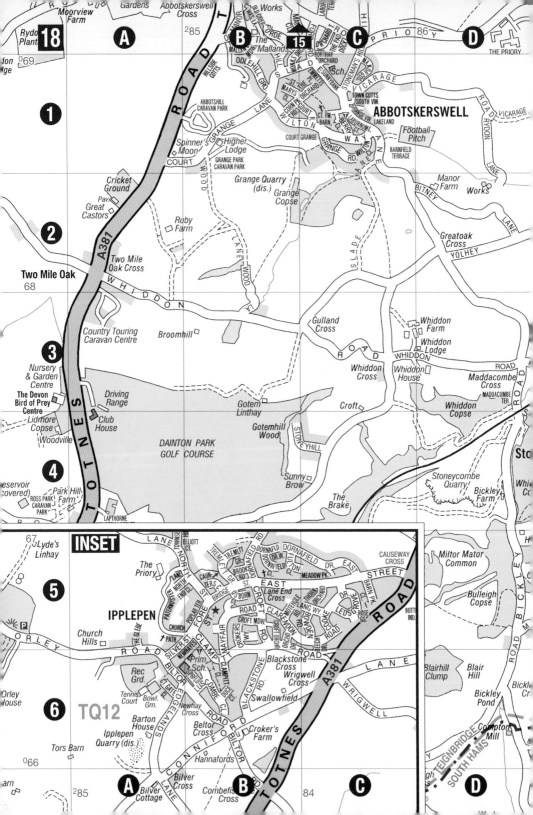

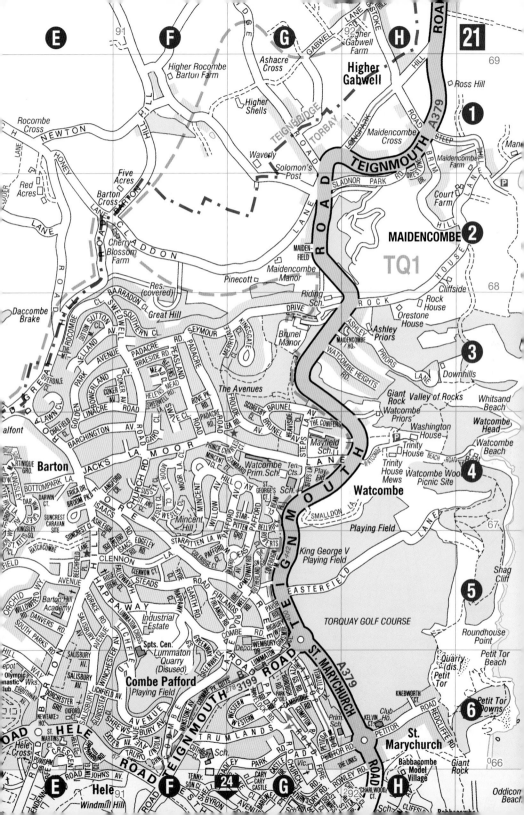

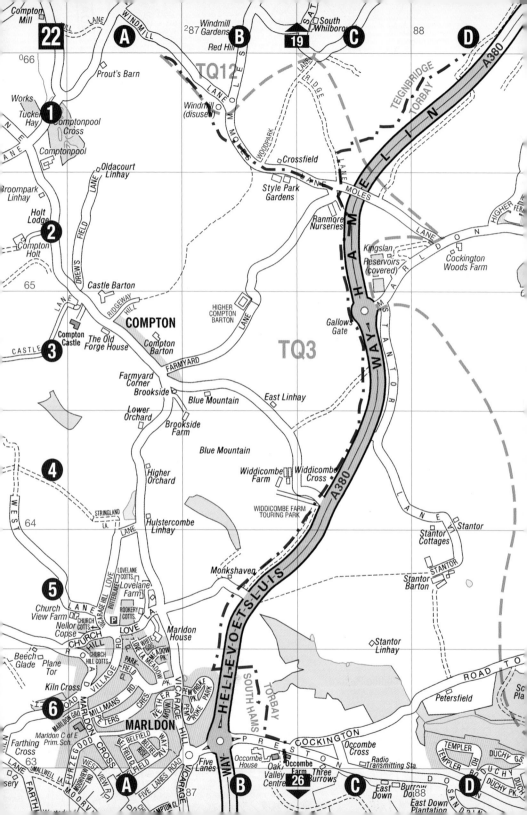

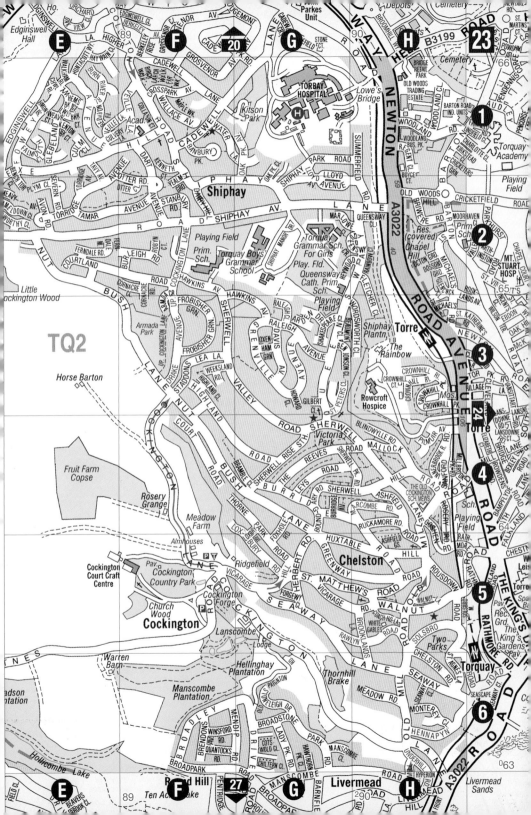

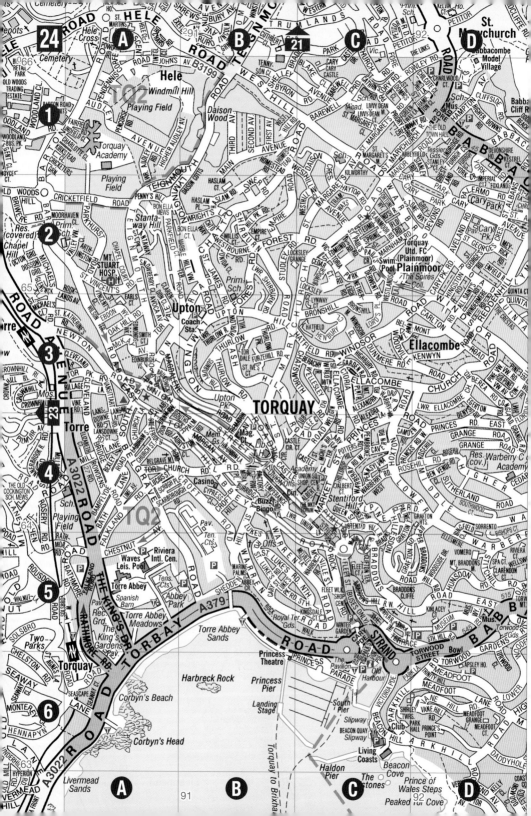

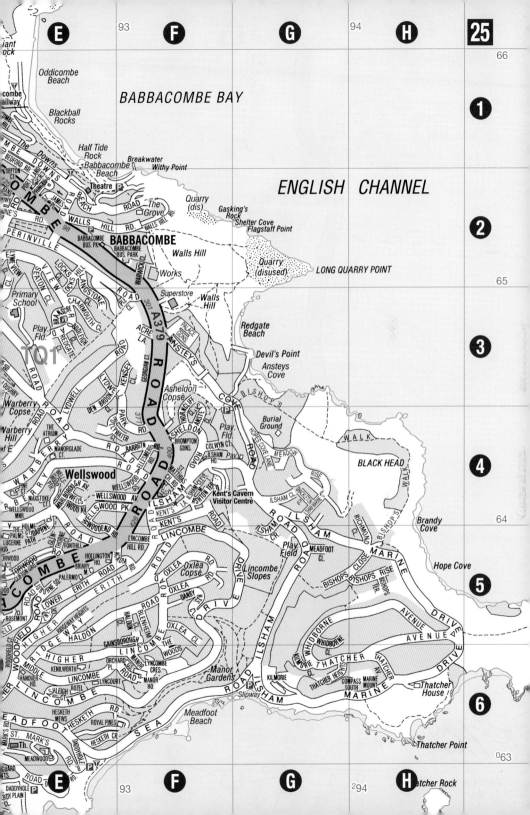

BABBACOMBE BAY

Oddicombe Beach

Blackball Rocks

ENGLISH CHANNEL

Half Tide Rock
Babbacombe Beach
Breakwater
Withy Point

Theatre P

The Grove

Quarry (dis)
Gasking's Rock
Shelter Cove
Flagstaff Point

BABBACOMBE
BABBACOMBE BUS. PK.
BABBACOMBE BUS. PARK

Walls Hill

Works

Quarry (disused)

LONG QUARRY POINT

65

Superstore

Walls Hill

Primary School

Play. Fld.

Redgate Beach

TQ1

Devil's Point
Ansteys Cove

Warberry Copse

Warberry Hill

THE ATRIUM

Asheldon Copse

Burial Ground

BLACK HEAD

Play. Fld.

Wellswood

WELLSWOOD AV.
WELLSWOOD PK.

Kent's Cavern Visitor Centre

Brandy Cove

64

Lincombe Slopes

Play Field

MEADFOOT CL.

Hope Cove

Oxlea Copse

Lincombe Slopes

Danby

The Woods

GAINSBOROUGH

Manor Gardens

KILMORIE

WHIDBORNE CL.

THATCHER

COMPASS SOUTH

MARINE MOUNT

Thatcher House

Meadfoot Beach

Slipway

MARINE DRIVE

HESKETH

ROYAL PINES

MEADWOOD

Th.

DADDYHOLE

Thatcher Point

0 63

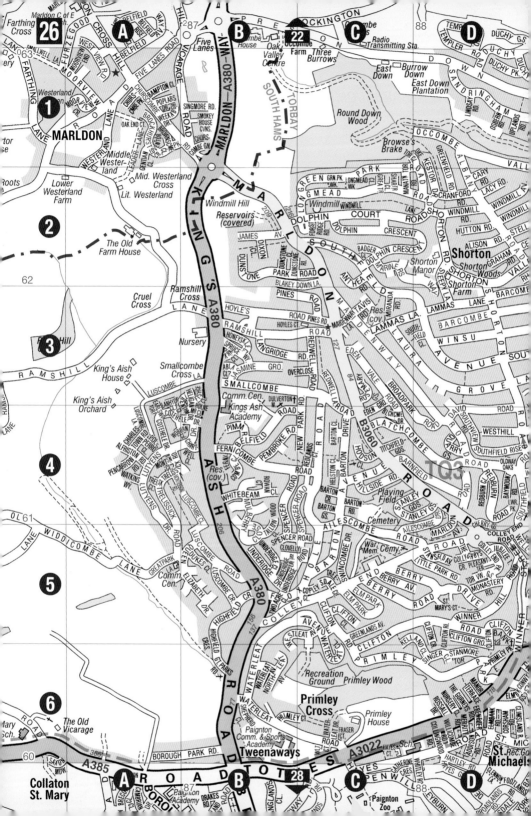

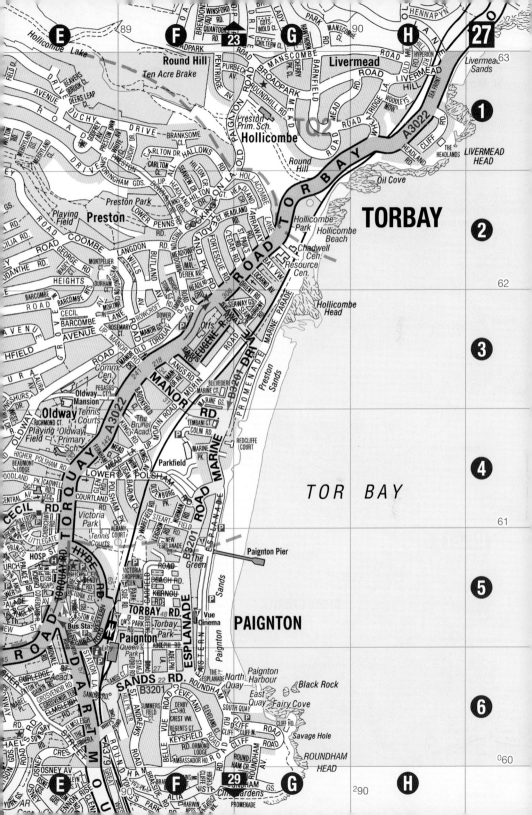

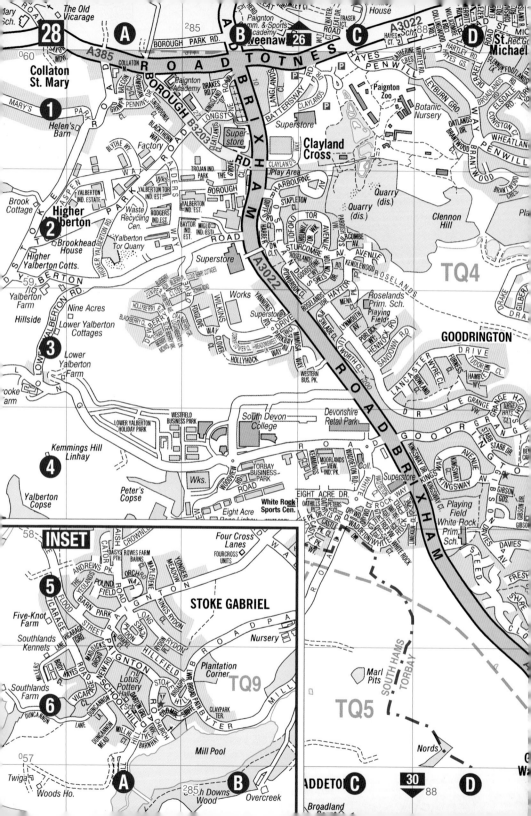

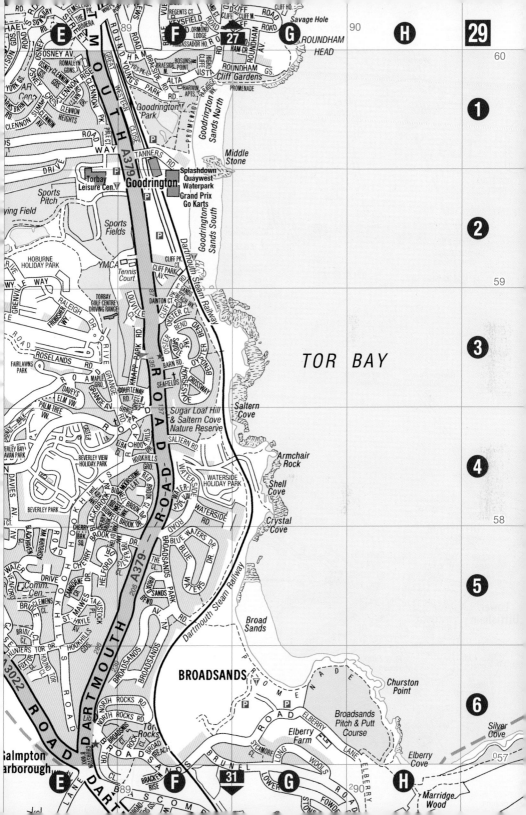

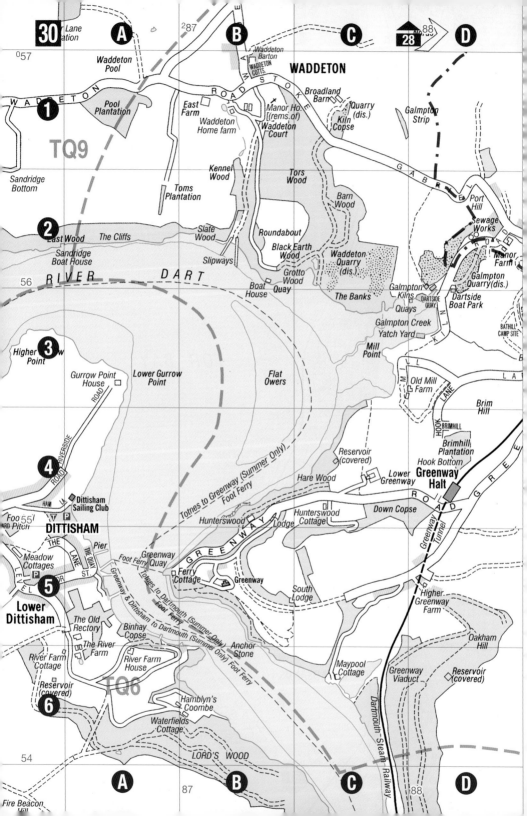

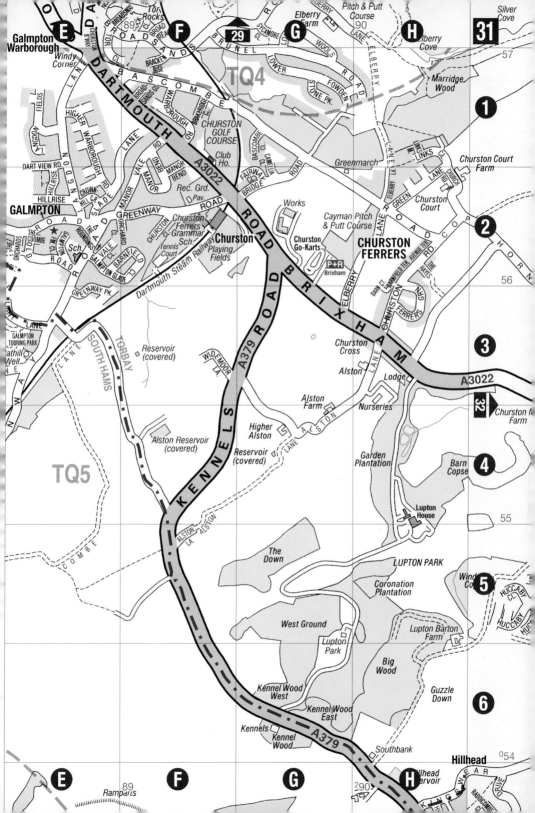

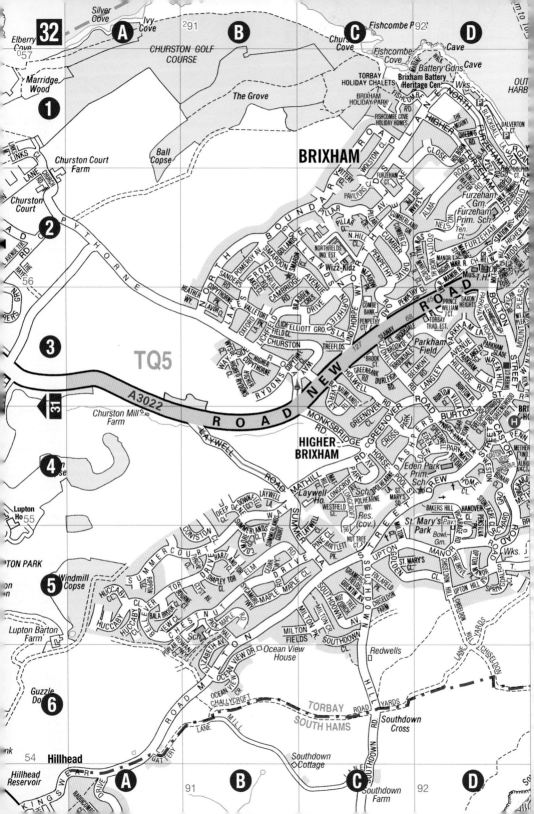

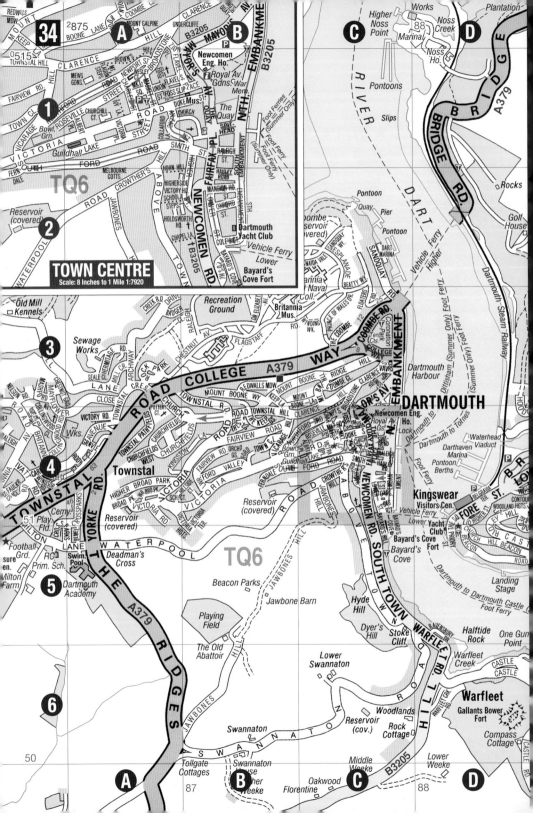

34

TOWN CENTRE

Scale: 8 Inches to 1 Mile 1:7920

TQ6

TQ6

DARTMOUTH

Kingswear

Warfleet

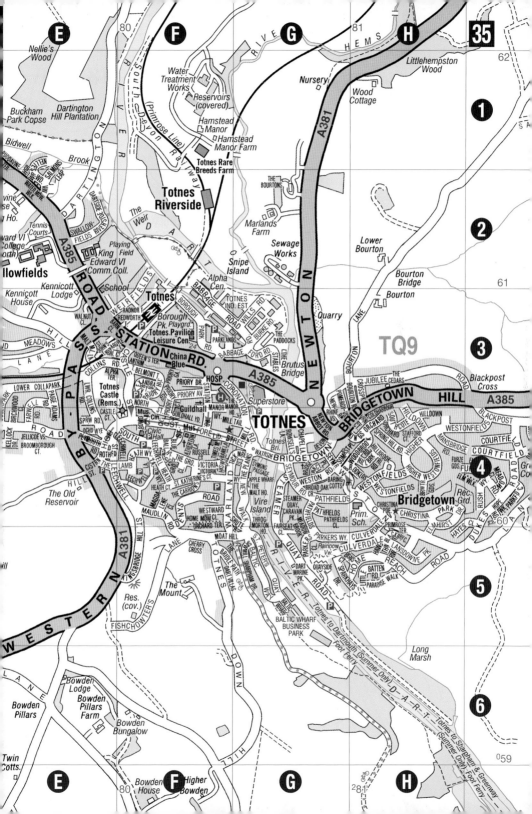

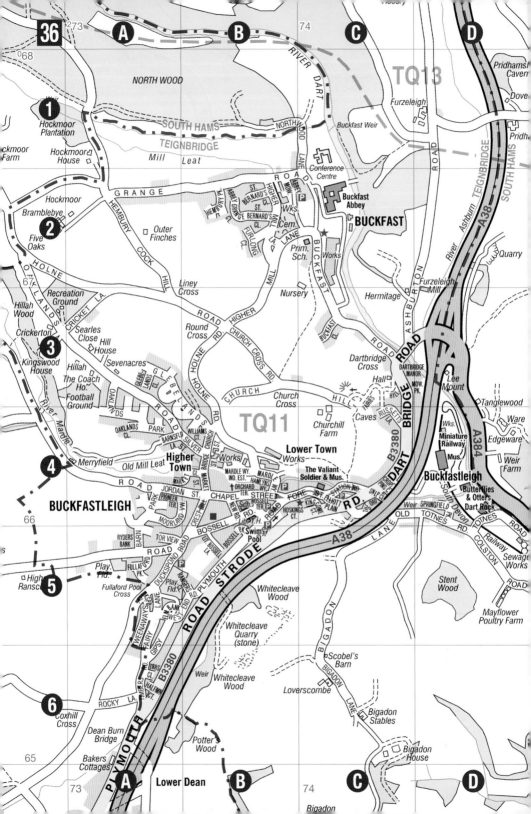

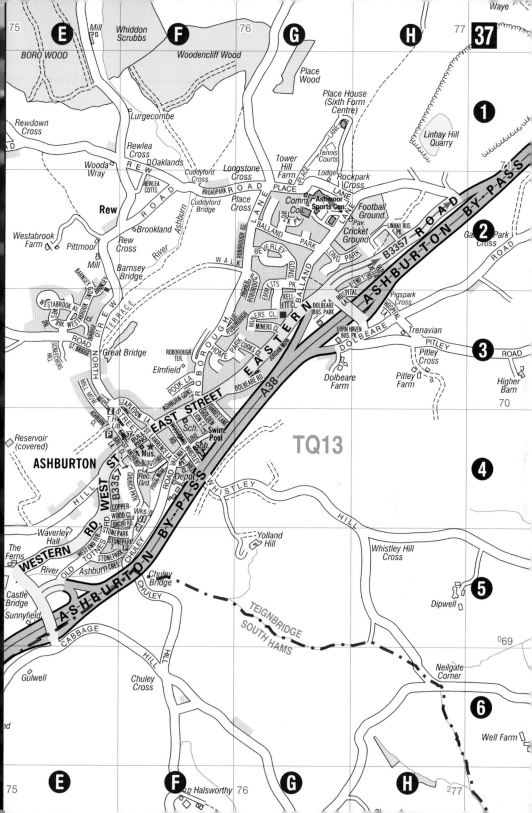

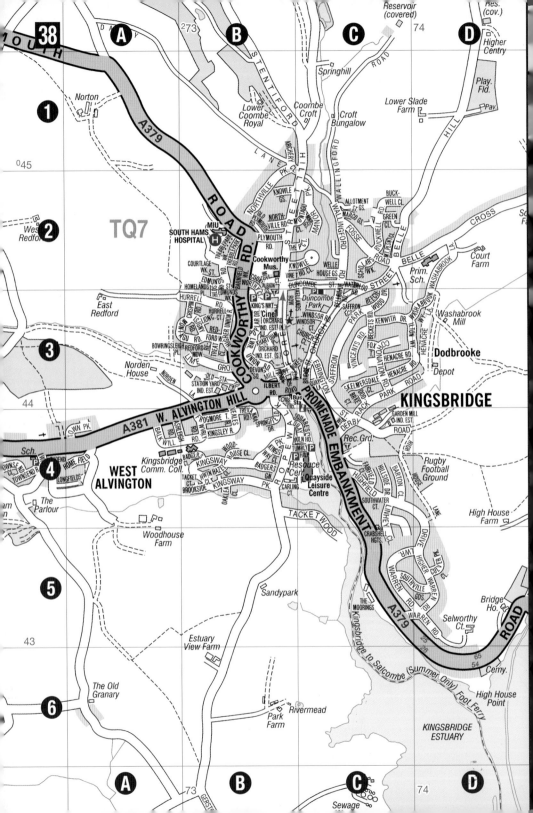

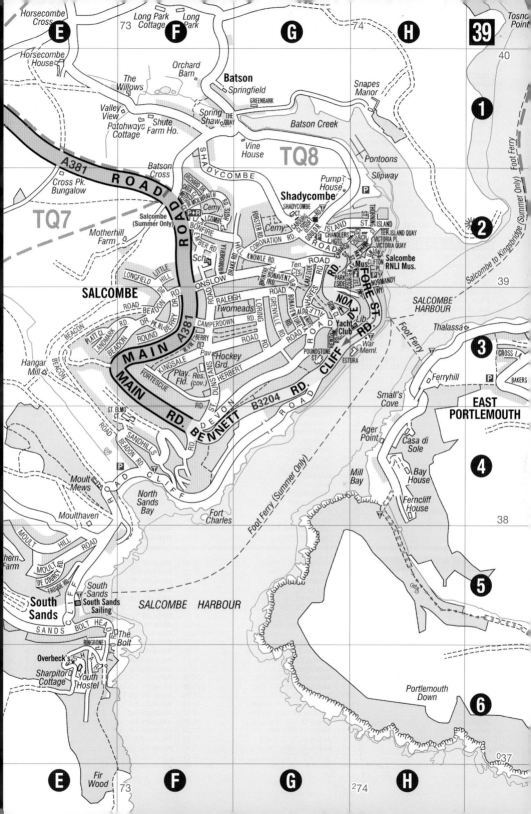

INDEX

Including Streets, Places & Areas, Hospitals etc., Industrial Estates,
Selected Flats & Walkways, Stations and Selected Places of Interest.

HOW TO USE THIS INDEX

1. Each street name is followed by its Postcode District, then by its Locality abbreviation(s) and then by its map reference; e.g. **Abbey Rd.** TQ2: Torq.....4B **24** is in the TQ2 Postcode District and the Torquay Locality and is to be found in square 4B on page **24**. The page number is shown in bold type.

2. A strict alphabetical order is followed in which Av., Rd., St., etc. (though abbreviated) are read in full and as part of the street name; e.g. **Broad Leaf Pk.** appears after **Broadlands Rd.** but before **Broadley Dr.**

3. Streets and a selection of flats and walkways that cannot be shown on the mapping, appear in the index with the thoroughfare to which they are connected shown in brackets; e.g. **Abbeyfield Ho.** TQ14: Teignm.....4E **13** (off Heywoods Rd.)

4. Addresses that are in more than one part are referred to as not continuous.

5. Places and areas are shown in the index in BLUE TYPE and the map reference is to the actual map square in which the town centre or area is located and not to the place name shown on the map; e.g. ASHBURTON.....4F **37**

6. An example of a selected place of interest is Torre Abbey.....5A **24**

7. Transport hub examples: Dawlish Station (Rail).....4E **5**; Kingsbridge Bus Station.....3B **38**; Brixham Park & Ride.....2G **31**

8. An example of a Hospital, Hospice or selected Healthcare facility is BRIXHAM COMMUNITY HOSPITAL.....4D **32**

9. Map references for entries that appear on the large scale page **34** are shown first, with small scale map references shown in brackets; e.g. **Above Town** TQ6: Dartm.....2A **34** (4C **34**)

GENERAL ABBREVIATIONS

Apts. : Apartments	**Cl.** : Close	**Flds.** : Fields	**La.** : Lane	**Nth.** : North	**St.** : Street
App. : Approach	**Cnr.** : Corner	**Gdn.** : Garden	**Lit.** : Little	**Pde.** : Parade	**Ter.** : Terrace
Arc. : Arcade	**Cotts.** : Cottages	**Gdns.** : Gardens	**Lwr.** : Lower	**Pk.** : Park	**Trad.** : Trading
Av. : Avenue	**Ct.** : Court	**Ga.** : Gate	**Mnr.** : Manor	**Pas.** : Passage	**Up.** : Upper
Bri. : Bridge	**Cres.** : Crescent	**Gt.** : Great	**Mans.** : Mansions	**Pl.** : Place	**Va.** : Vale
B'way. : Broadway	**Cft.** : Croft	**Grn.** : Green	**Mkt.** : Market	**Pct.** : Precinct	**Vw.** : View
Bus. : Business	**Dr.** : Drive	**Gro.** : Grove	**Mdw.** : Meadow	**Ri.** : Rise	**Vs.** : Villas
Cvn. : Caravan	**E.** : East	**Hgts.** : Heights	**Mdws.** : Meadows	**Rd.** : Road	**Vis.** : Visitors
Cen. : Centre	**Ent.** : Enterprise	**Ho.** : House	**M.** : Mews	**Shop.** : Shopping	**Wlk.** : Walk
Chu. : Church	**Est.** : Estate	**Ind.** : Industrial	**Mt.** : Mount	**Sth.** : South	**W.** : West
Cir. : Circus	**Fld.** : Field	**Info.** : Information	**Mus.** : Museum	**Sq.** : Square	**Yd.** : Yard

LOCALITY ABBREVIATIONS

Abbotskerswell: TQ12:................A'well	**Dartmouth:** TQ6:.....................Dartm	**Lower Dean:** TQ11:................Lwr D
Ashburton: TQ13:.......................Ashb	**Dawlish Warren:** EX7:............Daw W	**Maidencombe:** TQ1:................. Maid
Batson: TQ8:.................................Bat	**Dawlish:** EX7:..............................Daw	**Marldon:** TQ3:...........................Marl
Bickington: TQ12:........................ Bick	**Denbury:** TQ12:............................Den	**Netherton:** TQ12:....................N'ton
Bishopsteignton: TQ14:..........Bi'ton	**Dittisham:** TQ6:............................Ditt	**Newton Abbot:** TQ12:.............New A
Bovey Tracey: TQ13:..............Bov T	**East Ogwell:** TQ12:..................E Ogw	**North Whilborough:** TQ12:...N Whil
Brixham: TQ5:............................Brixh	**East Portlemouth:** TQ8:...........E Port	**Paignton:** TQ3,TQ4:..................Paig
Broadsands: TQ4:....................Broads	**Galmpton:** TQ5:........................Galm	**Preston:** TQ3:...........................Pres
Buckfast: TQ11:.........................Buck	**Goodrington:** TQ4:.....................Good	**Salcombe:** TQ8:..........................Salc
Buckfastleigh: TQ11:...............B'leigh	**Haccombe:** TQ12:.......................Hacc	**Shaldon:** TQ14:..........................Shal
Chudleigh Knighton: TQ13:....Chud K	**Heathfield:** TQ12:.....................H'fld	**Stoke Gabriel:** TQ9:..................Sto G
Chudleigh: TQ13:.......................Chud	**Holcombe:** EX7:...........................Holc	**Stokeinteignhead:** TQ12:........S'head
Churston Ferrers: TQ5:.............Chur F	**Ipplepen:** TQ12:............................Ipp	**Teigngrace:** TQ12:....................Teigng
Coffinswell: TQ12:......................Coff	**Kingsbridge:** TQ7:...................Kingsb	**Teignmouth:** TQ14:...................Teignm
Collaton St Mary: TQ4:............Coll M	**Kingskerswell:** TQ12:...............Kingsk	**Torquay:** TQ1,TQ2:......................Torq
Combeinteignhead: TQ12:......C'head	**Kingsteignton:** TQ12:................Kingst	**Totnes:** TQ9:.................................Tot
Compton: TQ3:..........................Comp	**Kingswear:** TQ6:......................Kingsw	**Two Mile Oak:** TQ12:...............Two O
Daccombe: TQ12:.......................Dacc	**Littlehempston:** TQ9:.................L'ton	**Waddeton:** TQ5:.........................Wadd
Dartington: TQ9:.........................Darti	**Liverton:** TQ12:............................Live	**West Alvington:** TQ7:................W Alv

A

	Acacia Cl. TQ12: Kingst.............6D **10**	**Albert Rd.** TQ1: Torq........................4C **24**
	Acadia Rd. TQ1: Torq.....................5F **25**	**Albert St.** EX7: Daw.........................4D **4**
Abbey Cl. NR10: Hor F........................3A **12**	**Acland Rd.** TQ8: Salc.....................3G **39**	**Albert Ter.** TQ12: New A.................2H **15**
Abbey Cl. TQ13: Bov T.........................3B **6**	**Acre La.** TQ1: Torq..........................3F **25**	**Albert Ter.** TQ13: Bov T...................3B **6**
Abbey Cl. TQ14: Teignm.....................2E **13**	**Addison Rd.** TQ12: New A..............3B **16**	**Albion Ct.** TQ5: Brixh......................4D **32**
Abbey Cres. TQ2: Torq.......................5B **24**	**Addison Rd.** TQ4: Paig...................6D **26**	**Albion Gdns.** TQ7: Kingsb................2B **38**
Abbeyfield TQ1: Torq...........................1C **24**	**Adelphi La.** TQ4: Paig....................6F **27**	**Albion Hill** TQ12: New A..................3H **15**
..................................(off Heywoods Rd.)	**Adelphi Mans.** TQ4: Paig................6F **27**	**Albion St.** TQ14: Shal......................6C **12**
Abbey Grange Cl. TQ11: Buck.............2B **36**	...................................(off Adelphi Rd.)	**Alder Cl.** TQ12: New A.....................5C **16**
Abbey Mdw. TQ11: Buck.....................2B **36**	**Adelphi Rd.** TQ4: Paig....................5F **27**	**Alder Cl.** TQ14: Teignm....................3D **12**
Abbey Pk....5A **24**	**Admirals Wlk.** TQ14: Teignm..........1C **12**	**Alders Way** TQ4: Paig.......................2A **28**
Abbey Rd. TQ13: Bov T.........................2B **6**	**Admiral Swimming Cen.**................3E **33**	**Alexandra Cinema Scott Cinema, The**.....2G **15**
Abbey Rd. TQ2: Torq...........................4B **24**	**Aggett Gro.** TQ13: Bov T...................1E **7**	**Alexandra Ho.** TQ12: New A.............3B **16**
ABBOTSBURY...2G **15**	**Ailescombe Dr.** TQ3: Paig...............5C **26**	**Alexandra La.** TQ1: Torq...................4C **24**
Abbotsbury Rd. TQ12: New A..............1G **15**	**Ailescombe Rd.** TQ3: Paig...............5C **26**	**Alexandra Rd.** EX7: Daw...................4D **4**
Abbotshill Cvn. Pk. TQ12: A'well.........1B **18**	**Aish Rd.** TQ9: Sto G........................5A **28**	**Alexandra Rd.** TQ1: Torq..................3C **24**
ABBOTSKERSWELL...............................1C **18**	**Alandale Cl.** TQ14: Teignm.............3E **13**	**Alexandra Rd.** TQ12: New A.............3A **16**
Abbotsridge Dr. TQ12: E Ogw..............4E **15**	**Alandale Rd.** TQ14: Teignm............3E **13**	**Alexandra Ter.** TQ12: New A.............3H **15**
Abbotswood TQ12: E Ogw....................4E **15**	**Albany Ct.** TQ3: Paig.......................4E **27**	**Alexandra Ter.** TQ14: Teignm...........5D **12**
Abbotswood TQ12: Kingst....................3E **11**	**Albany Rd.** TQ3: Pres......................2D **26**	**Alexandra Ter.** TQ9: Tot..................3F **35**
Abbrook Av. TQ12: Kingst....................2C **10**	**Albany St.** TQ12: New A..................2H **15**	**Alfriston Rd.** TQ3: Paig....................4A **26**
Abelia Cl. TQ3: Paig.............................3B **26**	**Alberta Cl.** TQ14: Teignm...............4E **13**	**Alison Rd.** TQ3: Pres.......................2D **26**
Above Town TQ6: Dartm 2A **34** (4C **34**)	**Albert Ct.** TQ1: Torq........................4C **24**	**Alive Fitness & Sport**......................3D **12**
	Albert Pl. TQ6: Dartm 1A **34** (4C **34**)	**Allenhayes La.** TQ8: Salc................3G **39**

Allenhayes Rd. TQ8: Salc 3G **39**
ALLER 1G **19**
Aller Brake Rd. TQ12: New A 5B **16**
Aller Cl. TQ12: Kingsk 1G **19**
Aller Hill EX7: Daw 5B **4**
Aller Mills TQ12: Kingsk 1G **19**
ALLER PK. 4C **16**
Aller Pk. Rd. TQ12: New A 5C **16**
Aller Rd. TQ12: Kingsk 1G **19**
All Hallows Rd. TQ3: Pres 1F **27**
Allotment Gdns. TQ7: Kingsb 2C **38**
All Saint's Rd. TQ1: Torq 3D **24**
Alma Rd. TQ5: Brixh 2D **32**
Alma Steps TQ6: Kingsw 5D **34**
 .... (off Beacon Rd.)
Alpha Ter. TQ9: Tot 3E **35**
Alpine Rd. TQ1: Torq 4C **24**
Alston La. TQ5: Chur F 5F **31**
Alta Vista Cl. TQ14: Teignm 2F **13**
Alta Vista Rd. TQ4: Good 1F **29**
Aluric Ri. TQ12: New A 1C **16**
Alvington Ter. TQ7: Kingsb 4B **38**
 .... (off W. Alvington Hill)
Alwyns Cl. TQ14: Teignm 4E **13**
 .... (off Lwr. Brimley Rd.)
Ambassador Ho. TQ4: Paig 6F **27**
Amethyst Dr. TQ14: Teignm 2E **13**
AMF Bowling Torquay 5D **24**
Anchorage, The TQ4: Paig...............6F **27**
 .... (off Belle Vue Rd.)
Anchorage Cl. TQ5: Brixh 2F **33**
Anchor Cen., The TQ7: Kingsb 3C **38**
 ....(off Bridge St.)
Andor Av. TQ12: Kingst 4C **10**
Andrea Ct. TQ14: Teignm 4D **12**
 .... (off Yannon Dr.)
Andrews Pk. TQ9: Sto G 5A **28**
Ansteys Cl. TQ1: Torq 4F **25**
Anstey's Cove Rd. TQ1: Torq 3F **25**
Anthea Rd. TQ3: Pres 2C **26**
Antrim Ter. TQ9: Tot 3F **35**
Anzac St. TQ6: Dartm 1A **34** (4C **34**)
Applegarth Av. TQ1: New A 6F **9**
Applegarth Cl. TQ12: New A 1D **14**
Apple Tree Cl. TQ13: Chud K 2H **7**
Apple Wharf TQ9: Tot 4G **35**
Apsley Ho. TQ1: Torq 6D **24**
Apters Hill TQ5: Brixh 2D **32**
 .... (off Middle St.)
Arch Cotts. TQ12: Kingst 4C **10**
Archery Cl. TQ7: Kingsb 1B **38**
Arch St. TQ14: Shal 6C **12**
Archway Dr. TQ6: Dartm 3A **34**
Arden Dr. TQ2: Torq 3G **23**
Argyle Ter. TQ9: Tot 3E **35**
Armada Cres. TQ2: Torq 3F **23**
Armada Dr. TQ14: Teignm 1C **12**
Arran Cl. TQ2: Torq.......................5D **20**
Arthington TQ1: Torq......................2A **24**
Ascension Way TQ2: Torq 5E **21**
Ashburn Cl. TQ13: Ashb 4E **37**
Ashburn Gdns. TQ13: Ashb 3F **37**
Ashburn Wlk. TQ4: Good 5E **29**
ASHBURTON 4F **37**
Ashburton By-Pass TQ13: Ashb 5E **37**
Ashburton Cl. TQ13: Bov T 5B **6**
Ashburton Info. Cen. 4E **37**
Ashburton Mus. 4F **37**
Ashburton Rd. TQ11: B'leigh 3C **36**
Ashburton Rd. TQ13: Bov T 5B **6**
Ashburton Swimming Pool 4F **37**
Ashcombe Rd. EX7: Daw 1A **4**
Asheldon Rd. TQ1: Torq 4F **25**
Ashfield Gdns. TQ2: Torq 5H **23**
Ashfield Rd. TQ2: Torq 4H **23**
Ashgrove Rd. TQ13: Bov T 6B **6**
ASH HILL 5H **13**
Ash Hill Rd. TQ1: Torq 3B **24**
Ashleigh Cl. TQ14: Teignm 2D **12**
Ashleigh Cl. TQ1: Torq 4E **21**
Ashleigh Ct. TQ1: Torq 6E **25**
Ashleigh Dr. TQ14: Teignm 2D **12**

Ashleigh Mt. TQ14: Teignm 2D **12**
Ashleigh Pk. TQ14: Teignm 2D **12**
Ashleigh Ri. TQ14: Teignm 2D **12**
Ashleigh Rd. TQ7: Kingsb 4A **38**
Ashleigh Vs. TQ9: Tot 4E **35**
 .... (off Plymouth Rd.)
Ashleigh Way TQ14: Teignm 2D **12**
Ashley Priors La. TQ1: Torq 3H **21**
Ashley Way EX7: Daw 3F **5**
Ashmill Ct. TQ12: New A 1E **15**
Ashmoor Sports Cen. 2G **37**
Ash Pk. EX7: Holc 1G **13**
Ashridge Gdns. TQ12: Kingst 6E **11**
Ash Rd. TQ12: Kingst 5D **10**
Ashton Ct. TQ12: Kingst 2D **10**
Ashton Ter. TQ1: Torq 4F **25**
Ash Way TQ12: New A 4C **16**
Ashwood Ct. TQ12: New A 3B **16**
 .... (off Marychurch Rd.)
Aspen Dr. TQ12: New A 5C **16**
Aspen Way TQ4: Paig 2A **28**
Astley Pk. 3E **33**
Atherton La. TQ9: Tot 4F **35**
Atrium, The TQ1: Torq 4E **25**
Atway Cl. TQ13: Bov T 2B **6**
Audley Av. TQ2: Torq 1A **24**
Audley Ri. TQ12: New A 4D **16**
Aveland Rd. TQ1: Torq 2D **24**
Avenue, The TQ12: New A 2H **15**
Avenue Rd. TQ12: Kingsk 2H **19**
Avenue Rd. TQ2: Torq 3B **6**
Avenue Rd. TQ13: Bov T 3B **6**
Avenue Ter. TQ5: Chur F 2H **31**
Avery Hill TQ12: Kingst 3D **10**
Avoca Av. TQ1: Torq 3A **24**
Avon Rd. TQ2: Torq 2E **23**

BABBACOMBE 2E **25**
Babbacombe Bus. Pk. TQ1: Torq 2E **25**
 .... (not continuous)
Babbacombe Cliff Railway 1D **24**
Babbacombe Corinthian Sailing Club ..1C **24**
 ....(off Fore St.)
Babbacombe Downs Rd. TQ1: Torq ...1D **24**
Babbacombe Model Village 1D **24**
Babbacombe Rd. TQ1: Torq 1D **24**
Babbacombe Theatre 2E **25**
Babbage Rd. TQ9: Tot 3F **35**
Back Rd. TQ12: New A 2G **15**
 .... (not continuous)
Badger Cl. TQ3: Pres 2C **26**
Badger Cl. TQ6: Dartm 3A **34**
Badgers Cl. TQ12: Kingst 3C **10**
Badgers Cl. TQ7: Kingsb 4B **38**
Badgers Grn. TQ7: Kingsb 4B **38**
Badgers Way TQ13: Bov T 3C **6**
Badlake Cl. EX7: Daw 3C **4**
Badlake Hill EX7: Daw 3C **4**
Bakers Hill TQ12: New A 2G **15**
Bakers Hill TQ5: Brixh 4D **32**
Bakers Piece TQ8: E Port 3H **39**
Bakers Vw. TQ1: Torq 2F **15**
Bala Brook Cl. TQ5: Brixh 5A **32**
Balkwill Rd. TQ7: Kingsb 4A **38**
Balland La. TQ13: Ashb 3G **37**
Balland Pk. TQ13: Ashb 2G **37**
Balmoral Cl. TQ12: New A 3B **16**
Baltic Way TQ9: Tot 5G **35**
Baltic Wharf TQ9: Tot 5G **35**
Baltic Wharf Bus. Pk. TQ9: Tot 5G **35**
Bampfylde Rd. TQ2: Torq 4A **24**
Bampton Cl. TQ3: Marl 1A **26**
Banbury Pk. TQ2: Torq 1F **23**
Bank La. TQ5: Brixh 2D **32**
Bank La. TQ9: Tot 4F **35**
Bank St. TQ14: New A 2G **15**
Bank St. TQ14: Teignm 5E **13**
Banner Ct. TQ3: Paig 5D **26**
 .... (off Winner St.)
Baptist La. TQ7: Kingsb 3B **38**
 ....(off Fore St.)

Baptist La. TQ8: Salc 3G **39**
 .... (off Devon Rd.)
Barchington Av. TQ2: Torq 4E **21**
Barcombe Hgts. TQ3: Pres 3D **26**
Barcombe La. TQ3: Pres 3E **27**
Barcombe M. TQ3: Pres 3E **27**
Barcombe Rd. TQ3: Pres 3D **26**
Barewell Cl. TQ1: Torq 1C **24**
Barewell Rd. TQ1: Torq 1C **24**
Barham Av. TQ14: Teignm 2F **13**
Baring Cotts. TQ9: Tot 4G **35**
Barn Cl. TQ9: Tot 3E **35**
Barn Ct. TQ5: Chur F 3H **31**
Barnfield Cl. TQ5: Galm 3F **31**
Barnfield Cl. TQ2: Torq 1G **27**
Barnfield Rd. TQ3: Paig 4C **26**
Barnfield Rd. TQ5: Brixh 4E **33**
Barnfield Ter. TQ12: A'well 1C **18**
Barnfield Ter. TQ5: Chur F 2H **31**
Barnfield Wlk. TQ7: Kingsb 2B **38**
Barnha, The TQ9: Sto G 6A **28**
Barnhill Rd. TQ12: Kingsk 3H **19**
Barn Owl Cl. TQ2: Torq 4C **20**
Barn Pk. TQ11: B'leigh 5A **36**
Barn Pk. TQ12: Live 1A **8**
Barn Pk. TQ9: Sto G 5A **28**
Barn Pk. Cl. TQ12: Ipp 5C **18**
Barnpark Cl. TQ14: Teignm 3E **13**
Barnpark Rd. TQ14: Teignm 4E **13**
Barnpark Ter. TQ14: Teignm 3E **13**
Barn Rd. TQ4: Good 3F **29**
Barns Cl. TQ12: Kingst 5D **10**
Barnsey Gdns. TQ13: Ashb 2E **37**
Barnsfield La. TQ11: B'leigh 4A **36**
Barnsley Cl. TQ14: Teignm 4E **13**
Barnsley Dr. TQ14: Teignm 4E **13**
Baron Way TQ12: New A 2C **16**
Barradon Cl. TQ2: Torq 2F **21**
Barrington Ho. TQ1: Torq 4F **25**
 .... (off Barrington Rd.)
Barrington Rd. TQ1: Torq 4F **25**
BARTON 5E **21**
Barton Acorn Youth Community & Sports Cen.
 ....5F **21**
Barton Av. TQ3: Paig 5C **26**
Barton Cl. TQ3: Paig 4C **26**
Barton Cl. TQ7: Kingsb 4C **38**
Barton Cres. EX7: Daw 4C **4**
Barton Cres. TQ3: Paig 4C **26**
Barton Dr. TQ12: New A 2E **15**
Barton Dr. TQ3: Paig 4C **26**
Barton Gdns. TQ3: Paig 4C **26**
Barton Hill EX7: Daw 4D **4**
Barton Hill TQ17: S'head 2F **21**
Barton Hill Rd. TQ2: Torq 6E **21**
Barton Hill Way TQ2: Torq 5D **20**
Barton La. EX7: Daw 4C **4**
Barton Rd. TQ1: Torq 2H **23**
Barton Rd. TQ2: Torq 1H **23**
Barton Rd. TQ3: Paig 4C **26**
Barton Rd. Ind. Units TQ2: Torq 1H **23**
Barton Ter. EX7: Daw 4D **4**
Barton Ter. EX7: Daw 4C **4**
Barum Cl. TQ3: Paig 4F **27**
Bascombe Cl. TQ5: Chur F 1G **31**
Bascombe Rd. TQ5: Chur F 1F **31**
Bathill Camp Site TQ5: Galm 3D **30**
Bath La. TQ2: Torq 4A **24**
Bath Ter. TQ14: Teignm 5E **13**
BATSON 1F **39**
Batson Gdns. TQ4: Paig 1D **28**
Battersway Rd. TQ4: Paig 1B **28**
Battery Gdns. 1D **32**
Battle Rd. TQ12: H'fld 5E **7**
Bayard's Cove TQ6: Dartm 2B **34** (4C **34**)
Bayard's Cove Fort 2B **34** (5C **34**)
Bayards Cove Steps TQ6: Dartm .. 2B **34** (4C **34**)
 .... (off Lower St.)
Bayard's Hill TQ6: Dartm 2B **34** (4C **34**)
Baymount Rd. TQ3: Paig 4D **26**
Baythorpe Lodge TQ2: Torq 1H **27**
 .... (off Livermead Hill)
Baytor Ind. Est. TQ4: Paig 2B **28**

Bay Vw. TQ3: Pres.................................2G 27
Bay Vw. Dr. TQ14: Teignm 3E 13
Bay Vw. Steps TQ5: Brixh.........................2E 33
....(off King St.)
Beach App. TQ5: Brixh 2E 33
....(off Pump St.)
Beach Rd. EX7: Daw W.............................1H 5
Beach Rd. TQ1: Torq...............................2E 25
Beach Rd. TQ4: Paig...............................5F 27
Beach St. EX7: Daw................................4E 5
Beach Wlk. TQ4: Good.............................3F 29
Beacon Dr. TQ12: New A...........................6F 9
Beacon Hill TQ1: Torq.............................6C 24
Beacon La. TQ6: Kingsw...........................5D 34
Beacon Quay TQ1: Torq............................6C 24
Beacon Rd. TQ6: Kingsw...........................5D 34
Beacon Rd. TQ8: Salc..............................3E 39
Beacon Ter. TQ1: Torq.............................6C 24
....(off Beacon Hill)
Beadon Dr. TQ8: Salc..............................3E 39
Beadon Rd. TQ8: Salc..............................3F 39
Beal Farm M. TQ13: Chud K........................2H 7
Beanhay Cl. TQ12: Live 1A 8
Bearne's La. TQ12: New A 2G 15
....(off Bank St.)
Beatty Way TQ6: Dartm............................2C 34
Beaumont Cl. TQ12: Live...........................1A 8
Beaumont Cl. TQ2: Torq............................3G 23
Beaumont Lodge TQ3: Paig.........................4E 27
Beaumont Rd. TQ12: New A.........................3H 15
Beavers Brook Cl. TQ3: Pres.......................1E 27
Becket Rd. TQ13: Bov T............................3C 6
Beckets Rd. TQ7: Kingsb...........................3C 38
Bedford Rd. TQ1: Torq.............................1E 25
Beech Dr. TQ12: Ipp...............................5C 18
Beechfield Av. TQ2: Torq..........................5D 20
Beechfield Pl. TQ2: Torq...........................5E 21
Beechwood Av. TQ12: New A........................4B 16
Beechwood Av. TQ13: Bov T........................6B 6
Beechwood Ct. TQ14: Teignm 2B 12
Beechwood Dr. TQ7: Kingsb........................3C 38
Belfield Av. TQ3: Marl.............................1A 26
Belfield Cl. TQ3: Marl.............................6A 22
Belfield Ri. TQ3: Marl.............................6A 22
Belfield Rd. TQ3: Paig.............................4B 26
Belfield Way TQ3: Marl............................6A 22
Belgrave M. TQ2: Torq.............................4A 24
Belgrave Rd. TQ12: New A.........................4C 16
Belgrave Rd. TQ2: Torq............................4A 24
Belgrave Ter. TQ14: Teignm 4E 13
Belgravia Ter. TQ6: Kingsw........................4D 34
Bella Vista Rd. TQ5: Brixh........................1D 32
Belle Cross Rd. TQ7: Kingsb.......................2D 38
Belle Hill TQ7: Kingsb.............................2C 38
Bellever Tor Dr. TQ5: Brixh.......................5A 32
Belle Vue Rd. TQ4: Paig...........................6F 27
Belle Vue Rd. TQ7: Kingsb.........................3C 38
Bellrock Cl. TQ2: Torq.............................4G 21
Belmont Cl. TQ12: Kingst..........................2D 10
Belmont Rd. TQ1: Torq.............................3C 24
Belmont Rd. TQ5: Brixh............................3D 32
Belmont Ter. TQ9: Tot.............................3F 35
Belvedere TQ3: Pres...............................3F 27
Belvedere Ct. EX7: Daw............................4E 5
....(off High St.)
Belvedere Rd. TQ12: New A........................6F 9
Bench Tor Cl. TQ2: Torq...........................1E 23
Benedict Cl. TQ14: Teignm 2E 13
Benedicts Cl. TQ12: Live...........................1A 8
Benedicts Rd. TQ12: New A 1A 8
Ben Jonson Cl. TQ2: Torq..........................3G 23
Benlears Acre TQ12: Live..........................1A 8
Bennett Rd. TQ8: Salc.............................4F 39
Ben Venue Cl. TQ1: Torq...........................4D 24
Berachah Rd. TQ1: Torq............................3C 24
Berea Rd. TQ1: Torq...............................3D 24
Bere Cotts. EX7: Daw.............................3B 4
Bere Hill EX7: Daw................................4B 4
Berkeley Av. TQ2: Torq............................6B 20
Berkeley Ri. TQ2: Torq.............................6B 20
Berkshire Cl. TQ12: E Ogw.........................5E 15
Berman Ct. TQ12: New A...........................2G 15
....(off Clarendon Rd.)

Berretts Way TQ12: Live...........................1B 8
Berry Av. TQ3: Paig...............................5C 26
Berry Cl. TQ12: A'well.............................1C 18
Berry Cl. TQ8: Salc................................3F 39
Berry Dr. TQ3: Paig...............................5C 26
Berry Head Country Pk............................2G 33
Berry Head Fortifications 1H 33
Berry Head Nat. Nature Reserve 3G 33
Berry Head Rd. TQ5: Brixh........................2E 33
Berry Hill TQ14: Bi'ton............................5G 13
Berry La. TQ12: Kingst............................4D 10
Berry Mdw. TQ12: Kingst..........................5D 10
Berry Rd. TQ3: Paig...............................5C 26
Berry Sq. TQ4: Paig...............................5F 27
....(off Beach Rd.)
Berrys Wood TQ12: New A.........................2E 15
Besigheim Way TQ12: New A.......................2B 16
Bethel Ter. TQ1: Torq.............................4C 24
....(off Princes Rd.)
Beverley Bay Cvn. Pk. TQ4: Good.................4E 29
Beverley Gdns. TQ13: Ashb........................2G 37
Beverley Pk. TQ4: Good...........................4E 29
Beverley Ri. TQ5: Brixh...........................3C 32
Beverley Vw. Holiday Pk. TQ4: Good 4E 29
Beverley Way TQ12: New A........................3F 15
Bexley La. TQ2: Torq.............................4A 24
Bickford La. TQ14: Teignm.........................5E 13
Bickfords Grn. TQ12: Live.........................1A 8
Bickington Steam Railway 2B 8
Bidwell Brook Dr. TQ4: Good......................4E 29
Bidwell Wlk. TQ4: Good...........................4E 29
Bigadon La. TQ11: B'leigh.........................5B 36
Bigbury Way TQ2: Torq............................5G 21
Bilberry Pl. TQ4: Paig.............................3A 28
Biltor Rd. TQ12: Ipp..............................6A 18
Bingfield Cl. TQ1: Torq............................4D 24
Birchlea Cl. TQ13: Bov T..........................6B 6
Birch Rd. TQ12: New A............................4C 16
Birch Wlk. TQ2: Torq.............................1F 23
Birchwood Cl. TQ9: Tot...........................4E 35
Birdwood Cl. TQ9: Tot............................4F 35
Bishops Av. TQ14: Bi'ton..........................6G 13
Bishops Cl. TQ1: Torq.............................5G 25
Bishops Cl. TQ1: Torq.............................4D 24
Bishops Ct. TQ14: Bi'ton..........................5G 13
Bishops Pl. TQ3: Paig.............................5E 27
Bishops Ri. TQ1: Torq.............................5H 25
BISHOPSTEIGNTON 5G 13
Bishopsteignton Ho. TQ14: Bi'ton 5F 13
Bishopsteignton Mus. of Rural Life 5H 13
Bishopsteignton Rd. TQ14: Teignm 5A 12
Bishopstone Gdns. TQ3: Pres.....................3F 27
Bishop's Wlk. TQ1: Torq...........................3G 25
Bishop Wilfrid Rd. TQ14: Teignm 3B 12
Bitney La. TQ12: A'well...........................2D 18
Bitton Av. TQ14: Teignm...........................4D 12
Bitton Ct. TQ14: Teignm...........................4C 12
Bitton Pk. Rd. TQ14: Teignm......................4C 12
....(not continuous)
Blackball La. TQ5: Brixh...........................1D 32
Blackberry Cl. TQ4: Paig 3A 28
Blackberry Ct. TQ9: Tot...........................5H 35
Blackberry Way TQ12: Kingst 2D 10
Blackbrook Av. TQ4: Good.........................4E 29
Blackbrook Wlk. TQ4: Good.......................4E 29
Blackenway La. TQ12: Coff........................6E 17
Blackhaven Cl. TQ4: Good.........................5E 29
Blackpost La. TQ9: Tot............................4H 35
Blackstone Rd. TQ12: Ipp.........................6B 18
Blackthorn Way TQ4: Paig.........................1A 28
Bladon Cl. TQ12: New A...........................4A 16
Blake Cl. TQ1: Torq...............................1C 24
Blakey Down La. TQ3: Paig........................2B 26
Blatchcombe Dr. TQ3: Paig........................4C 26
Blatchcombe Rd. TQ3: Paig........................4C 26
Blatchmore La. TQ6: Dartm.......................5A 34
Blenheim Cl. TQ1: Torq............................5F 25
Blenheim Cl. TQ2: Torq............................1F 15
Blenheim Ter. TQ13: Bov T........................3B 6
Bligh Cl. TQ14: Teignm............................1C 12
Blindwell Av. TQ12: Kingst........................4D 10
Blindwylle Rd. TQ2: Torq..........................4H 23
Blogishay La. TQ13: Ashb.........................4F 37

Blue Ball Hill TQ9: Tot.............................4F 35
Blueberry Row TQ4: Paig..........................3A 28
Blue Ridge Rd. TQ13: Bov T.......................6B 6
Bluewater Holiday Homes EX7: Daw W............1H 5
Blue Waters TQ13: Bov T..........................6B 6
Blue Waters Dr. TQ4: Broads......................5F 29
Blue Waters Ind. Est. TQ13: Bov T.................5B 6
Blythe Way TQ2: Torq.............................1A 28
Blythswood Cres. TQ1: Torq.......................2C 24
Body Hayes Cl. TQ9: Sto G........................6A 28
Bogons Cl. TQ9: Tot...............................5G 35
Bolt Head TQ8: Salc...............................5E 39
Bolton Ct. TQ5: Brixh..............................3D 32
....(off Windmill Hill)
Bolton St. TQ5: Brixh..............................3D 32
Bonair Cl. TQ5: Brixh..............................4D 32
Bonaventure Cl. TQ8: Salc.........................2G 39
Bonaventure Rd. TQ8: Salc........................2G 39
Bonds Mdw. TQ13: Bov T.........................2B 6
Bon Ella Ct. TQ1: Torq.............................2A 24
Bon Ella M. TQ1: Torq.............................2A 24
Bonfire Hill TQ8: Salc..............................2F 39
Boon's La. TQ7: Kingsb............................3B 38
....(off Ropewalk)
Borough Cl. TQ4: Paig.............................2B 28
Borough Pk. Rd. TQ3: Paig........................6A 26
Borough Pk. Rd. TQ9: Tot..........................3F 35
Borough Rd. TQ1: Torq............................6G 21
Borough Rd. TQ4: Paig............................1A 28
Borthay Orchard TQ12: A'well.....................1C 18
Boscawen Pl. TQ14: Teignm.......................4D 12
Bossell Ho. TQ11: B'leigh..........................5B 36
....(off Bossell Pk.)
Bossell Pk. TQ11: B'leigh..........................5B 36
Bossell Rd. TQ11: B'leigh..........................5B 36
Bossell Ter. TQ11: B'leigh..........................4B 36
Bosuns Point TQ4: Good..........................1F 29
Bottompark La. TQ2: Torq.........................4E 21
Bottoms La. TQ12: Dacc...........................3D 20
Boundary Cl. TQ12: Kingsk........................1G 19
Boundary Rd. TQ2: Torq...........................4G 23
Bourne Ct. TQ5: Brixh..............................5A 32
Bourne Rd. TQ12: Kingsk..........................2H 19
Bourton La. TQ9: Tot..............................3G 35
Bourton Rd. TQ9: Tot..............................3H 35
Bourtons, The TQ9: Tot...........................2G 35
Bove Pk. Rd. TQ2: Torq...........................3F 21
BOVEY TRACEY 3B 6
Bovey Tracey Golf Course 1A 6
Bovey Tracey Heritage Cen. 3B 6
Bovey Tracey Info. Cen. 3B 6
Bovey Tracey Rd. TQ12: New A 4F 9
Bovey Tracey Swimming Pool 4B 6
Bowden Hill TQ12: New A.........................3H 15
Bowden Rd. TQ12: Ipp.............................5C 18
Bowdens Cl. TQ13: Bov T..........................3B 6
Bowerland Av. TQ2: Torq..........................3E 21
Bowland Cl. TQ4: Paig.............................3D 28
Bowling Grn. TQ13: Ashb..........................4F 37
....(off Whistley Hill)
Bowringsleigh Pl. TQ7: Kingsb....................3A 38
Boyce Ct. TQ2: Torq...............................1H 23
Boyds Dr. TQ14: Teignm..........................4E 13
Bracken Cl. TQ12: New A..........................4C 16
Bracken Ri. TQ4: Broads...........................1F 31
Bradden Cres. TQ5: Brixh.........................3B 32
Braddons Cliffe TQ1: Torq.........................5C 24
Braddons Hill Rd. E. TQ1: Torq....................5C 24
Braddons Hill Rd. W. TQ1: Torq...................5C 24
Braddons St. TQ1: Torq............................5C 24
Bradley...3E 15
BRADLEY.......................................2E 7
Bradley Ct. TQ12: New A..........................2G 15
Bradley La. TQ12: New A..........................2F 15
Bradley Pk. Rd. TQ1: Torq.........................1B 24
Bradley Rd. TQ12: New A..........................4F 15
Bradley Rd. TQ13: Bov T...........................2D 6
Braeburn Pl. TQ5: Brixh...........................4D 32
Braeside M. TQ4: Good...........................1F 29
Braeside Rd. TQ2: Torq............................3F 21
Braeside Rd. TQ4: Good...........................1F 29
Brakeridge Cl. TQ5: Chur F........................1F 31
Bramble Cl. TQ2: Torq.............................4G 23

Branksome Cl. – Cadewell Pk. Rd.

Branksome Cl. TQ3: Pres 1F **27**
Branscombe Cl. TQ1: Torq 3E **25**
Brantwood Cl. TQ4: Good 1D **28**
Brantwood Cres. TQ4: Good 2D **28**
Brantwood Dr. TQ4: Good 1D **28**
Breakneck Hill TQ14: Teignm 1D **12**
Breakwater Ct. TQ5: Brixh 1F **33**
Brecon Cl. TQ4: Coll M 1A **28**
Brendons Av. TQ2: Torq 6F **23**
Brent Rd. TQ3: Paig 5D **26**
Brewery Ct. EX7: Daw 4E **5**
(off High St.)
Brewery La. TQ5: Brixh 2D **32**
(off Market St.)
Briary La. TQ1: Torq 4C **24**
Briary M. TQ1: Torq 5E **25**
Bridge Ct. TQ13: Bov T 5C **6**
Bridge Ct. TQ9: Tot 3E **35**
Bridge Cft. TQ13: Ashb 3E **37**
Bridge Retail Pk. Torquay 1H **23**
Bridge Rd. TQ14: Shal 6C **12**
Bridge Rd. TQ2: Torq 4A **24**
Bridge Rd. TQ5: Chur F 2G **31**
Bridge Rd. TQ6: Kingsw 1D **34**
Bridge St. TQ11: B'leigh 4B **36**
Bridge St. TQ12: Ipp 5B **18**
Bridge St. TQ7: Kingsb 3C **38**
Bridge St. Ho. TQ12: New A 2G **15**
(off Bank St.)
BRIDGETOWN 4H **35**
Bridgetown TQ9: Tot 4G **35**
Bridgetown Ct. TQ9: Tot 4G **35**
Bridgetown Hill TQ9: Tot 4G **35**
Bridgewater Gdns. TQ9: Tot 4H **35**
Bridle Cl. TQ4: Good 5E **29**
Bridle Path, The TQ9: Tot 5F **35**
Brim Brook Ct. TQ2: Torq 1E **23**
(off Chinkwell Ri.)
Brim Hill TQ1: Maid 1H **21**
Brimlands TQ5: Brixh 3C **32**
Brimlands Ct. TQ5: Brixh 3C **32**
(off New Rd.)
Brimley Bus. Pk. TQ13: Bov T 5B **6**
Brimley Ct. TQ13: Bov T 5A **6**
Brimley Cross TQ13: Bov T 5A **6**
Brimley Dr. TQ14: Teignm 4E **13**
Brimley Gdns. TQ13: Bov T 5B **6**
Brimley Grange TQ13: Bov T 5A **6**
Brimley Halt TQ13: Bov T 5B **6**
Brimley Pk. TQ13: Bov T 5B **6**
Brimley Rd. TQ13: Bov T 5A **6**
Brimley Va. TQ13: Bov T 4B **6**
Briseham Cl. TQ5: Brixh 4E **33**
Briseham Rd. TQ5: Brixh 4E **33**
Britannia Mus. 3B **34**
Briwere Rd. TQ1: Torq 2H **23**
BRIXHAM 2E **33**
Brixham Battery Heritage Cen. 1C **32**
BRIXHAM COMMUNITY HOSPITAL 4D **32**
Brixham Ent. Est. TQ5: Brixh 3E **33**
Brixham Heritage Mus. 2D **32**
Brixham Holiday Pk. TQ5: Brixh 1C **32**
Brixham Leisure Cen. 3E **33**
Brixham Park & Ride 2G **31**
Brixham Rd. TQ4: Good 1B **28**
Brixham Rd. TQ4: Paig 1B **28**
Brixham Rd. TQ5: Brixh 2G **31**
Brixham Rd. TQ5: Chur F 2G **31**
Brixham Theatre 2D **32**
Brixham Yacht Club 1E **33**
Broadacre Dr. TQ5: Brixh 2E **33**
Broadgate Cres. TQ12: Kingsk 3G **19**
Broadgate Rd. TQ12: Kingsk 2G **19**
BROADLANDS 2E **15**
Broadlands TQ14: Shal 6C **12**
Broadlands Av. TQ12: New A 2F **15**
Broadlands Ct. TQ12: New A 2F **15**
Broadlands Rd. TQ4: Paig 1D **28**
Broad Leaf Pk. TQ14: Teignm 2G **13**
Broadley Dr. TQ2: Torq 6F **23**
Broadmeade Ct. TQ12: New A 3A **16**
Broadmeadow Ind. Est. TQ14: Teignm 4B **12**
Broadmeadow La. TQ14: Bi'ton 3A **12**
Broadmeadow La. TQ14: Teignm 3A **12**
Broadmeadow Sports Cen. 4B **12**
Broadmeadow Vw. TQ14: Teignm 3B **12**
Broad Oak Cres. TQ9: Tot 4G **35**
Broad Pk. TQ6: Dartm 4A **34**
Broadpark TQ13: Ashb 2F **37**
Broadpark TQ13: Bov T 5A **6**
Broadpark Rd. TQ2: Torq 6F **23**
Broadpark Rd. TQ3: Paig 3C **26**
Broadpath TQ9: Sto G 6A **28**
(not continuous)
Broad Reach TQ4: Broads 6F **29**
Broadridge Cl. TQ12: New A 1C **14**
BROADSANDS 6E **29**
Broadsands Av. TQ4: Broads 6F **29**
Broadsands Bend TQ4: Broads 5F **29**
Broadsands Ct. TQ4: Broads 6E **29**
Broadsands Gdns. TQ5: Chur F 1F **31**
Broadsands Pk. Rd. TQ4: Broads 5F **29**
Broadsands Pitch & Putt Course 6H **29**
Broadsands Rd. TQ4: Broads 6E **29**
Broad Steps TQ5: Brixh 2D **32**
(off Higher St.)
Broadstone TQ6: Dartm 1A **34** (3C **34**)
Broadstone Pk. Rd. TQ2: Torq 6G **23**
Broadway Av. TQ12: Kingst 3C **10**
B'way. Rd. TQ12: Kingst 3B **10**
Brockhurst Pk. TQ3: Marl 1A **26**
Brocks La. TQ12: Teigng 6G **7**
Brompton Gdns. TQ1: Torq 4F **25**
Bronescombe Av. TQ14: Bi'ton 5H **13**
Bronshill M. TQ1: Torq 3C **24**
Bronshill Rd. TQ1: Torq 3C **24**
Bronzerock Vw. EX7: Holc 1G **13**
Brook Cl. EX7: Holc 1G **13**
Brook Cl. TQ13: Bov T 3B **6**
Brook Ct. TQ5: Brixh 3C **32**
Brookdale Cl. TQ5: Brixh 3C **32**
Brookdale Ct. TQ5: Brixh 3C **32**
Brookdale Pk. TQ5: Brixh 3C **32**
Brookdale Ter. EX7: Daw 4E **5**
BROOKEADOR 2G **19**
Brookedor TQ12: Kingsk 2G **19**
Brookedor Gdns. TQ12: Kingsk 2G **19**
Brookfield Cl. TQ12: Kingst 3D **10**
Brookfield Cl. TQ3: Pres 3F **27**
Brookfield Dr. TQ14: Teignm 2E **13**
Brookfield Orchard TQ12: Kingst 4D **10**
Brook Haven Cl. TQ12: Kingsk 2G **19**
Brook Ho. EX7: Daw 4C **4**
(off Church St.)
Brooklands EX7: Daw 4D **4**
(off Alexandra Rd.)
Brooklands TQ9: Tot 4H **35**
Brooklands La. TQ2: Torq 5H **23**
Brook La. TQ14: Shal 6B **12**
Brook Orchard TQ12: Kingsk 2G **19**
Brook Rd. TQ12: Ipp 5B **18**
Brookside TQ7: Kingsb 4B **38**
Brookside Cl. TQ14: Teignm 4C **12**
Brookside Pathway TQ9: Darti 1E **35**
(off Nellies Wood Vw.)
Brook St. EX7: Daw 4D **4**
Brookvale Cl. TQ14: Shal 6B **12**
Brookvale Orchard TQ14: Shal 6B **12**
Brook Way TQ12: Kingst 1C **10**
Broomborough Ct. TQ9: Tot 4E **35**
Broom Cl. EX7: Daw 1F **5**
Broomhill Way TQ2: Torq 6D **20**
Broom Pk. TQ2: Torq 4E **21**
Brow Hill TQ12: H'fld 5F **7**
Brownhills Rd. TQ12: New A 2F **15**
Brownings End TQ12: E Ogw 4E **15**
Brownings Wlk. TQ12: E Ogw 4E **15**
Browns Bri. Rd. TQ2: Torq 5C **20**
Brownscombe Cl. TQ3: Marl 1A **26**
Brown's Hill TQ6: Dartm 1A **34** (4C **34**)
(off Clarence Hill)
Brunel Av. TQ2: Torq 3G **21**
Brunel Cl. TQ14: Teignm 3E **13**
Brunel Ct. EX7: Daw 4E **5**
Brunel M. TQ2: Torq 5A **24**
(off Solsbro Rd.)
Brunel Rd. TQ12: New A 2A **16**
Brunel Rd. TQ4: Broads 6F **29**
Brunswick Pl. EX7: Daw 4D **4**
Brunswick Sq. TQ1: Torq 3A **24**
(off Teignmouth Rd.)
Brunswick St. TQ14: Teignm 5E **13**
Brunswick Ter. TQ1: Torq 3A **24**
Brutus Cen. TQ9: Tot 4F **35**
(off Station Rd.)
Buckeridge Av. TQ14: Teignm 3D **12**
Buckeridge Rd. TQ14: Teignm 2D **12**
BUCKFAST 2B **36**
Buckfast Cl. TQ11: Buck 3C **36**
BUCKFASTLEIGH 4B **36**
Buckfastleigh Station South Devon Railway 4D **36**
Buckfastleigh Swimming Pool 5B **36**
Buckfast Rd. TQ11: Buck 2C **36**
BUCKLAND 3C **16**
Buckland Brake TQ12: New A 3B **16**
Buckland Hgts. TQ12: New A 2C **16**
Buckland Rd. TQ12: New A Buckland Brake 3B **16**
(not continuous)
Buckland Rd. TQ12: New A Haytor Dr. 2C **16**
Buckland Vw. TQ12: New A 1A **16**
Buckley St. TQ8: Salc 2H **39**
Bucks Cl. TQ13: Bov T 3C **6**
Bucks La. TQ13: Bov T 3C **6**
Buckwell Cl. TQ7: Kingsb 2C **38**
Buckwell Rd. TQ7: Kingsb 2C **38**
Budleigh Cl. TQ1: Torq 3E **25**
Bugle Pl. TQ12: New A 6D **8**
Bullands Cl. TQ13: Bov T 2B **6**
Buller Rd. TQ12: New A 3A **16**
Bull Ring TQ13: Ashb 4F **37**
Bunting Cl. TQ12: E Ogw 4F **15**
Bunting Cl. TQ14: Teignm 3C **12**
Bunting Way EX7: Daw 6D **4**
Burch Gdns. EX7: Daw 1E **5**
Burdouns Way TQ12: Kingst 1D **10**
Burdouns Way TQ12: New A 1D **10**
Burke Rd. TQ9: Tot 3G **35**
Burleigh Rd. TQ2: Torq 2F **23**
Burnet Rd. TQ12: New A 6D **8**
Burnham Ct. TQ12: Kingst 4D **10**
(off Orchid Av.)
Burnley Cl. TQ12: New A 1C **14**
Burnley Rd. TQ12: New A 1C **14**
Burn River Ri. TQ2: Torq 1E **23**
Burnthouse Hill TQ12: N Whil 6F **19**
Burridge Av. TQ2: Torq 4G **23**
Burridge La. TQ2: Torq 4B **24**
Burridge Rd. TQ2: Torq 4G **23**
Bursledon Ct. EX7: Daw 4F **5**
(off E. Cliff Rd.)
Burton Pl. TQ5: Brixh 3D **32**
Burton St. TQ5: Brixh 4D **32**
Burton Villa Cl. TQ5: Brixh 3D **32**
Burwood Pl. TQ14: Teignm 3F **13**
Bury Rd. TQ12: New A 1G **15**
Bushell Rd. TQ12: New A 1F **15**
Bushmead Av. TQ12: Kingsk 2H **19**
Butland Av. TQ3: Pres 2F **27**
Butland Rd. TQ12: Kingst 3C **10**
Buttercombe Cl. TQ12: E Ogw 5E **15**
Buttercup Wlk. EX7: Daw 3E **5**
Buttercup Way TQ12: New A 6D **8**
Butterlake TQ3: Marl 5A **22**
Buttlands Ind. Est. TQ12: Ipp 5C **18**
Butt's La. TQ12: Coff 5F **17**
Buzz Bingo Torquay 4B **24**
Bygones Torquay 1D **24**
Byng Cl. TQ12: New A 1C **16**
Byron Rd. TQ1: Torq 1B **24**
Byter Mill La. TQ9: Sto G 6B **28**

C

Cabbage Hill TQ13: Ashb 5E **37**
Cabourg Cl. TQ8: Salc 2G **39**
Cadewell Cres. TQ2: Torq 6C **20**
Cadewell La. TQ2: Torq 1F **23**
Cadewell Pk. Rd. TQ2: Torq 6B **20**

Cad La. TQ13: Ashb 4F **37**
.................................(off Stapledon La.)
Cadwell Rd. TQ3: Paig...........................4E **27**
Calvados Pk. TQ12: Kingst 4E **11**
Camborne Cres. TQ4: Good 5E **29**
Cambrian Cl. TQ4: Coll M 1A **28**
Cambridge Rd. TQ1: Torq........................6G **21**
Cambridge Rd. TQ5: Brixh 3B **32**
Camden Rd. TQ1: Torq 4C **24**
Camellia Cl. TQ5: Chur F 1G **31**
Camomile Way TQ12: New A 6E **9**
Camperdown Rd. TQ8: Salc 3F **39**
Campion Pl. TQ12: New A 6D **8**
Canada Hill TQ12: E Ogw 4E **15**
Canal Way TQ12: Kingst 5C **10**
Cannon Rd. TQ12: H'fld 5F **7**
Canons Cl. TQ14: Bi'ton...........................5G **13**
Capra Cl. TQ12: New A 1C **16**
Captains Rd. TQ12: Kingst.......................3C **10**
Carew Gdns. TQ12: New A 2C **16**
Carey Rd. TQ6: Dartm 4A **34**
Carhaix Way EX7: Daw 2E **5**
Carlile Rd. TQ5: Brixh 2B **32**
Carling Ct. TQ7: Kingsb 4B **38**
Carlisle St. TQ12: New A 2H **15**
Carlton Cl. TQ3: Pres 1F **27**
Carlton Dr. TQ3: Pres................................1F **27**
Carlton Pl. TQ14: Teignm 5E **13**
Carlton Rd. TQ1: Torq..............................3D **24**
Carlton Ter. EX7: Daw 4E **5**
Carnac Dr. EX7: Daw 2E **5**
Caroline Cl. TQ12: Kingsk 4H **19**
Carpenters Ct. TQ12: New A 3H **15**
.................................(off Church Rd.)
Carr Cl. TQ8: Salc 2F **39**
Carrions, The TQ9: Tot 4F **35**
Carswells TQ12: Kingsk 2G **19**
Cartwright Cres. TQ14: Teignm 3B **12**
Cary Av. TQ1: Torq 2D **24**
Cary Castle TQ1: Torq 1C **24**
Cary Castle Dr. TQ1: Torq.......................1C **24**
Cary Pde. TQ2: Torq 5C **24**
Cary Pk. TQ1: Torq 2C **24**
Cary Pk. Rd. TQ1: Torq 2D **24**
Cary Rd. TQ2: Torq 5B **24**
Cary Rd. TQ3: Pres 2D **26**
Cassiobury Way TQ2: Torq 5D **20**
Castle Cir. TQ1: Torq 4B **24**
Castle Cir. Ct. TQ1: Torq........................4B **24**
Castle Ct. TQ9: Tot 4E **35**
Castle La. TQ1: Torq 4C **24**
.................................(not continuous)
Castle La. TQ3: Comp 3A **22**
Castle Pk. Cl. TQ4: Paig..........................4C **28**
Castle Rd. TQ1: Torq 4B **24**
Castle Rd. TQ6: Dartm 6D **34**
Castle Rd. TQ6: Kingsw 5D **34**
Castle St. TQ9: Tot...................................3F **35**
Castle Vw. Ter. TQ9: Tot 3F **35**
.................................(off Castle St.)
Castle Way TQ12: New A..........................1D **14**
Castlewood Av. TQ12: New A....................6F **9**
Castor Cl. TQ5: Brixh 4E **33**
Castor La. TQ4: Good...............................4E **29**
Castor M. TQ5: Brixh 4D **32**
Castor Rd. TQ5: Brixh 4D **32**
Catherine Cres. TQ4: Paig 1C **28**
Cator TQ9: Sto G 5A **28**
Caunters Cl. TQ12: Ipp 5B **18**
C'way. Cross TQ12: Ipp 5C **18**
Cavalier Rd. TQ12: H'fld 6D **6**
Cavalry Dr. TQ12: H'fld 6E **7**
Cavendish Cl. EX7: Daw 3C **4**
Cavern Rd. TQ1: Torq 4C **24**
Cavern Rd. TQ5: Brixh 3D **32**
Cayman Cl. TQ2: Torq 4D **20**
Cecil Av. TQ3: Pres 3E **27**
Cecilia Rd. TQ3: Pres 2E **27**
Cecil M. TQ3: Paig 4E **27**
Cecil Rd. TQ3: Paig 5D **26**
Cedar EX7: Daw W...................................1G **5**
Cedar Cl. TQ14: Teignm...........................2F **13**

Cedar Ct. Rd. TQ1: Torq...........................2C **24**
Cedar Rd. TQ12: New A 5C **16**
Cedar Rd. TQ3: Pres 2F **27**
Cedars, The TQ9: Tot..............................3H **35**
Cedars Rd. TQ1: Torq...............................4D **24**
Cedar Way TQ5: Brixh 5B **32**
Celtic Ct. EX7: Daw....................................3E **5**
.................................(off Celtic Flds.)
Celtic Flds. EX7: Daw 3E **5**
Centenary Way TQ13: Bov T 1E **7**
Centenary Way TQ12: New A 5B **20**
Central Av. TQ3: Paig 4E **27**
Centry Ct. TQ5: Brixh 3F **33**
Centry Rd. TQ5: Brixh 3F **33**
CHADWELL CEN. 2G **27**
Chalfield Cl. TQ2: Torq 4E **21**
Challabrook La. TQ13: Bov T....................4A **6**
Challycroft Rd. TQ5: Brixh.......................6B **32**
Chandlers Hgts. TQ8: Salc 2G **39**
Channel Vw. La. EX7: Holc 1G **13**
Chantry Cl. TQ14: Teignm 2F **13**
Chapel, The TQ9: Tot..............................4G **35**
.................................(off The Plains)
Chapel Ct. TQ1: Torq 2A **24**
Chapel Ct. TQ9: Sto G 5A **28**
Chapel Hill TQ12: New A 2G **15**
Chapel La. TQ12: Live..............................1A **8**
Chapel La. TQ6: Dartm 2A **34** (4C **34**)
.................................(off Newcomen Rd.)
Chapel La. TQ9: Tot 4G **35**
Chapel Rd. TQ12: New A 2A **16**
Chapel St. TQ11: B'leigh...........................4B **36**
Chapple Cross TQ13: Bov T 5A **6**
Chariot Dr. TQ12: Kingst...........................5E **11**
Charlemont Rd. TQ14: Teignm 1D **12**
Charles Rd. TQ12: Kingsk........................5H **19**
Charles St. TQ6: Dartm 1A **34** (4C **34**)
Charlestown Rd. TQ3: Paig 4A **26**
Charlotte Cl. TQ2: Torq 1A **24**
Charlton Ct. TQ14: Teignm 5E **13**
.................................(off Bank St.)
Charlton Ho. EX7: Daw 4E **5**
.................................(off E. Cliff Rd.)
Charlwood Ct. TQ1: Torq 1D **24**
Charmouth Cl. TQ1: Torq 3E **25**
Chartwell Cl. TQ3: Paig 4B **26**
Chartwell Dr. TQ12: New A 1F **15**
Chatsworth Rd. TQ1: Torq 3C **24**
Chatto Rd. TQ1: Torq 2B **24**
Chatto Way TQ1: Torq 2B **24**
Chelsea Pl. TQ14: Teignm 4D **12**
CHELSTON 5H **23**
Chelston Rd. TQ12: New A 1G **15**
Chelston Rd. TQ2: Torq 6H **23**
Chercombe Bri. Rd. TQ12: New A 2B **14**
Chercombe Cl. TQ12: New A 1D **14**
Chercombe Valley Rd. TQ12: New A 1D **14**
Cherry Brook Dr. TQ4: Good 5E **29**
Cherry Brook Sq. TQ4: Good 5E **29**
Cherry Brook Wlk. TQ4: Good 4E **29**
Cherry Cross TQ9: Tot 5F **35**
Cherry Gdns. TQ3: Paig 4D **26**
Cherry Pk. Cl. TQ2: Torq 1G **27**
Cherrywood Cl. TQ12: New A 1D **14**
Chestnut Av. TQ1: Torq 5A **24**
Chestnut Av. TQ6: Dartm 3B **34**
Chestnut Dr. TQ12: Kingst 5E **11**
Chestnut Dr. TQ12: New A 4D **16**
Chestnut Dr. TQ5: Brixh 5B **32**
Chestnut Gro. TQ6: Dartm 3A **34**
Chestnut Wlk. EX7: Daw...........................5C **4**
Chichester Cl. TQ14: Teignm 1C **12**
Chichester Way TQ12: New A 2B **16**
Chilcote Cl. TQ1: Torq 1D **24**
Chiltern Cl. TQ2: Torq 6G **23**
Chilton Av. TQ14: Teignm 3E **13**
China Blue 3F **35**
Chinkwell Ri. TQ2: Torq 1E **23**
Chiseldon Farm TQ5: Brixh 5C **32**
Chiseldon Hill TQ5: Brixh 5D **32**
Chiseldon La. TQ5: Brixh 6D **32**
Choak Wlk. TQ13: Bov T 1E **7**
Chockland Rd. TQ12: Kingst.....................2C **10**

Christina Pde. TQ9: Tot 4H **35**
Christina Pk. TQ9: Tot 4H **35**
CHUDLEIGH KNIGHTON..............................2H **7**
Chudleigh Knighton Heath Nature Reserve
....2G **7**
Chudleigh Rd. TQ12: Kingst......................2B **10**
Chuley Hill TQ13: Ashb 5F **37**
Chuley Rd. TQ13: Ashb 5F **37**
Church Cl. TQ6: Dartm..............1B **34** (4C **34**)
Church Cl. TQ7: Kingsb..............................3C **38**
Church Cl. TQ9: Tot 4F **35**
Church Cotts. TQ3: Marl 5A **22**
Church Ct. TQ12: Kingst 5D **10**
Church Ct. TQ12: New A 2G **15**
Church Cross Rd. TQ11: B'leigh 3B **36**
Church End Rd. TQ12: Kingsk 2G **19**
Churchfields TQ6: Dartm..........................4A **34**
Churchfields Dr. TQ13: Bov T 3C **6**
Churchfields W. TQ6: Dartm 4A **34**
Church Hill TQ11: B'leigh...........................3B **36**
Church Hill TQ13: Marl 6A **22**
Church Hill TQ6: Kingsw 5D **34**
Church Hill Cotts. TQ3: Marl 6A **22**
Church Hill E. TQ5: Brixh 2D **32**
Church Hill W. TQ5: Brixh 2D **32**
Church Ho. Cl. TQ13: Chud K 2H **7**
Churchill Av. EX7: Daw 5D **4**
Churchill Ct. TQ5: Brixh 3D **32**
.................................(off Bolton St.)
Churchill Ct. TQ6: Dartm 1A **34** (4C **34**)
.................................(off Victoria Rd.)
Churchill Dr. TQ14: Teignm 3E **13**
Churchills, The TQ12: New A 1F **15**
Church La. TQ2: Torq 4A **24**
Church La. TQ8: Salc 2H **39**
Church M. TQ12: Kingst 5D **10**
Church Path TQ12: Ipp 5A **18**
Church Path TQ12: New A 6H **9**
Church Path TQ13: Ashb 4F **37**
Church Path TQ3: Paig 5E **27**
Church Rd. TQ1: Torq 6G **21**
Church Rd. TQ12: E Ogw 4C **14**
Church Rd. TQ12: New A 3H **15**
Church Rd. TQ14: Bi'ton 5H **13**
Church Rd. TQ3: Paig 4F **21**
Church Rd. TQ5: Chur F 2H **31**
Church Rd. TQ6: Dartm 3A **34**
Church St. EX7: Daw 4C **4**
Church St. TQ11: B'leigh............................4B **36**
Church St. TQ12: Kingst 5D **10**
Church St. TQ2: Torq 4A **24**
Church St. TQ3: Paig 5E **27**
Church St. TQ5: Brixh 2D **32**
Church St. TQ7: Kingsb 3C **38**
Church St. TQ8: Salc 2G **39**
Church Vw. EX7: Daw 4C **4**
Church Vw. TQ12: Kingst...........................5D **10**
.................................(off Greenhill Rd.)
Church Wlk. TQ9: Sto G 6A **28**
Churchward Rd. TQ3: Paig 4E **27**
Church Way TQ12: Coff 2A **20**
Church Way TQ12: New A 4B **16**
Churchway TQ1: Torq................................2D **24**
Churscombe Grn. TQ3: Marl......................1B **26**
Churscombe Pk. TQ3: Marl 1A **26**
Churscombe Rd. TQ3: Marl 1A **26**
Churston B'way. TQ4: Broads 6E **29**
Churston Cl. TQ5: Galm............................2F **31**
CHURSTON FERRERS.................................2H **31**
Churston Go-Karts 2G **31**
Churston Golf Course 1F **31**
Churston Rd. TQ5: Chur F 3H **31**
Churston Station Dartmouth Steam Railway
....2F **31**
Churston Way TQ5: Brixh 3B **32**
Cistern St. TQ9: Tot 4E **35**
Claddon La. TQ1: Maid 2F **21**
Clampet La. TQ14: Teignm 5E **13**
.................................(off Fore St.)
Clampitt Cl. TQ12: Ipp 6B **18**
Clampitt Rd. TQ12: Ipp 5B **18**
Clanage St. TQ14: Bi'ton..........................5G **13**
Claremont Av. TQ12: Kingsk.....................3H **19**

Clarence Hill TQ6: Dartm.................. 1A **34** (4C **34**)
Clarence St. TQ6: Dartm............................3C **34**
Clarendon Cl. TQ1: Torq..........................2A **24**
Clarendon Ct. 1Q1: Torq..............................5D **24**
Clarendon Rd. TQ12: Ipp.............................5B **18**
Clarendon Rd. TQ12: New A.........................2G **15**
Clay Ho. TQ14: Teignm...............................4D **12**
.... (off Clay La.)
CLAYLAND CROSS...1B **28**
Claylands Dr. TQ4: Paig............................1C **28**
Claylands Way TQ4: Paig..........................1B **28**
Clay La. TQ13: Chud.....................................3H **7**
Clay La. TQ13: Chud K.................................3H **7**
Clay La. TQ14: Teignm................................4D **12**
Claypark Ter. TQ9: Sto G...........................6B **28**
Cleatlands Cl. TQ4: Paig............................1B **28**
Cleaveland Ri. TQ12: E Ogw......................4E **15**
Cleland Ct. TQ14: Bi'ton............................5G **13**
Clennon Av. TQ4: Good..............................1E **29**
Clennon Ct. TQ2: Torq................................5F **21**
Clennon Dr. TQ4: Good...............................1E **29**
Clennon Gdns. TQ4: Good.........................1E **29**
Clennon Hgts. TQ4: Good...........................1E **29**
Clennon La. TQ2: Torq................................5E **21**
Clennon La. TQ4: Paig.................................1D **28**
Clennon Pk. TQ4: Good..............................1E **29**
Clennon Ri. TQ4: Good...............................1E **29**
Clennon Summit TQ4: Good.....................1E **29**
Cleveland Cl. TQ4: Paig................................6F **27**
Cleveland Pl. EX7: Daw.................................4E **5**
....(off High St.)
Cleveland Rd. TQ2: Torq...............................3A **24**
Cleveland Rd. TQ4: Paig................................6F **27**
Cleve Ter. TQ1: Torq.....................................4F **25**
Cliffden Cl. TQ14: Teignm............................4E **13**
Cliff Ho. TQ4: Paig.......................................6G **27**
Cliff M. TQ4: Paig..6G **27**
Clifford Av. TQ12: Kingst.............................2C **10**
Clifford Cl. TQ12: Kingst..............................4D **10**
Clifford Cl. TQ14: Shal.................................6C **12**
Clifford Dr. TQ12: H'fld..................................5E **7**
Clifford St. TQ12: Kingst.............................4D **10**
Cliff Pk. Av. TQ4: Good...............................2F **29**
Cliff Pk. Ct. TQ4: Good...............................2F **29**
Cliff Pk. Rd. TQ4: Good...............................3F **29**
Cliff Rd. TQ14: Teignm.................................2F **13**
Cliff Rd. TQ2: Torq......................................1H **27**
Cliff Rd. TQ4: Paig.......................................6G **27**
Cliff Rd. TQ8: Salc......................................5E **39**
Cliffs, The EX7: Daw.....................................6E **5**
Cliffside Rd. TQ1: Torq................................1D **24**
Clifton Bank TQ3: Paig................................5D **26**
Clifton Cl. TQ3: Paig....................................5C **26**
Clifton Cres. TQ3: Paig.................................5D **26**
Clifton Gdns. TQ3: Paig................................5D **26**
Clifton Gro. TQ1: Torq.................................5E **25**
Clifton Gro. TQ3: Paig..................................5D **26**
Clifton Pl. EX7: Daw..4C **4**
Clifton Pl. TQ8: Salc...................................2H **39**
Clifton Ri. TQ3: Paig....................................5D **26**
Clifton Rd. TQ3: Paig...................................5C **26**
Clifton Ter. TQ1: Torq..................................5C **24**
Climsland Rd. TQ4: Paig..............................6D **26**
Close, The EX7: Holc....................................1H **13**
Close, The TQ4: Broads...............................5F **29**
Close, The TQ5: Brixh.................................2C **32**
Cloud Berry Cotts. TQ4: Paig.....................2B **28**
Clovelly Ri. EX7: Daw....................................5D **4**
Clovelly Ri. TQ3: Paig..................................5B **26**
Clover Cl. TQ4: Paig.....................................3B **28**
Clover Dr. EX7: Daw.......................................3D **4**
Clover Way TQ12: New A.............................6E **9**
Clyst Av. TQ5: Brixh....................................5B **32**
Coach Ho., The TQ3: Paig...........................4F **27**
.... (off Steartfield Rd.)
Coach Ho. La. TQ2: Torq............................5H **23**
Coach Pl. TQ12: New A..............................3H **15**
Coach Rd. TQ12: New A..............................4G **15**
Coastguard Cotts. EX7: Daw........................4F **5**
Coastguard Cotts. TQ1: Torq......................6D **24**
Coburg Pl. TQ2: Torq...................................5C **24**
....(off Warren Rd.)

Cockhaven Cl. TQ14: Bi'ton..........................6G **13**
Cockhaven Mead TQ14: Bi'ton....................6G **13**
Cockhaven Rd. TQ14: Bi'ton.......................6G **13**
COCKINGTON...5F **23**
Cockington Country Pk..............................5F **23**
Cockington Court Craft Cen.......................5E **23**
Cockington La. TQ2: Torq............................4F **23**
Cockington La. TQ3: Pres............................2F **27**
Cockington Rd. TQ3: Marl............................6C **22**
COFFINSWELL...1B **20**
Coffinswell La. TQ12: Kingsk.......................3H **19**
Coker Av. TQ2: Torq....................................3E **21**
COLDEAST..1A **8**
Coldharbour TQ9: Tot...................................4H **35**
Coleman Av. TQ14: Teignm.........................3C **12**
Coleridge Ct. TQ2: Torq..............................5F **21**
Cole's Ct. TQ6: Dartm 2B **34** (4C **34**)
Cole's La. TQ12: Kingsk..............................2G **19**
Colin Rd. TQ3: Pres......................................4F **27**
Collaford La. TQ6: Dartm............. 1A **34** (4C **34**)
....(off Sth. Ford Rd.)
Collaton Ct. TQ2: Torq.................................1F **23**
Collaton Ho. TQ1: Torq................................5E **25**
.... (off Old Torwood Rd.)
Collaton M. TQ4: Coll M...............................1A **28**
Collaton Rd. TQ2: Torq................................6A **20**
COLLATON ST MARY......................................1A **28**
College TQ13: Bov T......................................2D **6**
College Rd. TQ12: New A.............................4G **15**
College Way TQ6: Dartm.............................3B **34**
Collett Way TQ12: New A..............................2B **16**
Colleybrook Cl. TQ12: Kingst......................1C **10**
Colley Cres. TQ3: Paig.................................5D **26**
Colley End Pk. TQ3: Paig.............................5D **26**
Colley End Rd. TQ3: Paig.............................5B **26**
Collingwood Cl. TQ1: Torq...........................6D **24**
Collingwood Cl. TQ6: Dartm.......................4A **34**
Collingwood Rd. TQ4: Paig.........................6D **26**
Collingwood Rd. TQ6: Dartm......................4A **34**
Collins Rd. TQ9: Tot.....................................3E **35**
Colston Rd. TQ11: B'leigh............................5D **36**
Colwyn Ct. TQ1: Torq..................................4F **25**
Combe Bank TQ5: Brixh..............................3C **32**
COMBEINTEIGNHEAD....................................1H **17**
Combe La. TQ5: Galm.................................5E **31**
COMBE PAFFORD..6F **21**
Combe Rd. TQ2: Torq..................................5G **21**
Commanders Cut TQ6: Dartm....................3B **34**
.... (off Chestnut Av.)
Commercial Rd. EX7: Daw.............................4E **5**
Commercial Rd. TQ4: Paig...........................5E **27**
Common La. TQ12: N Whil...........................4E **19**
Commons La. EX7: Daw.................................3D **4**
Commons La. TQ14: Shal..............................6B **12**
Commons Old Rd. TQ14: Shal......................6C **12**
.... (not continuous)
Compass Sth. TQ1: Torq..............................6G **25**
COMPTON...3A **22**
Compton Castle..3A **22**
Compton Ho. TQ1: Torq................................2D **24**
.... (off Palermo Rd.)
Compton Pl. TQ1: Torq.................................6G **21**
Condor Dr. TQ2: Torq...................................5C **20**
Condor Way TQ2: Torq.................................5C **20**
Congella Rd. TQ1: Torq................................3D **24**
Conifers, The TQ13: Bov T............................5C **18**
Conifers, The TQ2: Torq...............................4G **21**
Coniston Cl. TQ5: Brixh................................5B **32**
Coniston Ct. TQ4: Paig.................................1D **28**
Coniston Rd. TQ12: E Ogw...........................5E **15**
Conniford La. TQ12: Ipp...............................6B **18**
Connybear La. TQ12: Coff.............................6E **17**
Contour Hgts. TQ6: Kingsw.........................4D **34**
Conway Cres. TQ4: Paig..............................6E **27**
Conway Rd. TQ4: Paig.................................6E **27**
Cooke Dr. TQ12: Ipp....................................5C **18**
Cooks Cl. TQ12: Kingst................................4E **11**
Cooks Cl. TQ13: Ashb..................................3G **37**
Cookworthy Ct. TQ7: Kingsb.......................2B **38**
Cookworthy Mus...2B **38**
Cookworthy Rd. TQ7: Kingsb......................3B **38**
COOMBE...2C **12**
Coombe, The TQ5: Galm.............................2E **31**

Coombe, The TQ6: Dartm............................3C **34**
Coombe Av. TQ14: Teignm...........................4C **12**
Coombe Cl. TQ13: Bov T...............................3D **6**
Coombe Cl. TQ6: Dartm................................3C **34**
Coombe Cross TQ13: Bov T............................3D **6**
Coombe La. TQ13: Bov T................................3D **6**
Coombe La. TQ14: Teignm............................2C **12**
Coombe La. TQ2: Torq..................................6F **21**
Coombe Mdw. TQ13: Bov T...........................3D **6**
Coombe Pk. Cotts. TQ1: Torq......................6F **21**
Coombe Pk. TQ14: Teignm..........................3C **12**
Coombe Rd. TQ14: Shal..............................6A **12**
Coombe Rd. TQ3: Pres.................................2E **27**
Coombe Rd. TQ6: Dartm..............................3C **34**
Coombesend Rd. TQ12: Kingst....................4E **11**
.... (not continuous)
Coombesend Rd. E. TQ12: Kingst................4F **11**
Coombeshead Rd. TQ12: New A..................1E **15**
Coombe Shute TQ9: Sto G..........................6A **28**
Coombe Va. Rd. TQ14: Teignm.....................3C **12**
Coombe Vw. TQ14: Teignm.........................2B **12**
Copley Cl. TQ3: Paig....................................5C **26**
Copperwood Cl. TQ13: Ashb........................4E **37**
Coppice, The EX7: Daw...................................6D **4**
Copp Path EX7: Daw.......................................5C **4**
.... (off Taylor Cl.)
Copse, The TQ12: New A...............................3D **16**
Copythorne Cl. TQ5: Brixh...........................3B **32**
Copythorne Pk. TQ5: Brixh...........................3B **32**
Copythorne Rd. TQ5: Brixh..........................2H **31**
Copythorne Rd. TQ5: Chur F.........................2H **31**
Corfe Cres. TQ2: Torq...................................1A **24**
Cormorant Cl. TQ2: Torq.............................4C **20**
Cornacre Cl. TQ2: Torq.................................2F **23**
Cornacre Rd. TQ2: Torq...............................3F **23**
Cornerstones TQ9: Tot.................................4F **35**
.... (off Warland)
Cornfield Grn. TQ2: Torq.............................5G **21**
.... (off Bellrock Cl.)
Cornflower Cl. TQ4: Paig..............................3B **28**
Cornflower Way TQ12: New A......................6E **9**
Corn Pk. Rd. TQ12: A'well............................1B **18**
Coronation Av. EX7: Daw...............................5D **4**
Coronation Rd. TQ12: Kingst.......................4D **10**
Coronation Rd. TQ12: New A........................2F **15**
Coronation Rd. TQ7: Kingsb.........................3C **38**
Coronation Rd. TQ8: Salc.............................2G **39**
Coronation Rd. TQ9: Tot...............................3F **35**
Coronation St. TQ14: Shal...........................6C **12**
Corsham Rd. TQ4: Paig...............................6D **26**
Coryton Cl. EX7: Daw.....................................4D **4**
Cotehele Dr. TQ3: Paig.................................4A **26**
Cotmore Cl. TQ5: Brixh.................................5B **32**
Cotswold Cl. TQ2: Torq................................6G **23**
Cottey Mdw. TQ12: Kingst...........................5D **10**
County Court Torquay & Newton Abbot.....6D **20**
Courtenay Gdns. TQ12: New A....................3H **15**
Courtenay Mnr. TQ1: Torq...........................5D **24**
.... (off Grafton Rd.)
Courtenay Pk. TQ12: New A.........................2A **16**
Courtenay Pl. TQ14: Teignm........................5E **13**
.... (off Den Promenade)
Courtenay Rd. TQ12: New A.........................3G **15**
Courtenay Rd. TQ4: Good............................3F **29**
Courtenay St. TQ12: New A..........................2G **15**
Courtenay St. TQ8: Salc..............................2G **39**
Courtenay Ter. TQ8: Salc.............................2G **39**
.... (off Devon Rd.)
Court Farm Barn TQ12: A'well.....................1C **18**
Courtfield TQ9: Tot.......................................4H **35**
Court Ga. Cl. TQ12: Ipp...............................6A **18**
Court Grange TQ12: A'well...........................1A **18**
Court Grange La. TQ12: A'well.....................1A **18**
Courtlage Wlk. TQ7: Kingsb.........................2B **38**
Courtland Rd. TQ2: Torq..............................2E **23**
Courtland Rd. TQ3: Paig...............................4E **27**
Courtlands Rd. TQ12: New A........................3A **16**
Court M. TQ12: New A..................................2G **15**
.... (off Wolborough St.)
Court Rd. TQ12: A'well.................................1C **18**
Court Rd. TQ2: Torq.....................................4F **23**
Courtyard, The TQ12: New A........................2G **15**
.... (off Wolborough St.)

Cousens Cl. EX7: Daw 2F **5**
Coventry Farm Trad. Est. TQ12: Kingsk.......5H **19**
Coverdale Ct. TQ3: Paig..............................5E **27**
....(off Bishops Pl.)
Coverdale Rd. TQ3: Paig.............................5E **27**
Cowslip Cres. TQ12: New A 6D **8**
Cowslip Mdw. EX7: Daw 2E **5**
Coxs Steps TQ6: Dartm 1A **34** (4C **34**)
....(off Clarence Hill)
Crabshell Hgts. TQ7: Kingsb..........................5C **38**
Cranberry Gro. TQ4: Paig 3A **28**
Cranesbill Way TQ12: New A 6D **8**
Cranford Rd. TQ3: Pres 2D **26**
Creek Rd. TQ6: Dartm 3A **34**
Crescent, The TQ5: Brixh.............................4E **33**
Crescent Ct. TQ6: Dartm..............................4A **34**
....(off Townstal Cres.)
Cresswell Cl. TQ12: Kingsk 2H **19**
Crestas, The TQ1: Torq...............................3D **24**
Crest Hill TQ11: B'leigh................................4B **36**
Crest Vw. TQ4: Paig 6F **27**
Cricketers Grn. TQ2: Torq.............................1H **23**
Cricket Fld. Rd. TQ12: New A..........................1H **15**
Cricketfield Ct. TQ2: Torq.............................2H **23**
Cricket La. TQ11: B'leigh.............................3A **36**
Crispin Rd. TQ7: Kingsb...............................3B **38**
Croft, The TQ12: E Ogw 4C **14**
Croft Cl. TQ12: E Ogw 4C **14**
Croft Ct. TQ2: Torq....................................4B **24**
....(off Abbey Rd.)
Croft Hill TQ2: Torq....................................4B **24**
Croft Mdw. TQ12: Ipp 5B **18**
Croft Orchard TQ12: Ipp 5B **18**
Croft Rd. TQ12: E Ogw 4B **14**
Croft Rd. TQ12: Ipp 5B **18**
Croft Rd. TQ2: Torq....................................4B **24**
Croft Rd. TQ8: Salc 2G **39**
Croftview Ter. TQ8: Salc 2G **39**
....(off Island St.)
Croker's Mdw. TQ13: Bov T 2B **6**
Crokers Way TQ12: Ipp 5B **18**
Cromartie Point TQ2: Torq 1H **27**
....(off Livermead Hill)
Cromwells Way TQ13: Bov T..........................2B **6**
Croppins Cl. TQ11: B'leigh............................4C **36**
Cross Grange Trad. Est. TQ12: H'fld 4E **7**
Cross Hill TQ12: C'head................................2F **17**
Cross Hill TQ2: N'ton 2F **17**
Cross La. TQ12: N'ton 1G **17**
Cross La. TQ8: E Port.................................3H **39**
Crossley Cl. TQ12: Kingst 3D **10**
Crossley Moor Rd. TQ12: Kingst 4D **10**
Cross Pk. TQ12: N'ton 1G **17**
Cross Pk. TQ5: Brixh..................................4C **32**
Crosspark TQ9: Tot 3H **35**
Crosspark Av. TQ2: Torq..............................1F **23**
Crossparks TQ6: Dartm 5A **34**
Crossway TQ4: Good 3F **29**
Crown & Anchor Way TQ3: Paig 5E **27**
Crownhill Ct. TQ2: Torq...............................3H **23**
Crownhill Cres. TQ5: Galm 2E **31**
Crownhill Pk. TQ2: Torq...............................3H **23**
Crownhill Ri. TQ2: Torq...............................3H **23**
Crownley La. TQ9: Sto G 5A **28**
Crown Sq. TQ14: Shal 6C **12**
Crowther's Hill TQ6: Dartm 2A **34** (4C **34**)
Crystal Cl. TQ4: Good 3F **29**
Cudhill Rd. TQ5: Brixh................................3C **32**
Culm Cl. TQ2: Torq....................................1E **23**
Culverdale TQ9: Tot 5H **35**
Culver Pk. Cl. TQ7: Kingsb...........................5D **38**
Culver Rd. TQ2: Torq..................................1E **23**
Culvery Grn. TQ2: Torq...............................1E **23**
Cumber Cl. TQ5: Brixh................................2C **32**
Cumber Dr. TQ5: Brixh................................2C **32**
Cumberland Grn. TQ5: Brixh 2C **32**
Cummings Cross TQ12: Live..........................1A **8**
Curledge St. TQ4: Paig 6E **27**
Curlew Cl. TQ2: Torq..................................4B **20**
Custom Ho. Hill TQ14: Teignm 5D **12**
Cuthbert Cl. TQ1: Torq................................6F **21**
Cypress Cl. TQ2: Torq.................................4B **24**
Cypress Ct. TQ4: Paig 6E **27**
....(off Fisher St.)

D

Daccabridge Rd. TQ12: Kingsk 3G **19**
DACCOMBE 3D **20**
Daccombe Hill TQ12: Dacc...........................3D **20**
Daccombe Mill La. TQ12: Coff 3H **19**
Daccombe Mill La. TQ12: Kingsk 3H **19**
Daddyhole Plain TQ1: Torq............................6E **25**
Daddyhole Rd. TQ1: Torq 6D **24**
....(not continuous)
Daggers Copse TQ12: New A 2E **15**
Dagmar St. TQ14: Shal 6C **12**
Daimonds La. TQ14: Teignm 4D **12**
Dainton Bus. Pk. TQ12: H'fld.........................4G **7**
Dainton Ct. TQ4: Good 3F **29**
Dainton M. TQ4: Paig.................................6E **27**
Dainton Pk. Golf Course 4A **18**
Dairy Hill TQ12: Torq.................................2F **23**
Daison Cotts. TQ1: Torq..............................1C **24**
Daison Cres. TQ1: Torq...............................1C **24**
Daisy La. TQ12: New A 6D **8**
Daisys Path TQ9: Sto G 5A **28**
Dalverton Ct. TQ5: Brixh..............................1D **32**
Danby Hgts. Cl. TQ1: Torq............................5F **25**
Dandelion Pl. TQ12: New A.............................6D **8**
Dane Heath Bus. Pk. TQ12: H'fld 4E **7**
Danvers Rd. TQ2: Torq 5E **21**
Daphne Cl. TQ1: Torq.................................5E **25**
D'arcy Ct. TQ12: New A 1H **15**
Darky La. TQ7: Kingsb................................1A **38**
Darracombe Cres. TQ12: New A 6F **9**
Darran Cl. TQ12: Kingst...............................4E **11**
Darran Rd. TQ12: Kingst...............................4E **11**
Dart Av. TQ2: Torq 1F **23**
Dartbridge Mnr. TQ11: B'leigh 3C **36**
Dart Bri. Rd. TQ11: B'leigh............................4C **36**
Dartington La. TQ9: Darti 2E **35**
Dart Marina TQ6: Dartm 2C **34**
Dart Marine Pk. TQ9: Tot 5G **35**
....(off Station Rd.)
Dartmoor Ct. TQ13: Bov T..............................3B **6**

Dartmoor Otters & Buckfast Butterflies
....4D **36**
DARTMOUTH......................1B **34** (4C **34**)
Dartmouth Ct. TQ6: Dartm...... 2B **34** (4C **34**)
....(off Oxford St.)
Dartmouth Mus. 1B **34** (4C **34**)

Dartmouth Outdoor Heated Swimming Pool
....5A **34**
Dartmouth Rd. TQ4: Broads..........................5E **27**
Dartmouth Rd. TQ4: Good 5E **27**
Dartmouth Rd. TQ4: Paig 5E **27**
Dartmouth Rd. TQ5: Chur F...........................1E **31**

Dartmouth Steam Railway Churston Station
....2F **31**

Dartmouth Steam Railway Goodrington Station
....1F **29**

Dartmouth Steam Railway Greenway Halt
....4D **30**

Dartmouth Steam Railway Kingswear Station
....4D **34**

Dartmouth Steam Railway Paignton Station
....6E **27**
Dartmouth Steam Railway Vis. Cen.......... 4D **34**
Dartmouth to Dartmouth Castle Foot Ferry
.....................................1B **34** (5D **34**)
Dartmouth to Dittisham Foot Ferry
...................................1B **34** (4C **34**)
Dartmouth to Totnes Foot Ferry
...................................1B **34** (4D **34**)
Dartmouth Visitor Cen.................1B **34** (4C **34**)
Dartmouth Yacht Club.................2B **34** (4C **34**)
....(off South Embankment)
Darton Gro. TQ9: Sto G 6A **28**
Dart Rock Climbing Cen..............................4D **36**
Dartside TQ9: Tot 2E **35**
Dartside Ct. TQ6: Dartm...............................3C **34**
....(off Clarence St.)
Dartside Quay TQ5: Galm 3D **30**
Dart Vw. Rd. TQ5: Galm 1E **31**
Dart Vs. TQ9: Tot 5F **35**
Darwin Ct. TQ2: Torq..................................4E **21**

Darwin Cres. TQ2: Torq...............................4E **21**
Dashpers TQ5: Brixh..................................4C **32**
Daveys Elm Vw. TQ4: Good...........................3E **29**
David Rd. TQ3: Paig...................................4D **26**
Davies Av. TQ4: Good 4E **29**
Davis Av. TQ2: Torq...................................3G **23**
Davis Ct. TQ12: New A 1F **15**
Dawes Cl. TQ12: E Ogw................................5E **15**
DAWLISH 4E **5**
Dawlish Bus. Pk. EX7: Daw............................1F **5**
DAWLISH COMMUNITY HOSPITAL 4D **4**
Dawlish Leisure Cen..................................2F **5**
Dawlish Mus. 4D **4**
Dawlish Rd. TQ14: Teignm 4E **13**
Dawlish Station (Rail) 4E **5**
Dawlish St. TQ14: Teignm 4E **13**
Dawlish Tourist Info. Cen..............................4E **5**
Daws Mdw. TQ2: Kingst 5D **10**
Daymond Dr. TQ13: Bov T.............................1E **7**
Deans Cl. TQ14: Bi'ton................................5G **13**
De Courcy Rd. TQ8: Salc 5E **39**
Decoy Country Pk. 4H **15**
Decoy Discovery Cen.................................4A **16**
Decoy Ind. Est. TQ12: New A 5A **16**
Decoy Rd. TQ12: New A...............................3A **16**
Deep Dene Cl. TQ5: Brixh.............................4B **32**
Deer Pk. Av. TQ14: Teignm 3C **12**
Deer Pk. Cl. TQ14: Teignm 3C **12**
Deer Pk. Dr. TQ14: Teignm 3C **12**
Deerpark La. TQ12: Hacc.............................6G **17**
Deers Leap Cl. TQ3: Pres.............................1E **27**
Dell Ct. TQ12: New A 2H **15**
Den, The TQ14: Teignm 5E **13**
Den Brook Cl. TQ1: Torq..............................3E **25**
Denby Ho. TQ4: Paig..................................6F **27**
Den Cres. TQ14: Teignm 5E **13**
Dendy Rd. TQ4: Paig..................................5E **27**
Den Prom. TQ14: Teignm 5E **13**
Den Rd. TQ14: Teignm 5E **13**
Denys Rd. TQ1: Torq..................................3D **24**
Denys Rd. TQ9: Tot 4F **35**
Derby Rd. TQ7: Kingsb................................4C **38**
Derncleugh Gdns. EX7: Holc.........................1H **13**
Derrell Rd. TQ4: Paig.................................1D **28**
Derwent Rd. TQ1: Torq................................2C **24**
De Tracey Pk. TQ13: Bov T.............................3C **6**
Devon Bird of Prey Cen., The 3A **18**
Devoncourt TQ5: Brixh................................1F **33**
Devondale Ct. EX7: Daw W............................1H **5**
Devon Guild of Craftsmen, The 3C **6**
Devon Heath TQ13: Chud K...........................2H **7**
Devon Ho. Dr. TQ13: Bov T.............................2D **6**
Devon Ho. Flats TQ13: Bov T..........................2D **6**
Devon M. TQ13: Chud K................................2H **7**
....(off Devon Heath)
Devon Pl. TQ9: Tot....................................4G **35**
....(off Bridgetown)
Devon Rd. TQ8: Salc..................................4F **39**
Devonshire Ho. TQ1: Torq............................1D **24**
Devonshire Retail Pk. TQ4: Paig 4C **28**
Devon Sq. TQ12: New A...............................2H **15**
Devon Sq. TQ7: Kingsb................................3B **38**
Devons Rd. TQ1: Torq.................................2D **24**
Devon Ter. TQ9: Tot...................................4G **35**

Devon Valley Holiday Village
TQ14: Shal..6A **12**
Devon Vw. EX7: Daw W................................1H **5**
Devon Windsurf & Canoe Cen.......................4H **15**
Dewberry Dr. TQ4: Good..............................2A **28**
Diane Cl. TQ4: Good...................................4C **28**
Diane Ct. TQ4: Good...................................4C **28**
....(off Diane Cl.)
Dickers Ter. TQ12: Kingst.............................4D **10**
Diptford Cl. TQ4: Paig.................................2B **28**
Dittisham Sailing Club................................4A **30**
Divett Ct. TQ12: Live...................................1A **8**
Dixon Cl. TQ3: Paig...................................2B **26**
Dobbin Arch TQ12: Kingsk 3G **19**
Doctors Rd. TQ5: Brixh................................4D **32**
DODBROOKE 3D **38**
Dodbrooke Ct. TQ7: Kingsb...........................3C **38**
Dolbeare Bus. Pk. TQ13: Ashb 3G **37**

Dolbeare Rd. TQ13: Ashb 3G 37
....(not continuous)
Dolphin Ct. TQ14: Shal 6C 12
....(off Albion St.)
Dolphin Ct. TQ5: Brixh 2D 32
Dolphin Ct. Rd. TQ3: Pres 2C 26
Dolphin Cres. TQ3: Pres 2C 26
Dolphion Sq. TQ13: Bov T 3B 6
Dorchester Gro. TQ2: Torq 6E 21
Dornafield Ct. TQ12: Ipp 5B 18
Dornafield Dr. E. TQ12: Ipp 5B 18
Dornafield Dr. W. TQ12: Ipp 5B 18
Dornafield Rd. TQ12: Ipp 5B 18
Dosson Gro. TQ1: Torq 2H 23
Douglas Av. TQ5: Brixh 3F 33
Douglas Ho. TQ14: Teignm 4D 12
....(off Bitton Pk. Rd.)
Dower Ct. TQ3: Pres 3F 27
Dower Rd. TQ1: Torq 2B 24
Downaway La. TQ12: Dacc 1D 20
Downfield Cl. TQ5: Brixh 4B 32
Dragoon Cl. TQ12: H'fld 6D 6
Drake Av. TQ14: Teignm 1C 12
Drake Av. TQ2: Torq 3F 23
Drake Dr. TQ4: Good 3D 28
Drake La. TQ13: Bov T 3D 6
Drake Rd. TQ12: New A 2C 16
Drake Rd. TQ13: Bov T 3D 6
Drake Rd. TQ8: Salc 2F 39
Drakes Rd. TQ4: Paig 1B 28
Drew's Fld. La. TQ3: Comp 2A 22
Drew St. TQ5: Brixh 4D 32
Drive, The EX7: Daw 4E 5
Drive, The TQ14: Bi'ton 5F 13
Drive, The TQ5: Brixh 5D 32
Drum Way TQ12: H'fld 5E 7
Duchy Av. TQ3: Pres 1D 26
Duchy Dr. TQ3: Pres 1D 26
Duchy Gdns. TQ3: Pres 6D 22
Duchy Pk. TQ3: Pres 1D 26
Duckspond Cl. TQ11: B'leigh 5A 36
Duckspond Rd. TQ11: B'leigh 5A 36
Dukes Cl. TQ3: Paig 5B 26
Dukes Rd. TQ9: Tot 4H 35
Duke St. TQ6: Dartm 1A 34 (4C 34)
Duke St. TQ7: Kingsb 3B 38
Dulverton M. TQ3: Paig 3B 26
Dunboyne Ct. TQ1: Torq 1C 24
....(off St Marychurch Rd.)
Duncannon Cl. TQ9: Sto G 6A 28
Duncannon Mead TQ9: Sto G 6A 28
Duncombe St. TQ7: Kingsb 2C 38
Dunley La. TQ13: Bov T 1G 7
Dunmere Rd. TQ1: Torq 3C 24
Dunmore Ct. TQ14: Shal 6D 12
Dunmore Dr. TQ14: Shal 6D 12
Dunning Rd. TQ14: Teignm 2C 12
Dunning Wlk. TQ14: Teignm 2C 12
....(off Lake Av.)
Dunstone Cl. TQ3: Paig 2B 26
Dunstone Pk. Rd. TQ3: Paig 2B 26
Dunstone Rd. TQ3: Paig 2B 26
Durham Cl. TQ3: Pres 2E 27
Durleigh Rd. TQ5: Brixh 3C 32

E

Eagle Cl. TQ12: Kingst 1C 10
Eaglewood Cl. TQ2: Torq 5B 20
Ealing Cl. TQ5: Brixh 4E 33
Earls Ct. TQ1: Torq 3A 24
Earlswood Dr. TQ3: Paig 4A 26
East Cliff Cl. EX7: Daw 3E 5
Eastcliffe Ho. TQ14: Teignm 3F 13
East Cliff Gdns. EX7: Daw 3E 5
East Cliff Rd. EX7: Daw 3E 5
Eastcliff Wlk. TQ14: Teignm 4F 13
East End Ter. TQ13: Ashb 2H 37
Easterfield La. TQ1: Torq 5G 21
Eastern Backway TQ7: Kingsb 3C 38
....(off Church St.)
Eastern Esplanade TQ4: Paig 6F 27
Eastern Rd. TQ13: Ashb 3G 37

EAST OGWELL 4C 14
East Pafford Av. TQ2: Torq 5G 21
EAST PORTLEMOUTH 3H 39
East St. TQ12: Den 6A 14
East St. TQ12: Ipp 5B 18
East St. TQ12: New A 2G 15
East St. TQ13: Ashb 4F 37
East St. TQ13: Bov T 2C 6
East St. TQ2: Torq 3A 24
Eastwood Cres. TQ12: New A 1D 14
Eaton Ct. TQ14: Teignm 2D 12
Eaton Hall Dr. TQ6: Dartm 3B 34
....(off Flagstaff Rd.)
Eaton Pl. TQ4: Paig 6E 27
Ebdon Way TQ1: Torq 3A 24
Ebenezer Rd. TQ3: Paig 6D 26
Ebrington St. TQ7: Kingsb 3C 38
Eden Cl. TQ5: Brixh 4D 32
Eden Gro. TQ3: Paig 4C 26
Edenhurst Ct. TQ1: Torq 3C 24
....(off Parkhill Rd.)
Eden Pk. TQ5: Brixh 4D 32
Edens Ct. TQ14: Teignm 4E 13
....(off Heywoods Rd.)
Eden Vale Rd. TQ3: Paig 3C 26
Edgelands La. TQ12: Ipp 6A 18
Edgeley Rd. TQ2: Torq 5F 21
EDGINSWELL 1F 23
Edginswell Cl. TQ2: Torq 6B 20
Edginswell La. TQ12: Kingsk 4G 19
Edginswell La. TQ2: Torq 6B 20
Edinburgh Rd. TQ5: Brixh 4E 33
Edinburgh Vs. TQ1: Torq 3A 24
Edmonds Wlk. TQ1: Torq 3A 24
Egerton Rd. TQ1: Torq 3D 24
Eight Acre Dr. TQ4: Paig 4C 28
Elba Cl. TQ4: Good 4F 29
Elberry La. TQ4: Broads 6G 29
Elberry La. TQ5: Chur F 3G 31
Elizabethan Way TQ14: Teignm 2F 13
Elizabeth Av. TQ5: Brixh 6B 32
Elizabeth Ct. TQ2: Torq 4A 24
Elizabeth Ct. TQ9: Tot 4H 35
Elizabeth Sq. TQ12: New A 3C 16
Elkins Hill TQ5: Brixh 2E 33
Ellacombe Chu. Rd. TQ1: Torq 3C 24
Ellacombe Rd. TQ1: Torq 3C 24
Ellerslie Ho. TQ14: Shal 6D 12
....(off Marine Pde.)
Ellesmere TQ1: Torq 5D 24
Ellesmere Rd. TQ1: Torq 4F 25
Ellington Ct. TQ2: Torq 5B 24
....(off St Luke's Rd. Sth.)
Elliott Ct. TQ12: Ipp 5B 18
Elliott Gro. TQ5: Brixh 3B 32
Elliott Plain TQ11: B'leigh 4C 36
Elm Bank TQ11: B'leigh 5A 36
Elm Dr. TQ12: Kingst 4D 10
Elmfield Way TQ12: Kingst 5D 10
Elm Gro. TQ14: Teignm 1D 12
Elm Gro. Cl. EX7: Daw 3E 5
Elm Gro. Dr. EX7: Daw 3E 5
Elm Gro. Rd. EX7: Daw 2E 5
Elmhirst Dr. TQ9: Tot 4H 35
Elmhurst Ct. TQ14: Teignm 4D 12
El Monte Cl. TQ14: Teignm 3D 12
Elm Pk. TQ3: Paig 6C 26
Elm Rd. TQ12: New A 2H 15
Elm Rd. TQ5: Brixh 5B 32
Elmsleigh Ct. TQ4: Paig 6E 27
....(off Elmsleigh Rd.)
Elmsleigh Pk. TQ4: Paig 6E 27
Elmsleigh Rd. TQ4: Paig 6E 27
Elm Tree Cl. TQ12: Torq 5B 20
Elm Wlk. TQ9: Tot 4H 35
Elmwood Av. TQ12: New A 1D 14
Elmwood Cres. EX7: Daw 3E 5
Elsdale Rd. TQ4: Paig 1D 28
Embankment, The TQ14: Shal 6B 12

Embankment Rd. TQ7: Kingsb 4C 38
Ember Rd. TQ8: Salc 2F 39
Emblett Dr. TQ12: New A 1D 14
Emblett Hill Vw. TQ12: E Ogw 4E 15
Embury Cl. TQ12: Kingsk 3H 19
Emlyn Pl. TQ13: Bov T 3C 6
Emmetts Pk. TQ13: Ashb 3G 37
Emmetts Pl. TQ12: A'well 1C 18
Empire Ct. TQ1: Torq 2B 24
Empire Rd. TQ1: Torq 2B 24
Empsons Cl. EX7: Daw 4C 4
Empsons Hill EX7: Daw 4C 4
Enfield Rd. TQ1: Torq 2D 24
English Riviera Visitor Info. Cen. 6C 24
Erica Dr. TQ2: Torq 4E 21
Esplanade TQ14: Teignm 5E 13
Esplanade, The TQ4: Paig 6F 27
Esplanade Rd. TQ3: Paig 5F 27
Esplanade Rd. TQ4: Paig 6F 27
Estuary Ct. TQ14: Teignm 4B 12
Estuary Vw. TQ12: Kingst 5E 11
Estura TQ8: Salc 3G 39
Eugene Rd. TQ3: Pres 3F 27
Eureka Ter. TQ13: Bov T 2C 6
Eveleigh Cl. TQ5: Brixh 4D 32
Exe Hill TQ2: Torq 1E 23
Exeter Av. TQ2: Torq 6E 21
Exeter Cross TQ12: Live 1B 8
Exeter Rd. TQ12: Kingst 1C 10
Exeter Rd. TQ12: Kingst 5A 10
Exeter Rd. TQ12: New A 5A 10
Exeter Rd. TQ12: New A 6G 9
Exeter Rd. TQ14: Teignm 2C 12
Exeter St. TQ14: Teignm 4D 12
Explorer Wlk. TQ2: Torq 4E 21
....(off Kingsley Av.)

F

Factory Row TQ2: Torq 4B 24
Fairfax Pl. TQ6: Dartm 2B 34 (4C 34)
Fairfax Rd. TQ12: H'fld 6D 6
Fairfield Cl. TQ13: Bov T 3B 6
Fairfield Cl. TQ7: Kingsb 4C 38
Fairfield Rd. TQ12: Kingsk 4H 19
Fairfield Rd. TQ2: Torq 1A 24
Fairfield Ter. TQ2: Torq 2H 15
Fairies Hill TQ11: B'leigh 3C 36
Fair Isle Cl. TQ2: Torq 5D 20
Fairlawns Pk. TQ4: Good 3E 29
Fairlea Cl. EX7: Daw 1F 5
Fairlea Rd. EX7: Daw 2E 5
Fair Oaks TQ14: Teignm 3C 12
Fairseat Cl. TQ9: Tot 4G 35
Fairview Pk. TQ13: Bov T 5B 6
Fairview Rd. TQ12: Kingst 6A 14
Fairview Rd. TQ6: Dartm 1A 34 (4B 34)
Fairwater Cl. TQ12: Kingst 4E 11
Fairwaters TQ12: Kingst 3D 10
Fairway Cl. TQ5: Chur F 2G 31
Fairy La. TQ11: B'leigh 5A 36
Falkland Dr. TQ12: Kingst 3E 11
Falkland Rd. TQ2: Torq 5A 24
Falkland Way TQ14: Teignm 2C 12
Falloway Cl. TQ2: Torq 5F 21
Fallowfield Cl. TQ12: New A 2C 16
Falmouth Cl. TQ2: Torq 1E 23
Farleigh TQ12: New A 6C 8
Farm Cl. TQ12: Kingsk 1G 19
Farm Ct. TQ5: Brixh 2F 33
Farmyard La. TQ3: Comp 3A 22
Farthing La. TQ3: Marl 1A 26
Farwell Rd. TQ9: Tot 4E 35
Fay Rd. EX7: Daw 4E 5
Fern Cl. TQ5: Brixh 3E 33
Ferncombe Cl. TQ12: Kingst 1D 10
Ferncombe Dr. TQ12: Kingst 1D 10
Ferndale TQ6: Dartm 2A 34 (4B 34)
Ferndale M. TQ2: Torq 2E 23
Ferndale Rd. TQ14: Teignm 3D 12
Ferndale Rd. TQ2: Torq 2E 23
Fernham Ter. TQ3: Paig 4E 27
Fernicombe Cl. TQ3: Paig 4B 26

Fernicombe Rd. TQ3: Paig..................4B 26
Fern Rd. TQ12: New A.....................5C 16
Fernworthy Cl. TQ2: Torq................2D 22
Ferrers Grn. TQ5: Chur F.................3H 31
Ferrymans Reach TQ14: Shal 6D 12
....(off Marine Pde.)
Field Cl. TQ3: Pres.........................1E 27
Finistere Av. EX7: Daw...................2E 5
Firbank Rd. EX7: Daw.....................1F 5
Firestone La. TQ12: A'well 6F 15
Firlands TQ14: Teignm....................2D 12
Firlands Rd. TQ2: Torq....................5F 21
Firleigh Rd. TQ12: Kingst.................2C 10
First Av. EX7: Daw..........................5C 4
First Av. TQ1: Torq..........................1B 24
First Av. TQ14: Teignm....................4C 12
First Dr. TQ14: Teignm Second Dr. 4D 12
First Dr. TQ14: Teignm The Rowdens 3F 13
Fir Wlk. TQ2: Torq..........................1F 23
Fishacre Cl. TQ3: Paig.....................3B 26
Fishchowter's La. TQ9: Tot 5F 35
Fishcombe Cove Holiday Homes TQ5: Brixh ...1C 32
Fishcombe Rd. TQ5: Brixh...............1C 32
Fisher Rd. TQ12: New A..................2G 15
Fisher St. TQ4: Paig........................6E 27
Five Acres TQ13: Bov T...................6B 6
Five Lanes Rd. TQ3: Marl 1A 26
Flagstaff Rd. TQ6: Dartm.................3B 34
Flats, The EX7: Daw........................1E 5
Flavel Arts Cen., The...............1A 34 (4C 34)
....(off Mayor's Av.)
Flavel Pl. TQ6: Dartm 1A 34 (4C 34)
....(off Mayor's Av.)
Flavel St. TQ6: Dartm 1A 34 (4C 34)
....(off Foss St.)
Fleet Ct. TQ1: Torq.........................5C 24
Fleet St. TQ1: Torq.........................5C 24
Fleet St. TQ2: Torq.........................5C 24
Fleet Wlk. TQ2: Torq.......................5C 24
....(off Fleet St.)
Flemons Ct. TQ4: Paig....................6D 26
....(off St Michael's Rd.)
Fletcher Cl. TQ2: Torq....................2H 23
Flete Av. TQ12: New A....................3C 16
Flete Cl. TQ12: New A.....................3C 16
Floaters Rd. TQ6: Dartm.................3C 34
Flood St. TQ9: Sto G.......................5A 28
Florence Pl. TQ12: New A...............3A 16
Florida Rd. TQ1: Torq.....................4D 24
Flowers Mdw. TQ12: Live................1A 8
....(off Divett Dr.)
Flow La. TQ14: Bi'ton 6G 13
....(not continuous)
Fluder Cres. TQ12: Kingsk..............4A 20
Fluder Hill TQ12: Kingsk.................3H 19
Fluder La. TQ12: Dacc....................2E 21
Fluder Ri. TQ12: Kingsk..................4A 20
Foales Ct. TQ13: Ashb....................4F 37
....(off North St.)
Follafield Pk. TQ5: Brixh.................5C 32
Folly Ct. TQ13: Bov T.....................5C 6
Folly La. TQ8: Salc.........................2H 39
....(off Fore St.)
Fonthill TQ1: Torq..........................5E 25
Football La. TQ12: Kingst................3D 10
Footland La. TQ12: Dacc................2D 20
Footlands Rd. TQ4: Paig.................1D 28
Forbes Cl. TQ12: H'fld....................5E 7
Forches Cross TQ12: New A...........4D 8
FORCHES CROSS.............................4F 9
Ford TQ6: Dartm.............................4B 34
Forde Cl. TQ12: A'well....................6F 15
Forde Cl. TQ12: New A...................2A 16
Fordens La. EX7: Holc....................1G 13
Forde Pk. TQ12: New A..................3A 16
Forde Pl. TQ12: New A....................3A 16
Forde Rd. TQ12: New A..................2A 16
Forde Vs. TQ12: New A...................3A 16
Ford Pk. TQ13: Chud K...................2H 7
Ford Rd. TQ12: A'well.....................6G 15
Ford Rd. TQ9: Tot...........................3G 35
Ford Valley TQ6: Dartm...................4B 34
Foredown La. TQ12: Kingsk............3F 19

Foresters Ter. TQ14: Teignm...........5D 12
Fore St. TQ1: Torq..........................1C 24
Fore St. TQ11: B'leigh....................4B 36
Fore St. TQ12: Ipp..........................5B 18
Fore St. TQ12: Kingsk.....................3G 19
Fore St. TQ12: Kingst......................4D 10
Fore St. TQ13: Bov T.......................3C 6
Fore St. TQ14: Bi'ton.......................5G 13
Fore St. TQ14: Shal.........................6C 12
Fore St. TQ14: Teignm.....................4B 12
....(not continuous)
Fore St. TQ2: Torq..........................4E 21
Fore St. TQ5: Brixh.........................2D 32
Fore St. TQ6: Kingsw......................4D 34
Fore St. TQ7: Kingsb.......................3B 38
Fore St. TQ8: Salc...........................2H 39
Fore St. TQ9: Tot............................4F 35
Forest Ridge Rd. TQ3: Pres.............2C 26
Forest Rd. TQ1: Torq.......................3B 24
Forge Pl. TQ13: Bov T.....................3B 6
Forgeway Cl. TQ2: Torq...................5G 23
Forster Rd. TQ8: Salc......................2G 39
Fortescue Rd. TQ3: Pres.................2F 27
Fortescue Rd. TQ8: Salc..................3F 39
Fosse Rd. TQ7: Kingsb....................2C 38
Foss Slip TQ6: Dartm............1A 34 (4C 34)
....(off Mayor's Av.)
Foss St. TQ6: Dartm.............1A 34 (4C 34)
Fountain Ct. TQ13: Bov T.................3C 6
....(off Fore St.)
Fountain Ct. TQ14: Teignm..............5E 13
....(off Triangle Pl.)
Fouracre Way TQ12: Kingst.............3E 11
Fourcross Units TQ9: Sto G..............5B 28
Fourth Av. TQ14: Teignm.................3C 12
Fourview Cl. TQ5: Brixh...................3F 33
Fowey Av. TQ2: Torq.......................1E 23
Foxglove Cl. TQ12: New A...............6E 9
Foxglove Way TQ12: New A.............3B 28
Foxglove Way TQ4: Paig..................3B 28
Foxhole Rd. TQ2: Torq....................5G 23
Foxhole Rd. TQ3: Paig.....................5C 26
Foxhollows TQ12: New A.................3D 16
Foxlands TQ1: Torq.........................2D 24
Foxlands Wlk. TQ1: Torq.................1D 24
....(off Fore St.)
Foxley Cres. TQ12: New A...............2E 15
Fox Tor Cl. TQ4: Good.....................6E 29
Foxwell La. TQ12: New A.................1F 15
Franeth Cl. TQ12: Kingst.................3C 10
Fraser Ct. TQ3: Paig.......................6C 26
Fraser Dr. TQ14: Teignm.................3C 12
Frederick Ter. EX7: Daw...................4D 4
....(off Stockton Rd.)
Freestone Rd. TQ12: Kingst............3C 10
French St. TQ14: Teignm.................4E 13
Freshwater Dr. TQ4: Good...............5D 28
Frobisher Cl. TQ14: Teignm.............1C 12
Frobisher Grn. TQ2: Torq.................3F 23
Frobisher La. TQ8: Salc...................2F 39
Frobisher Rd. TQ12: New A..............1C 16
Frogmore Ter. TQ7: Kingsb..............4B 38
Froude Av. TQ2: Torq......................3G 21
Froude Rd. TQ8: Salc......................5E 39
Fullaford Pk. TQ11: B'leigh..............5A 36
Fulton Cl. TQ12: Ipp.......................5B 18
Furlong Cl. TQ11: Buck...................2B 36
Furness Cl. TQ4: Paig.....................3D 28
Furrough Cl. TQ1: Torq....................1D 24
Furrough Cross TQ1: Torq................1D 24
Furzebrake Cl. TQ2: Torq.................5B 20
Furze Cap TQ12: Kingst..................1C 10
Furzedown Rd. TQ12: Kingsk...........2H 19
Furze Gdns. TQ9: Tot......................4H 35
Furzeham Ct. TQ5: Brixh.................2C 32
Furzeham Green..............................2D 32
Furzeham Pk. TQ5: Brixh................2D 32
Furzehill Rd. TQ1: Torq...................3B 24
Furze La. TQ5: Brixh.......................2E 33
Furzeleigh La. TQ13: Bov T.............2B 6
Furze Rd. TQ9: Tot.........................4H 35

G

Gabwell La. TQ12: S'head................1G 21
Gainsborough Cl. TQ1: Torq.............5E 25
Gales Crest TQ13: Chud K................2H 7
Gallants Bower Fort.........................6D 34
Gallery, The TQ2: Torq.....................5C 24
....(off Fleet St.)
Galloway Dr. TQ14: Teignm.............2B 12
GALMPTON.......................................2E 31
Galmpton Ct. TQ5: Galm.................2E 31
....(off Galmpton Farm Cl.)
Galmpton Farm Cl. TQ5: Galm 2E 31
Galmpton Glade TQ5: Galm.............2E 31
Galmpton Touring Pk. TQ5: Galm 3E 31
GALMPTON WARBOROUGH.............6E 29
Ganders Pk. TQ2: Torq....................6H 19
Gard Cl. TQ2: Torq..........................4F 21
Garden Cl. TQ8: Salc......................3G 39
Garden Mill Ind. Est. TQ7: Kingsb 4C 38
Garden Rd. TQ1: Torq.....................5B 24
Garfield Rd. TQ4: Paig.....................5F 27
Garlic Rea TQ5: Brixh......................2E 33
....(not continuous)
Garners Cl. TQ12: E Ogw.................4C 14
Garners La. TQ12: E Ogw................4C 14
Garrow Cl. TQ5: Brixh.....................4D 32
Garston Av. TQ12: New A.................1G 15
Garth Rd. TQ2: Torq.........................5F 21
Gascon Cl. TQ12: Kingst.................5E 15
Gatehouse Barns EX7: Daw..............2E 5
Gatehouse Cl. EX7: Daw...................3D 4
Gatehouse Hill EX7: Daw...................3E 5
Gatehouse Ri. EX7: Daw...................3E 5
Gate Tree Cl. TQ12: Kingst..............4E 11
Gattery La. TQ5: Brixh....................6A 32
Gaze Hill TQ12: New A.....................6G 9
Gentian Cl. TQ3: Marl.....................1A 26
Genting Casino Torquay..................4B 24
George Rd. TQ3: Pres.....................2E 27
George St. TQ12: New A..................2G 15
George St. TQ14: Teignm.................5E 13
Georgian Ct. TQ1: Torq....................3F 25
Gerston La. TQ7: Kingsb..................6B 38
Gerston Pl. TQ3: Paig......................5E 27
Gerston Rd. TQ4: Paig.....................5E 27
Gerstons, The TQ3: Paig..................5E 27
Gestridge Rd. TQ12: Kingst.............3C 10
Gibson Cl. TQ4: Good......................4D 28
Gibson Dr. TQ4: Good......................4D 28
Gibson Gdns. TQ4: Good..................4D 28
Gibson Rd. TQ4: Good......................4D 28
Gilbert Av. TQ14: Teignm.................2C 12
Gilbert Cl. TQ2: Torq........................3G 23
Gilbert Rd. TQ12: New A..................2B 16
Gilbert Way TQ4: Good....................3D 28
Gillard Rd. TQ5: Brixh......................3F 33
Gilley Cl. TQ13: Bov T.....................1E 7
Gills Nursery TQ9: Tot....................4F 35
....(off South St.)
Gilpin Cl. EX7: Daw.........................2F 5
Gipsy La. TQ11: B'leigh...................6A 36
Gladstone Pl. TQ12: New A..............2H 15
Gladstone Ter. TQ14: Teignm...........4E 13
Glebe, The TQ12: Ipp......................5A 18
Glebe Cl. TQ12: New A.....................2E 15
Glebelands TQ11: B'leigh.................3A 36
Glebeland Way TQ2: Torq.................1E 23
Glen, The TQ12: New A....................3C 16
Glenarm Ter. TQ9: Tot.....................3F 35
....(off Castle St.)
Glencarnock Cl. TQ1: Torq...............2H 23
Glendale Ter. TQ9: Tot....................3F 35
....(off Castle St.)
Glendaragh Rd. TQ14: Teignm.........4E 13
Glen Lyn Pk. TQ13: Bov T...............5C 6
Glenmore Rd. TQ5: Brixh.................3D 32
Glen Rd. TQ3: Paig.........................4E 27
Glenside Cl. TQ14: Teignm..............3D 12
Glenthorne Cl. TQ1: Torq.................5E 25
Gloucester Cl. TQ2: Torq..................6E 21
Gloucester Rd. TQ12: New A............3H 15

Gloucester Rd. TQ14: Teignm 4D 12
Godfrey Av. TQ3: Pres 1E 27
Golden Cl. TQ5: Brixh...............................5C 32
Golden Hind Museum Ship 2E 33
Golden Lion Ct. TQ13: Ashb 4F 37
Golden Pk. Av. TQ2: Torq 4E 21
Golden Sands Holiday Pk. EX7: Daw W
   Dawlish Warren 1G 5
Golden Ter. EX7: Daw................................4D 4
Goldfinch Cl. TQ12: Kingst.........................3B 10
Gollands TQ5: Brixh..................................2C 32
Gollands Cl. TQ5: Brixh.............................2B 32
Golvers Hill Cl. TQ12: Kingst 4D 10
Golvers Hill Rd. TQ12: Kingst 4D 10
Goodridge Cl. EX7: Daw 2E 5
GOODRINGTON 4D 28
Goodrington Orchard TQ4: Good................3F 29
   ....(off Hookhills Rd.)
Goodrington Rd. TQ4: Good.......................4D 28
Goodrington Station Dartmouth Steam Railway
   ....1F 29
Goodstone Way TQ4: Paig..........................2C 28
Gorway TQ14: Teignm 3E 13
Goshen Rd. TQ2: Torq 4H 23
Gothic Rd. TQ12: New A.............................3G 15
Gould Pl. TQ12: New A 1C 16
Gould Rd. TQ8: Salc....................................2G 39
Gourders La. TQ12: Kingsk..........................5G 19
Grace Gdns. TQ14: Teignm..........................3C 12
Grafton Ct. TQ1: Torq 5C 24
   ....(off Grafton Rd.)
Grafton Hgts. TQ1: Torq 4D 24
Grafton Rd. TQ1: Torq 5C 24
Grafton Rd. TQ12: New A 2G 15
Grafton Ter. TQ1: Torq 5C 24
Graham Rd. TQ3: Pres 2D 26
Gramercy Flds. TQ5: Brixh 5C 32
Grampian Cl. TQ4: Coll M 1A 28
Grandison Av. TQ14: Bi'ton 5H 13
Grand Pier Teignmouth, The 5E 13
Grand Prix Go Karts Dawlish Warren 1H 5
Grand Prix Go Karts Paignton 2F 29
Grange Av. TQ4: Good 3E 29
Grange Cl. TQ12: New A 4A 16
Grange Dr. TQ14: Teignm 3D 12
Grange Hgts. TQ4: Good 3D 28
Grange Hgts. Cl. TQ4: Good........................3D 28
Grange Pk. TQ14: Bi'ton 5F 13
Grange Pk. Cvn. Pk. TQ12: A'well 1B 18
Grange Rd. TQ1: Torq 4D 24
Grange Rd. TQ11: Buck 2A 36
Grange Rd. TQ12: A'well..............................1C 18
Grange Rd. TQ4: Good 4D 28
Grange Vw. TQ12: A'well..............................1C 18
Grange Vw. TQ4: Good.................................3D 28
Grasmere Cl. TQ2: Torq 5G 21
Great Bri. TQ13: Ashb..................................3E 37
Great Cliff EX7: Daw....................................5E 5
Great Furlong TQ14: Bi'ton 5F 13
Great Gate La. TQ3: Paig 5E 27
   ....(off Littlegate Rd.)
Great Headland Cres. TQ3: Pres 2F 27
Great Headland Rd. TQ3: Pres 2F 27
Great Hill Rd. TQ2: Torq 3E 21
Grea Tor Cl. TQ3: Pres.................................2C 26
Great Pk. Cl. TQ14: Bi'ton...........................6G 13
Greatpark La. TQ3: Paig..............................5A 26
Great Parks Rd. TQ3: Paig...........................6B 26
Great Rea Rd. TQ5: Brixh.............................2E 33
Great Tree Cl. TQ4: Good.............................4D 28
Great Tree Ct. TQ4: Good.............................5C 28
Great Tree Pl. TQ4: Paig...............................4C 28
Great Tree Vw. TQ4: Paig.............................4C 28
Great Western Cl. TQ4: Good 1E 29
Great Western Rd. TQ4: Paig 5E 27
Grebe Way TQ12: Kingst..............................3B 10
Greebys, The TQ3: Paig...............................5D 26
Green, The TQ13: Ashb................................4F 37
   ....(off St Andrews Cl.)
Green, The TQ14: Shal................................6C 12
Greenaway La. TQ12: Coff...........................1A 20
Greenaway Rd. TQ12: New A 1F 15
Greenbank TQ8: Bat....................................1G 39

Greenbank Av. TQ12: Kingst 3C 10
Greenbank Rd. TQ5: Brixh..........................3C 32
Green Cl. TQ7: Kingsb................................2C 38
Greenfield Rd. TQ3: Pres 1D 26
Greenhill TQ12: Kingst 5D 10
Greenhill Gdns. TQ12: Kingsk.....................3G 19
Greenhill La. TQ12: Den 6A 14
Greenhill Rd. TQ12: Kingsk.........................3G 19
Greenhill Rd. TQ12: Kingst 5D 10
Greenhill Way TQ12: Kingst........................5C 10
Greenlands Av. TQ3: Paig 5C 26
Green La. TQ5: Chur F 2H 31
Greenover Cl. TQ5: Brixh 4C 32
Greenover Rd. TQ5: Brixh 4C 32
Green Pk. Rd. TQ3: Pres 2C 26
Green Pk. Wlk. TQ3: Pres 2C 26
Greenswood Cl. TQ5: Brixh 4D 32
Greenswood Rd. TQ5: Brixh 4D 32
Greenway 5B 30
Greenway Cl. TQ2: Torq 6F 21
Greenway Gdns. TQ2: Torq 5F 21
Greenway Halt Dartmouth Steam Railway.....4D 30
Greenway La. TQ1: Torq................................1C 24
Greenway Pk. TQ5: Galm 3E 31
Greenway Rd. TQ1: Torq 1C 24
Greenway Rd. TQ2: Torq 5G 23
Greenway Rd. TQ5: Galm 5B 30
Grenadine Cl. TQ2: Torq 4D 20
Grendon Ct. TQ14: Teignm 4C 12
Grenville Av. TQ14: Teignm 2C 12
Grenville Av. TQ2: Torq 3G 23
Grenville Cl. TQ12: New A 2B 16
Grenville Cl. TQ6: Dartm 4A 34
Grenville Rd. TQ8: Salc.................................3G 39
Grenville Way TQ4: Good..............................3E 29
Greycoat La. TQ12: New A 4F 9
Greystone Way TQ1: Torq.............................2C 24
Grosvenor Av. TQ2: Torq 6B 20
Grosvenor Cl. TQ2: Torq 6B 20
Grosvenor Rd. TQ4: Paig 6E 27
Grosvenor Ter. TQ14: Teignm 3D 12
Grosvenor Ter. TQ4: Paig..............................6E 27
Grove, The TQ4: Paig....................................2B 28
Grove, The TQ9: Tot......................................4F 35
Grove Av. TQ14: Teignm 4D 12
Grove Cl. TQ9: Tot...4F 35
Grove Ct. EX7: Daw.......................................4F 5
Grove Ct. TQ14: Teignm 3E 13
Grove Cres. TQ14: Teignm............................4D 12
Grove M. TQ9: Tot...4F 35
   ....(off Grove Cl.)
Grove Ter. TQ14: Teignm 4D 12
Guardhouse Visitor Cen., The.......................2H 33
Guestland Rd. TQ1: Torq 2D 24
Guildhall Totnes 4F 35
Guildhall Yd. TQ9: Tot...................................4F 35
Gurneys, The TQ3: Paig................................6D 26

H

Haccombe Path TQ12: New A 3C 16
Haccombe Rd. TQ12: Hacc...........................2F 17
Haccombe Rd. TQ12: N'ton 2F 17
Haccombe Way TQ12: Kingst 5E 11
Hackney La. TQ12: Kingst 5E 11
   ....(not continuous)
Hackney La. TQ12: N'ton 6F 11
Hackney Marshes Local Nature Reserve... 6D 10
Haddon Ct. TQ3: Paig 4E 27
   ....(off Cecil Rd.)
Hadfield Ct. TQ13: Chud K............................2H 7
Halcyon Rd. TQ12: New A 2G 15
Haldon Av. TQ14: Teignm 3E 13
Haldon Cl. TQ1: Torq....................................5F 25
Haldon Cl. TQ12: New A 3C 16
Haldon Ho. TQ1: Torq 6G 21
   ....(off Teignmouth Rd.)
Haldon Ri. TQ12: New A 3C 16
Haldon Rd. TQ1: Torq....................................5E 25
Haldon Ter. EX7: Daw....................................4D 4
   ....(off High St.)
Halfmoon Ct. TQ11: B'leigh 6A 36
Hall La. EX7: Holc...1G 13

Hall's La. TQ12: Kingsk.................................3G 19
Halsteads Rd. TQ2: Torq 5F 21
Hambleton Way TQ4: Paig............................3D 28
Hameldown Cl. TQ2: Torq 2E 23
Hameldown Way TQ12: New A 1A 16
Hamelin Way TQ2: Torq.................................1C 22
Hamelin Way TQ3: Marl.................................2C 22
Hamilton Dr. TQ12: New A 1G 15
Hamiltons, The TQ14: Shal............................6C 12
Ham La. TQ6: Ditt 4A 30
Hamlyns Way TQ11: B'leigh 4B 36
Hampton Av. TQ1: Torq 1D 24
Hampton Cl. TQ1: Torq...................................1D 24
Hampton La. TQ1: Torq 1D 24
Hampton Rd. TQ12: New A.............................2H 15
Handley Ct. EX7: Holc....................................1H 13
Hanover Cl. TQ5: Brixh 4D 32
Hanover Ho. TQ1: Torq...................................6E 25
Happaway Cl. TQ2: Torq.................................5F 21
Happaway Rd. TQ2: Torq................................5E 21
Harberton Cl. TQ4: Paig.................................2B 28
Harbourne Av. TQ4: Paig...............................2B 28
Harbour Vw. Cl. TQ5: Brixh 2D 32
Hardy Cl. TQ1: Torq.......................................6E 25
Hares La. TQ13: Ashb 4F 37
Harewood TQ1: Torq......................................2D 24
   ....(off Cary Pk.)
Harlington Ct. TQ12: New A 1H 15
Harpins Ct. TQ12: Kingsk..............................1H 19
Hartland Tor Cl. TQ5: Brixh 5B 32
Hartley Rd. TQ4: Paig 6D 26
Hartop Rd. TQ14: Teignm 6G 21
Harts Cl. TQ14: Teignm 3C 12
Harveys Cl. TQ13: Chud K 2H 7
Harwin Apts. TQ4: Good 1F 29
Haslam Cl. TQ1: Torq.....................................2B 24
Haslam Rd. TQ1: Torq....................................2B 24
Hatchcombe La. TQ2: Torq............................5E 21
Hatcher St. EX7: Daw.....................................4D 4
Hatfield TQ1: Torq..3C 24
Hatfield Rd. TQ1: Torq 3C 24
Hauley Rd. TQ6: Dartm 2B 34 (4C 34)
Havelock Rd. TQ1: Torq 6G 21
Haven, The TQ14: Bi'ton 5G 13
Hawkes Way TQ9: Tot....................................4F 35
Hawkins Av. TQ2: Torq 2F 23
Hawkins Dr. TQ14: Teignm 3D 12
Hawkins Rd. TQ12: New A 2C 16
Hawksweed Cl. TQ12: New A.........................6E 9
Hawthorn Cl. TQ1: Torq.................................5C 16
Hawthorn Cl. TQ7: Kingsb 4B 38
Hawthorn Pk. Cl. TQ2: Torq 6G 23
Hawthorn Row TQ9: Tot.................................5H 35
Haycock La. TQ5: Brixh 2F 33
Hayes, The TQ5: Chur F 2H 31
Hayes Cl. TQ9: Tot...5H 35
Hayes Ct. TQ4: Paig 6C 26
Hayes Gdns. TQ4: Paig 1D 28
Hayes Rd. TQ4: Paig 1C 28
Hayle Av. TQ4: Good......................................5E 29
Hayley Pk. TQ12: Kingsk................................4G 19
Haytor Av. TQ4: Paig 3C 28
Haytor Cl. TQ14: Teignm................................3B 12
Haytor Dr. TQ12: New A 2C 16
Haytor Gro. TQ12: New A...............................2D 16
Haytor Pk. TQ12: Kingst 4D 10
Haytor Rd. TQ1: Torq......................................2C 24
Haytor Rd. TQ13: Bov T 3A 6
Haytor Ter. TQ12: New A 2G 15
Haytor Vw. TQ12: H'fld...................................4F 7
Haywain Cl. TQ2: Torq....................................6A 20
Hazel Cl. TQ12: New A....................................4D 16
Hazel Cl. TQ14: Teignm 1D 12
Hazel Cl. TQ7: Kingsb 4B 38
Hazeldown Rd. TQ14: Teignm 2D 12
Hazelwood TQ1: Torq......................................4E 25
   ....(off Lwr. Warberry Rd.)
Hazelwood Cl. TQ5: Brixh 3E 33
Headland Gro. TQ3: Pres 2F 27
Headland Pk. Rd. TQ3: Pres 2F 27
Headland Rd. TQ2: Torq 1H 27
Headlands, The TQ2: Torq..............................1H 27
Headway Cl. TQ14: Teignm............................4B 12

Headway Cross Rd. TQ14: Teignm............3B 12
Headway Ri. TQ14: Teignm.....................3B 12
Heath Cl. TQ12: H'fld..............................5F 7
Heath Ct. TQ5: Brixh.............................1F 33
Heath Ct. TQ9: Tot................................4F 35
Heather Cl. TQ12: New A........................1E 15
Heather Ct. TQ14: Teignm.....................2D 12
Heatherdene TQ13: Bov T.......................3B 6
Heather Est. TQ12: H'fld.........................4E 7
Heather Way TQ5: Brixh.........................3B 32
HEATHFIELD 5E 7
Heathfield Bus. Pk. TQ12: H'fld...............4E 7
Heathfield Cl. TQ13: Bov T......................5B 6
Heathfield Cotts. TQ12: H'fld...................4F 7
Heathfield Ho. TQ13: Bov T 4B 6
....(off Ashburton Rd.)
Heathfield Mdw. TQ13: Bov T...................5B 6
Heathfield Ter. TQ13: Bov T.....................4B 6
Heath Hill TQ12: H'fld..............................5F 7
Heathlands Ct. TQ14: Teignm 1C 12
Heathlands Ri. TQ14: Teignm....(off Heathlands Ri.)
Heathlands Ri. TQ14: Teignm...................1C 12
Heath Pk. TQ12: New A............................4D 16
Heath Pk. TQ5: Brixh..............................2F 33
Heath Ri. TQ5: Brixh...............................2F 33
Heath Rd. TQ5: Brixh...............................2E 33
Heath Wlk. TQ13: Bov T............................1E 7
Heath Way TQ9: Tot.................................4F 35
....(not continuous)
Heatree Cl. TQ14: Teignm........................1D 12
Heaviside Cl. TQ2: Torq............................4G 21
Hebditch Cl. TQ13: Bov T..........................3D 6
HELE 6E 21
Hele Cl. TQ2: Torq...................................6E 21
Helens Mead Cl. TQ2: Torq........................3F 21
Helens Mead Rd. TQ2: Torq.......................3F 21
Hele Pk. Development TQ12: New A.............6D 8
Hele Rd. TQ12: Kingst...............................2C 10
Hele Rd. TQ2: Torq...................................6D 20
Helford Dr. TQ4: Good...............................5E 29
Helford Wlk. TQ4: Good.............................5E 29
Heligan Dr. TQ3: Paig................................3B 26
Hellevoetsluis Way TQ3: Marl.....................6B 22
Helmdon Ri. TQ2: Torq...............................1E 23
Helston Cl. TQ3: Paig................................4C 26
Heltor Bus. Pk. TQ12: H'fld.........................3E 7
Hembury Cock Hill TQ11: B'leigh..................2A 36
Hembury Pk. TQ11: Buck.............................2B 36
Hems Brook Ct. TQ2: Torq 1E 23
Henacre La. TQ7: Kingsb.............................3D 38
Henacre Rd. TQ7: Kingsb.............................3C 38
Henbury Cl. TQ1: Torq.................................3C 24
Hennapyn Rd. TQ2: Torq..............................6H 23
Hennock Rd. TQ4: Paig................................3C 28
Henty Av. EX7: Daw.....................................3F 5
Henty Cl. EX7: Daw......................................2F 5
Herbert Rd. TQ2: Torq.................................5G 23
Herbert Rd. TQ8: Salc.................................3F 39
Heritage Way TQ5: Brixh.............................2F 33
Hermitage Rd. TQ6: Dartm..........................3A 34
Hermosa Gdns. TQ14: Teignm.....................4D 12
Hermosa Rd. TQ14: Teignm.........................4D 12
Heron Way TQ2: Torq..................................4B 20
Hesketh Cres. TQ1: Torq.............................6E 25
Hesketh M. TQ1: Torq.................................6E 25
Hesketh Rd. TQ1: Torq................................6E 25
Hestow Rd. TQ12: Kingst..............................1D 10
Hewett Cl. TQ12: New A...............................2D 16
Heywood Cl. TQ2: Torq.................................2G 23
Heywood Est. TQ12: Kingst...........................6C 10
Heywoods Cl. TQ14: Teignm.........................4E 13
....(off Heywoods Rd.)
Heywoods Rd. TQ14: Teignm........................4E 13
Highbury Rd. TQ1: Torq................................3C 24
Highcliff Ct. EX7: Daw..................................4E 5
....(off E. Cliff Rd.)
Highcliffe M. TQ4: Good................................1F 29
High Cl. TQ13: Bov T....................................3D 6
Higher Audley Av. TQ2: Torq.........................1A 24
Higher Bibbery TQ13: Bov T..........................3D 6
Higher Brimley TQ14: Teignm........................3D 12
Higher Brimley Rd. TQ14: Teignm..................4D 12
HIGHER BRIXHAM 4D 32

Higher Broad Pk. TQ6: Dartm........................4A 34
Higher Brook St. TQ14: Teignm......................4D 12
Higher Buckeridge Rd. TQ14: Teignm.............2D 12
Higher Budleigh Mdw. TQ12: New A...............2E 15
Higher Cadewell La. TQ2: Torq......................6A 20
Higher Compton Barton TQ3: Comp................3B 22
Higher Coombe Dr. TQ14: Teignm..................2C 12
Higher Copythorne TQ5: Brixh.......................3B 32
Higher Downs Rd. TQ1: Torq.........................1D 24
Higher Dr. EX7: Daw.....................................2F 5
Higher Edginswell La. TQ2: Torq....................2D 22
Higher Erith Rd. TQ1: Torq.............................5E 25
Higher French Pk. TQ12: New A.....................2E 15
Higher Furzeham Rd. TQ5: Brixh....................1D 32
HIGHER GABWELL 1H 21
Higher Holcombe Cl. TQ14: Teignm................2E 13
Higher Holcombe Dr. TQ14: Teignm...............1E 13
Higher Holcombe Rd. TQ14: Teignm...............1E 13
Higher Kingsdown Rd. TQ14: Teignm.............4B 12
Higher Lincombe Rd. TQ1: Torq....................6E 25
Higher Mnr. Rd. TQ5: Brixh...........................2D 32
Higher Mnr. Ter. TQ3: Paig............................6D 26
....(off Manor Ter.)
Higher Mill La. TQ11: Buck............................2B 36
....(not continuous)
HIGHER MORLEY 2A 14
Higher Penn TQ5: Brixh................................4E 33
Higher Polsham Rd. TQ3: Paig.......................4E 27
Higher Queen's Ter. TQ1: Torq......................4C 24
Higher Ranscombe Rd. TQ5: Brixh.................3E 33
Higher Ringmore Rd. TQ14: Shal...................6A 12
Higher Roborough TQ13: Ashb......................3G 37
Higher Rydons TQ5: Brixh.............................3B 32
Higher Sackery TQ12: C'head........................1G 17
Higher Sandygate TQ12: Kingst.....................1C 10
Higherside TQ6: Dartm...................2A (4C 34)
....(off Higher St.)
Higher Steps TQ5: Brixh...............................2D 32
....(off Higher St.)
Higher St. TQ5: Brixh....................................2D 32
Higher St. TQ6: Dartm ....1 B 34 (4C 34)
Higher St. TQ6: Kingsw.................................4D 34
HIGHER TOWN 4A 36
Higher Union La. TQ2: Torq...........................4B 24
Higher Union Rd. TQ7: Kingsb.......................3B 38
Higher Warberry Rd. TQ1: Torq.....................4D 24
Higher Warborough Rd. TQ5: Galm................1E 31
Higher Warren Rd. TQ7: Kingsb.....................5D 38
Higher Weir TQ9: Darti.................................2E 35
Higher Westonfields TQ9: Tot........................4H 35
Higher Woodfield Rd. TQ1: Torq....................6D 24
Higher Woodway Cl. TQ14: Teignm................2E 13
Higher Woodway Rd. TQ14: Teignm...............1D 12
HIGHER YALBERTON 2A 28
Higher Yalberton Rd. TQ4: Paig....................2A 28
Higher Yannon Dr. TQ14: Teignm..................3C 12
Highfield Cl. TQ5: Brixh................................3B 32
Highfield Cres. TQ3: Paig.............................5B 26
Highfield Dr. TQ7: Kingsb............................4C 38
Highgrove Pk. TQ14: Teignm.......................2E 13
High Ho. Cl. EX7: Daw.................................3E 5
High Ho. La. TQ7: Kingsb............................4C 38
Highland Cl. TQ2: Torq................................3F 23
Highland Rd. TQ2: Torq...............................3F 23
High St. EX7: Daw..4D 4
High St. TQ9: Tot..4E 35
HIGHWEEK 6G 9
Highweek Cl. TQ12: New A..........................6G 9
Highweek Rd. TQ12: New A.........................1F 15
....(not continuous)
Highweek St. TQ12: New A..........................2G 15
Highweek Village TQ12: New A....................6G 9
Highweek Way TQ12: New A........................2G 15
Highwood Grange TQ12: New A....................3G 15
....(not continuous)
Hillbrook Ri. TQ9: Tot.................................4H 35
Hillbrook Rd. TQ9: Tot................................4H 35
Hilldown TQ9: Tot.......................................4H 35
Hilldrop Ter. TQ1: Torq................................4C 24
Hiller La. TQ12: N'ton..................................3E 17
Hillesdon Rd. TQ1: Torq..............................4C 24
Hillfield TQ9: Sto G....................................6A 28
Hillmans Rd. TQ12: New A...........................3H 15

Hill Pk. Cl. TQ5: Brixh.................................3F 33
Hill Pk. Rd. TQ1: Torq.................................2B 24
Hill Pk. Rd. TQ12: New A..............................1E 15
Hill Pk. Rd. TQ5: Brixh.................................3F 33
Hill Pk. Ter. TQ4: Paig.................................6F 27
Hillrise TQ5: Galm.......................................2E 31
Hill Rd. TQ12: New A...................................3G 15
Hillsborough TQ1: Torq................................5C 24
....(off Hillesdon Rd.)
Hillside Cl. TQ14: Teignm............................2B 12
Hillside Cotts. TQ12: A'well.........................1B 18
Hillside Ct. TQ6: Dartm...............................4B 34
Hillside Dr. TQ7: Kingsb..............................4C 38
Hillside Rd. TQ3: Paig.................................4C 26
Hillside Rd. TQ5: Brixh................................3D 32
Hillside Ter. TQ3: Paig.................................5D 26
....(off Colley End Pk.)
Hill Vw. EX7: Holc......................................1G 13
Hill Vw. Ter. TQ1: Torq................................2B 24
Hilly Gdns. Rd. TQ1: Torq............................6G 21
Hilton Cres. TQ3: Pres................................1F 27
Hilton Dr. TQ3: Pres....................................2F 27
Hilton Rd. TQ12: New A...............................3H 15
Hind St. TQ13: Bov T....................................2C 6
Hingston Rd. TQ1: Torq...............................2D 24
HMP Channings Wood..................................6A 14
Hoburne Holiday Pk. TQ4: Good...................2E 29
Hockmore Dr. TQ12: New A..........................1C 16
Hodson Cl. TQ3: Paig..................................4C 26
Holbeam Cl. TQ12: New A............................1D 14
Holbeam La. TQ12: Bick...............................6A 8
Holbeam La. TQ12: E Ogw...........................6A 8
Holborn Rd. TQ5: Brixh................................1D 32
HOLCOMBE 1G 13
Holcombe Down Rd. EX7: Holc.....................6A 4
Holcombe Down Rd. TQ14: Teignm...............1D 12
Holcombe Dr. EX7: Holc...............................1H 13
Holcombe Rd. EX7: Holc..............................6C 4
Holcombe Rd. TQ14: Teignm........................2G 13
Holcombe Village EX7: Holc.........................1G 13
Holdsworth Ho. TQ6: Dartm 2A 34 (4C 34)
....(off Higher St.)
Hollacombe La. TQ3: Pres...........................2G 27
Hollam Way TQ12: Kingst............................3E 11
Hollands Rd. TQ14: Teignm.........................5E 13
HOLLICOMBE 1G 27
Hollington Ho. TQ1: Torq.............................5E 25
Hollyberry Rd. TQ1: Torq.............................3A 28
Hollyhock Way TQ4: Paig............................3B 28
Hollywater Cl. TQ1: Torq.............................4E 25
Holman Cl. EX7: Daw..................................2F 5
Holme Ct. TQ1: Torq...................................4E 25
Holmes Rd. TQ12: H'fld...............................5E 7
Holne Moor Cl. TQ3: Paig...........................4B 26
Holne Rd. TQ11: B'leigh.............................2A 36
Holwell Rd. TQ5: Brixh...............................3C 32
Holwill Tor Wlk. TQ4: Paig..........................2C 28
Homebourne Ho. TQ4: Paig........................6F 27
....(off Belle Vue Rd.)
Home Cl. TQ5: Brixh...................................4D 32
Homecombe Ho. TQ1: Torq.........................4E 25
....(off St Albans Rd.)
Home Fld. TQ7: W Alv.................................4A 38
Homelands Pl. TQ7: Kingsb........................2B 38
Homelands Rd. TQ7: Kingsb.......................2B 38
Home Mdw. TQ9: Tot..................................4F 35
Homepalms Ho. TQ1: Torq..........................3A 24
....(off Teignmouth Rd.)
Home Pk. TQ13: Ashb................................3F 37
Home Reach Rd. TQ9: Tot..........................5H 35
Homers Cl. TQ12: Kingst...........................5C 10
Homers Cres. TQ12: Kingst.......................5C 10
Homers La. TQ12: Kingst..........................5C 10
Homestead Rd. TQ1: Torq.........................1B 24
Homestead Ter. TQ1: Torq........................1B 24
Hometeign Ho. TQ12: New A......................1A 16
....(off Salisbury Rd.)
Homeyards, The TQ14: Shal......................6C 12
....(off Commons Old Rd.)
Homeyards Botanical Gdns.......................6C 12
Honey La. TQ12: S'head...........................1E 21
Honeysuckle Cl. TQ3: Paig.......................3B 26
Honeysuckle Dr. EX7: Daw........................2D 4

Honeywell TQ12: Kingst................................5D 10
Honeywell Rd. TQ12: Kingst 5D 10
Hoodown La. TQ6: Kingsw........................3D 34
Hookhills Dr. TQ4: Good..............................4F 29
Hookhills Gdns. TQ4: Good.......................5E 29
Hookhills Gro. TQ4: Good............................4F 29
Hookhills Rd. TQ4: Good.............................5E 29
Hook La. TQ5: Galm......................................4D 30
Hoopern Ter. EX7: Daw 4D 4
....(off Stockton Rd.)
Hope Cl. TQ9: Tot..4H 35
Hope's Cl. TQ14: Teignm............................3C 12
Hopes Cove La. TQ1: Torq..........................4G 25
Hope Wlk. TQ9: Tot......................................4H 35
Hopkins Ct. TQ12: New A 2H 15
....(off Hopkins La.)
Hopkins La. TQ12: New A 2H 15
Horace Rd. TQ2: Torq..................................5E 21
Horn Hill TQ6: Dartm 1A 34 (4C 34)
....(off Above Town)
Horns Pk. TQ14: Bi'ton 5F 13
Horse La. TQ14: Shal......................................6D 12
Horsepool St. TQ5: Brixh.............................4C 32
Horseshoe Bend TQ4: Good.........................3F 29
Hosegood Way TQ12: Kingst 4C 10
Hoskings Ct. TQ11: B'leigh..........................4B 36
Hospital Hill EX7: Daw 4D 4
Hospital La. TQ13: Ashb...............................3G 37
....(not continuous)
Hound Tor Cl. TQ4: Good.............................6E 29
House of Marbles...5C 6
Howard Cl. EX7: Daw Brook St. 4D 4
Howard Cl. EX7: Daw....................................4C 4
....(off Penfield Gdns.)
Howard Cl. TQ14: Teignm.............................2C 12
Howard Cl. TQ2: Torq....................................3G 23
Howard Cl. TQ12: Torq..................................2C 12
Howards Way TQ12: New A 1C 16
Howton La. TQ12: New A...............................6C 8
Howton Rd. TQ12: New A...............................5C 8
Hoxton Rd. TQ1: Torq...................................4C 24
Hoyles Cl. TQ3: Paig......................................3B 26
Hoyle's Rd. TQ3: Paig...................................3B 26
Huccaby Cl. TQ5: Brixh................................5A 32
Humber La. TQ12: Kingst.............................3E 11
Humber La. TQ14: Teignm...........................1H 11
Humpy, The EX7: Daw 3C 4
Hunsdon Rd. TQ1: Torq................................5D 24
Huntacott Way TQ2: Torq.............................1E 23
Hunter's Moon TQ1: Torq............................5E 25
....(off Babbacombe Rd.)
Hunters Tor Dr. TQ4: Good..........................6E 29
Hunterswell Rd. TQ12: New A 2F 15
Hurrell Ct. TQ7: Kingsb................................3B 38
Hurrell Rd. TQ7: Kingsb................................3B 38
Hutchings Way TQ14: Teignm......................3B 12
Hutton Rd. TQ3: Pres....................................2D 26
Huxley Va. TQ1: Kingsk.................................4G 19
Huxnor Rd. TQ12: Kingsk.............................4G 19
Huxtable Hill TQ2: Torq 5G 23
Hyde Rd. TQ4: Paig.......................................5E 27
Hyfield Gdns. TQ1: Torq...............................5C 24
....(off Grafton Rd.)
Hyperion TQ2: Torq.......................................1H 27

Iddesleigh Ter. EX7: Daw 4E 5
Idewell Rd. TQ2: Torq...................................5G 21
Ilbert Rd. TQ7: Kingsb..................................3B 38
Ilford Pk. TQ12: New A 1C 8
Ilsham Cl. TQ1: Torq.....................................4G 25
Ilsham Cres. TQ1: Torq.................................5G 25
Ilsham Ho. TQ1: Torq.....................................4F 25
Ilsham Marine Dr. TQ1: Torq........................4G 25
Ilsham M. TQ1: Torq......................................4F 25
Ilsham Rd. TQ1: Torq....................................4F 25
Ilton Way TQ7: Kingsb..................................3C 38
Imperial Ct. TQ1: Torq..................................2D 24
Imperial M. TQ12: New A 2H 15
....(off Lemon Rd.)
Indio Rd. TQ13: Bov T.....................................4B 6
Innerbrook Rd. TQ2: Torq............................4H 23

Inverteign Dr. TQ14: Teignm 4B 12
Inverteign Hgts. TQ14: Teignm 3B 12
IPPLEPEN...5B 18
Isaac Gro. TQ2: Torq.....................................4E 21
Isaacs Rd. TQ2: Torq.....................................4E 21
Isambard Ct. TQ2: Torq................................4G 21
Isigny Rd. TQ7: Kingsb.................................3B 38
Island Quay TQ8: Salc..................................2H 39
Island St. TQ8: Salc.......................................2G 39
Island Ter. TQ8: Salc.....................................2H 39
Ivatt Rd. TQ6: Dartm....................................4A 34
Ivy Ho. TQ14: Teignm....................................5D 12
....(off Ivy La.)
Ivy La. TQ14: Teignm....................................5D 12
Ivy La. TQ6: Dartm 1A 34 (4C 34)
....(off Roseville St.)

Jack's La. TQ2: Torq......................................4E 21
Jacolind Wlk. TQ5: Brixh.............................3E 33
Jacqueline Ho. TQ9: Tot..............................4F 35
....(off Ticklemore St.)
James Av. TQ3: Paig......................................2B 26
Jasmine Gro. TQ3: Paig................................3B 26
Jawbones Hill TQ6: Dartm 2A 34 (4C 34)
Jellicoe Rd. TQ12: New A 2C 16
Jellicoe Vs. TQ9: Tot.....................................4E 35
Jetty Marsh Local Nature Reserve.............6B 10
Jetty Marsh Rd. TQ12: New A 6A 10
John Nash Dr. EX7: Daw 5C 4
John's Av. TQ2: Torq.....................................1A 24
Jonida Cl. TQ1: Torq......................................2B 24
Jordan Dr. TQ14: Teignm.............................3B 12
Jordan Mdw. TQ13: Ashb.............................3G 37
Jordan Orchard TQ11: B'leigh......................4A 36
....(off Jordan St.)
Jordan St. TQ11: B'leigh...............................4A 36
Joslin Ct. TQ12: Kingst.................................3C 10
Jubilee Cl. TQ1: Torq....................................4C 24
Jubilee Cl. TQ14: Teignm.............................2F 13
Jubilee Cl. TQ6: Dartm.................................4A 34
Jubilee Rd. TQ12: New A 2G 15
Jubilee Rd. TQ9: Tot.....................................3H 35
Jubilee Ter. TQ3: Paig..................................5D 26
Juniper Cl. TQ4: Paig....................................3A 28
Jurys Cnr. Cl. TQ12: Kingsk..........................3H 19

Keatings La. TQ14: Teignm..........................4C 12
Keats Cl. TQ14: Teignm................................2B 12
Keep Gdns., The TQ6: Dartm........................4A 34
Keep La. TQ6: Dartm 1A 34 (3B 34)
Kelland Cl. TQ3: Paig.....................................5C 26
Kellett Cl. TQ13: Ashb..................................3G 37
Kellock Dr. TQ9: Tot......................................4E 35
Kelly Cl. TQ1: Torq..6D 24
Kelvin Ct. TQ1: Torq......................................6H 21
Kelvin Ct. TQ5: Brixh.....................................2E 33
Kemmings Cl. TQ4: Paig...............................4C 28
Kemp M. TQ13: Ashb....................................4F 37
....(off Bull Ring)
Kendlewood Cl. TQ4: Paig............................2C 28
Kenilworth TQ1: Torq...................................6E 25
Kennels Rd. TQ5: Chur F..............................4F 31
Kenneth Ct. TQ2: Torq.................................1F 23
Kenneth Ter. TQ2: Torq................................1F 23
....(off Kenneth Ct.)
Kensey Cl. TQ1: Torq......................................3F 25
Kenton Brook Ct. TQ2: Torq.........................1E 23
Kents Cavern...4F 25
Kent's Cavern Visitor Cen............................4F 25
Kent's La. TQ1: Torq......................................4F 25
Kent's Rd. TQ1: Torq.....................................4F 25
Kenwith Dr. TQ7: Kingsb..............................3C 38
Kenwyn Rd. TQ1: Torq..................................3D 24
Kernou Rd. TQ4: Paig....................................5F 27
Kerria Cl. TQ3: Paig.......................................3B 26
Kerswell La. TQ12: Coff................................2H 19
Kestor Dr. TQ3: Pres.....................................2D 26
Kestrel Ct. TQ1: Torq....................................1D 24
Keyberry Cl. TQ12: New A 4A 16

Keyberry Mill TQ12: New A 4A 16
Keyberry Pk. TQ12: New A 4A 16
Keyberry Rd. TQ12: New A 4A 16
Keysfield Rd. TQ4: Paig................................6F 27
Khartoum Pl. TQ7: Kingsb............................3R 38
Killerton Cl. TQ3: Paig..................................4E 27
Kilmorie TQ1: Torq..6G 25
Kilmorie Cl. TQ1: Torq..................................6G 25
Kiln Cl. TQ13: Bov T..5B 6
Kilnford Rd. TQ12: Kingst.............................4E 11
Kiln Forehead La. TQ12: Kingst...................4E 11
Kiln Ho. TQ7: Kingsb.....................................4C 38
Kiln Orchard TQ12: New A 2E 15
Kiln Path TQ5: Brixh.....................................3D 32
Kiln Rd. TQ13: Bov T.......................................5B 6
Kiln Rd. TQ5: Galm.......................................3D 30
Kilworthy TQ1: Torq......................................1C 24
King Charles Bus. Pk. TQ12: H'fld 3E 7
Kingcome Ct. TQ11: B'leigh.........................4C 36
Kingfisher Cl. TQ2: Torq...............................5C 20
Kingfisher Way TQ12: Kingst.......................3B 10
Kingsale Rd. TQ8: Salc.................................3F 39
Kings Arms Pas. TQ7: Kingsb.......................3B 38
....(off Fore St.)
King's Ash Rd. TQ3: Paig..............................2B 26
Kings Av. TQ3: Paig.......................................4F 27
KINGSBRIDGE...3B 38
Kingsbridge Bus Station...............................3B 38
Kingsbridge Cookworthy Mus.......................2B 38
Kingsbridge Hill TQ9: Tot.............................5F 35
Kingsbridge Info. Cen..................................3C 38
Kingsbridge La. TQ13: Ashb.........................4F 37
Kingsbridge La. M. TQ13: Ashb....................4E 37
....(off Kingsbridge La.)
Kings Cinema Kingsbridge...........................3B 38
Kings Coombe Dr. TQ12: Kingst..................2D 10
Kings Cotts. TQ12: New A 2H 15
Kings Ct. TQ12: Kingsk.................................3G 19
Kings Ct. TQ12: Kingst..................................5D 10
Kingsdale Ct. TQ2: Torq................................5C 24
Kingsdown Cl. EX7: Daw...............................3E 5
Kingsdown Cl. TQ14: Teignm.......................4B 12
Kingsdown Cres. EX7: Daw...........................3E 5
Kingsdown Rd. TQ14: Teignm......................4B 12
King's Dr. TQ5: Brixh.....................................3E 33
King's Dr., The TQ2: Torq..............................5A 24
Kingsgate Cl. TQ2: Torq................................3G 21
Kingshurst Dr. TQ3: Paig..............................3E 27
KINGSKERSWELL...3G 19
Kingskerswell By-Pass TQ12: Kingsk...........2F 19
Kingskerswell Rd. TQ12: Kingsk...................6B 20
Kingskerswell Rd. TQ12: New A 4A 16
Kingskerswell Rd. TQ2: Torq........................4C 20
Kingsland Dr. TQ4: Paig................................1B 28
Kingsleigh Mnr. TQ1: Torq...........................4D 24
....(off Lwr. Warberry Rd.)
Kingsley Av. TQ2: Torq..................................4E 21
Kingsley Ct. TQ2: Torq..................................4E 21
....(off Kingsley Av.)
Kingsley Rd. TQ7: Kingsb.............................4B 38
Kingsley Sq. TQ2: Torq.................................4E 21
King's Mkt. TQ7: Kingsb................................3B 38
Kings Mdw. TQ12: Kingsk..............................3G 19
Kings Orchard TQ9: Tot................................4H 35
Kings Quay TQ6: Dartm................................3C 34
Kings Rd. TQ3: Paig......................................4F 27
Kings Rydon Cl. TQ9: Sto G.........................5A 28
KINGSTEIGNTON...4D 10
Kingsteignton Retail Pk................................5C 10
Kingsteignton Rd. TQ12: New A 2H 15
Kingsteignton Swimming Pool.....................2C 10
Kingston Cl. TQ12: Kingsk............................3H 19
Kingston La. TQ6: Dartm..............................4A 34
King St. EX7: Daw...4D 4
King St. TQ12: New A 2H 15
King St. TQ5: Brixh..2E 33
King's Wlk. EX7: Daw.....................................5E 5
Kingswater Ct. TQ5: Brixh............................2D 32
Kingsway TQ14: Teignm................................4B 12
Kingsway Av. TQ4: Good...............................4D 28
Kingsway Cl. TQ4: Good...............................4D 28
Kingsway Cl. TQ7: Kingsb.............................4B 38
Kingsway Ct. TQ4: Good...............................4D 28

Kingsway Dr. TQ4: Good 4D 28
Kingsway Pk. TQ7: Kingsb 4B 38
KINGSWEAR..4D 34
Kingswear Station Dartmouth Steam Railway
....4D 34
Kingswood Ct. TQ4: Paig.....................6F 27
....(off Cleveland Rd.)
Kiniver Ct. TQ14: Teignm.....................2E 13
Kinlacey Ct. TQ1: Torq.........................5D 24
Kintyre Cl. TQ2: Torq...........................5D 20
Kirkham Ct. TQ3: Paig..........................5D 26
....(off Colley End Rd.)
Kirkham House 5D 26
....(off Cecil Rd.)
Kirkham St. TQ3: Paig...........................5E 27
Kirkstead Cl. TQ2: Torq.......................1H 23
Kistor Gdns. TQ9: Tot...........................3F 35
....(off Castle St.)
Kittersley Dr. TQ12: Live 1A 8
Kittiwake Dr. TQ2: Torq.........................4B 20
Knapp Pk. Rd. TQ4: Good......................3F 29
Knebworth Ct. TQ1: Torq......................6H 21
Knick Knack La. TQ5: Brixh 4D 32
Knights Mead TQ13: Chud K 2H 7
Knowle, The TQ12: Kingst 5E 11
Knowle Gdns. TQ7: Kingsb....................2B 38
Knowle Ho. Cl. TQ7: Kingsb.................2C 38
Knowle Rd. TQ8: Salc............................2G 39
KNOWLES HILL......................................1G 15
Knowles Hill Rd. TQ12: New A 1G 15

L

Laburnum Ct. TQ12: A'well......................1C 18
Laburnum Rd. TQ12: New A....................4B 16
Laburnum Row TQ2: Torq......................3A 24
Laburnum St. TQ2: Torq........................4A 24
Laburnum Ter. TQ12: A'well...................6G 15
Lacy Rd. TQ3: Pres.................................2D 26
Ladies Mile EX7: Daw.............................3G 5
Lady Pk. Rd. TQ2: Torq..........................6G 23
Lady's Mile Holiday Pk. EX7: Daw 1G 5
Lake Av. TQ14: Teignm...........................2C 12
Lakeland TQ12: A'well.............................1C 18
Lakes Cl. TQ5: Brixh..............................2B 32
Lakeside TQ8: Salc.................................2G 39
Lakeside Cl. TQ13: Bov T 6B 6
Lakes Rd. TQ5: Brixh.............................3B 32
Lake St. TQ6: Dartm 1A 34 (4C 34)
Lamacraft Cl. EX7: Daw..........................2F 5
Lamb, The TQ9: Tot................................4E 35
Lambert Cl. EX7: Daw.............................2F 5
Lamb Pk. Cl. TQ12: Kingst....................1D 10
Lammas La. TQ3: Pres............................3C 26
Lancaster Dr. TQ4: Paig.........................3C 28
Lancaster Ho. TQ4: Paig........................6F 27
....(off Belle Vue Rd.)
Landmark Rd. TQ8: Salc.........................3E 39
Landrace Cl. TQ12: E Ogw 5E 15
Landscore Cl. TQ14: Teignm..................4D 12
Landscore Rd. TQ14: Teignm.................4C 12
Landscove Holiday Pk. TQ5: Brixh.........3G 33
Lands Rd. TQ5: Brixh.............................1G 33
Lane, The TQ6: Ditt................................5A 30
Langaller Cl. TQ13: Bov T 5A 6
Langaller La. TQ13: Bov T 6A 6
Langdon Flds. TQ5: Galm.......................1E 31
Langdon La. TQ5: Galm..........................2E 31
Langdon Rd. EX7: Daw............................1C 4
Langdon Rd. TQ3: Pres..........................2F 27
Langford Cres. TQ2: Torq......................4E 21
Langlands Cl. TQ4: Paig.........................1B 28
Langley Av. TQ5: Brixh...........................3D 32
Langley Cl. TQ5: Brixh...........................3D 32
Langridge Rd. TQ3: Paig........................3B 26
Langs Rd. TQ3: Pres..............................3F 27
Langstone Cl. TQ1: Torq........................2E 25
Langstone Cl. TQ12: H'fld.......................5E 7
Lang Way TQ12: Ipp...............................5C 18
Lanherne EX7: Daw.................................4E 5
Lanhydrock Cl. TQ3: Paig......................3A 26
Lansdowne Ct. TQ2: Torq......................4A 24

Lansdowne La. TQ2: Torq......................3A 24
Lansdowne Pk. TQ9: Tot........................5H 35
Lansdowne Rd. TQ2: Torq.....................3A 24
Lapthorne Ind. Est. TQ12: Ipp...............4A 18
Larch Cl. TQ14: Teignm.........................1D 12
Larch Wlk. TQ2: Torq..............................1F 23
Larkin Cl. TQ13: Bov T 1E 7
Larks Cl. TQ14: Shal..............................6B 12
Larksmead Cl. TQ12: E Ogw 4F 15
Larksmead Way TQ12: E Ogw.................4E 15
Larkspur Cl. TQ4: Paig...........................3B 28
Larkspur Dr. TQ12: New A 6E 9
Laskeys Heath TQ12: Live 1A 8
Laura Av. TQ3: Paig................................3E 27
Laura Gro. TQ3: Pres.............................3C 26
Laura Pl. TQ3: Paig................................3C 26
....(off Well St.)
Laurel La. TQ3: Shal..............................6B 12
Laureston Rd. TQ12: New A....................3H 15
Laurie Av. TQ12: New A...........................1E 15
Lauriston Cl. TQ2: Torq..........................4A 24
Lavender Cl. TQ5: Brixh.........................3B 32
Lawn Cl. TQ2: Torq.................................4E 21
Lawn Hill EX7: Daw..................................4E 5
Lawns End TQ14: Bi'ton.........................5F 13
Lawn Ter. EX7: Daw.................................4E 5
Laywell Cl. TQ5: Brixh............................5C 32
Laywell La. TQ5: Brixh............................4B 32
Laywell Rd. TQ5: Brixh...........................4B 32
Lea, The TQ14: Bi'ton.............................5H 13
....(not continuous)
Lea, The TQ14: Teignm..........................5H 13
....(not continuous)
Lea Cliff Pk. EX7: Daw W 1H 5
Leader Cl. TQ5: Brixh.............................2F 33
Leader La. TQ3: Marl..............................1A 26
Leadstone Camping EX7: Daw................1H 5
Lealands TQ13: Bov T 4B 6
Lea Mt. TQ14: Bi'ton..............................5H 13
Lea Mt. Cl. EX7: Daw................................5E 5
Lea Mt. Dr. EX7: Daw................................5D 4
Lea Mt. Rd. EX7: Daw...............................5E 5
Leander Ct. TQ14: Teignm.....................5D 12
Lea Rd. TQ2: Torq..................................4G 21
Leat Cl. TQ12: Kingst............................4D 10
Leat Mdw. TQ12: Live...............................1A 8
Leat Ter. TQ12: Kingst...........................4D 10
Lea Va. Rd. TQ12: New A.........................2F 15
Leaze Rd. TQ12: Kingst.........................3C 10
Ledsgrove TQ12: Ipp.............................5C 18
Leechwell Ct. TQ9: Tot...........................4F 35
....(off The Lamb)
Leechwell La. TQ9: Tot...........................4F 35
....(not continuous)
Leechwell St. TQ9: Tot...........................4F 35
....(not continuous)
Lee Ct. TQ5: Brixh...................................3F 33
Leeward La. TQ2: Torq...........................4D 20
Leigham Ct. EX7: Daw..............................4E 5
Leigham Ter. TQ7: Kingsb.......................3B 38
....(off Fore St.)
Leighon Rd. TQ3: Paig...........................5F 27
Le Molay-Littry Way TQ13: Bov T 3C 6
Lemon Ct. TQ12: New A..........................2H 15
....(off Marsh Rd.)
Lemon M. TQ12: New A...........................2H 15
....(off The Avenue)
Lemon Pl. TQ12: New A...........................2H 15
Lemon Rd. TQ12: New A.........................2H 15
Lethbridge Ct. TQ12: New A...................2H 15
....(off Courtenay Pk. Rd.)
Leyburn Gro. TQ4: Paig..........................1D 28
Leyfield Wlk. EX7: Daw............................3E 5
Ley La. TQ12: Kingst..............................3C 10
Leys Rd. TQ2: Torq................................4G 23
Lichfield Av. TQ2: Torq...........................5F 21
Lichfield Cl. TQ5: Brixh..........................3B 32
Lichfield Dr. TQ5: Brixh..........................3B 32
Lidford Tor Av. TQ4: Paig.......................2B 28
Light La. TQ5: Galm................................3E 31
Lime Av. TQ5: Torq.................................4A 24
Lime Gro. TQ7: Kingsb...........................3B 38
Limekiln Cl. TQ4: Good..........................5C 28

Lime Tree Wlk. TQ12: New A 4B 16
Linacre La. TQ12: Coff...........................1B 20
Linacre Rd. TQ2: Torq............................4E 21
Lincoln Grn. TQ2: Torq...........................6F 21
Lincombe Dr. TQ1: Torq.........................5F 25
Lincombe Hill Rd. TQ1: Torq.................5F 25
Linden Rd. EX7: Daw................................5C 4
Linden Ter. TQ12: New A.........................2F 15
Lindisfarne Way TQ2: Torq.....................5D 20
Lindfield Cl. TQ2: Torq...........................1A 24
Lindridge Cl. TQ12: Kingst.....................1C 10
Lindridge Hill TQ12: Kingst....................1D 10
Lindridge La. TQ12: Kingst....................1C 10
....(not continuous)
Lindridge Rd. TQ1: Torq.........................1D 24
Lindsay Rd. TQ3: Pres...........................1D 26
Lindthorpe Way TQ5: Brixh....................3C 32
Linhay Bus. Pk. TQ13: Ashb..................2H 37
Linhay Cl. TQ12: Kingst.........................5E 11
Linhay Dr. TQ12: Kingst.........................5E 11
Linhey Cl. TQ7: Kingsb..........................4C 38
Links, The TQ1: Torq..............................6H 21
Links Cl. TQ5: Chur F.............................1H 31
Lion Cl. TQ7: Kingsb..............................3B 38
Lisburne Cres. TQ1: Torq.......................5E 25
Lisburne Pl. TQ1: Torq............................5E 25
....(off Lisburne Sq.)
Lisburne Sq. TQ1: Torq..........................5E 25
Little Barton TQ12: Kingst.....................2D 10
Little Batten Rd. TQ9: Tot.......................5H 35
Little Bossell La. TQ11: B'leigh 5B 36
Little Bradley Ponds Nature Reserve.....1E 7
Little Cl. TQ12: Kingst...........................2D 10
Littlefield TQ14: Bi'ton............................5F 13
Littlefield Cl. TQ2: Torq..........................6C 20
Littlegate Rd. TQ3: Paig.........................5E 27
Little Hayes TQ12: Kingst......................2D 10
Little Hill TQ8: Salc................................2F 39
Littlejoy Rd. TQ12: New A.......................2A 14
Little Park Rd. TQ3: Paig........................5D 26
Little Roborough TQ13: Ashb.................3F 37
Little Theatre Torquay, The...................6E 25
Little Triangle TQ14: Teignm..................5E 13
....(off Triangle Pl.)
Little Week Cl. EX7: Daw.........................1F 5
Little Week Gdns. EX7: Daw....................1F 5
Little Week La. EX7: Daw.........................1F 5
Little Week Rd. EX7: Daw.........................1F 5
LIVERMEAD...1H 27
Livermead Hill TQ2: Torq.......................1H 27
Living Coasts..6C 24
Livingstone Rd. TQ14: Teignm...............3E 13
Livvy Dean Cl. TQ1: Torq........................1C 24
Livvy Dean M. TQ1: Torq........................1C 24
Lloyd Av. TQ2: Torq................................1G 23
Locarno Av. TQ3: Pres............................2G 27
Locks Cl. TQ1: Torq................................2E 25
Locks Hill TQ1: Torq...............................2E 25
Locksley Cl. TQ1: Torq...........................2C 24
Locksley Grange TQ1: Torq....................2B 24
Lockyear Pl. TQ13: Bov T 1E 7
Loganberry La. TQ4: Paig.......................3A 28
Logan Rd. TQ2: Paig..............................4F 27
Long Barton TQ12: Kingst......................2D 10
Longcroft Av. TQ5: Brixh........................4C 32
Longcroft Dr. TQ5: Brixh........................4C 32
Longfield Av. TQ12: Kingst.....................4E 11
Longfield Dr. TQ8: Salc..........................2F 39
Longfields TQ7: W Alv.............................4A 38
Longfield Stables Cvn. & Camping Site
TQ12: Kingst...2E 11
Longford La. TQ12: Kingst.....................3D 10
Longford Pk. TQ12: Kingst.....................3D 10
Longlands EX7: Daw.................................4D 4
Long La. TQ12: Hacc..............................3E 17
Longmead Rd. TQ3: Pres.......................2C 26
Longmead Wlk. TQ3: Pres......................2C 26
Long Pk. TQ13: Ashb..............................2G 37
Longpark Hill TQ1: Maid.........................1H 21
Long Rydon TQ9: Sto G..........................5A 28
Longstone Rd. TQ4: Paig........................1B 28
Long Wools TQ4: Broads........................6G 29
Lonsdale Rd. TQ12: New A......................3A 16
Lonsee Gdns. TQ12: Kingsk...................2G 19

Lord Nelson Dr. TQ6: Dartm 4A 34
Lord's Pl. TQ1: Torq..................................3C 24
Loring Rd. TQ8: Salc...................................3G 39
Lorn Haven Bus. Pk. TQ13: Ashb 3G 37
Lorris Dr. TQ14: Teignm 3C 12
Louville Camp TQ5: Brixh 2G 33
Louville Cl. TQ4: Good 3F 29
Love La. TQ13: Ashb..................................4F 37
Love La. TQ14: Teignm 2F 13
Love La. TQ3: Marl....................................5A 22
                                          (not continuous)
Love La. Cl. TQ3: Marl 5A 22
Lovelane Cotts. TQ3: Marl...........................5A 22
Loventor Cres. TQ3: Marl 1A 26
Lower Audley Rd. TQ2: Torq........................1A 24
Lower Brimley Cl. TQ14: Teignm 4E 13
Lower Brimley Ter. TQ14: Teignm 3E 13
Lower Broad Pk. TQ6: Dartm 4A 34
Lower Broad Path TQ9: Sto G 6B 28
Lower Brook St. TQ14: Teignm 5E 13
Lower Budleigh Mdw. TQ2: New A 2E 15
Lower Cannon Rd. TQ12: H'fld.....................5E 7
Lower Collapark TQ9: Tot 3E 35
Lower Collins Rd. TQ9: Tot 3E 35
Lower Congella Rd. TQ1: Torq....................3D 24
Lower Coombe Rd. TQ12: Kingst 4E 11
Lower Dawlish Water EX7: Daw 2A 4
LOWER DEAN...6A 36
LOWER DITTISHAM...................................5A 31
Lower Dr. EX7: Daw...................................2F 5
Lower Ellacombe Chu. Rd. TQ1: Torq........3D 24
Lower Erith Rd. TQ1: Torq 5E 25
Lower Fairview Rd. TQ6: Dartm 4B 34
Lower Fern Rd. TQ12: New A 5C 16
Lower Fowden TQ4: Broads 1G 31
Lower French Pk. TQ12: New A 2E 15
Lower Kingsdown Rd. TQ14: Teignm...........4B 12
Lower Manor Rd. TQ5: Brixh 2D 32
Lower Meadow Ri. EX7: Daw 4C 4
LOWER NETHERTON..................................1E 17
Lower Pk. TQ3: Paig 4D 26
Lower Penns Rd. TQ3: Pres 2F 27
Lower Polsham Rd. TQ3: Paig 4E 27
Lower Rea Rd. TQ5: Brixh 2E 33
LOWER SANDYGATE...................................1C 10
Lower Sandygate TQ12: Kingst 1C 10
Lower Shirburn Rd. TQ1: Torq 2B 24
Lower St. TQ6: Dartm 2B 34 (4C 34)
Lower St. TQ7: W Alv..................................4A 38
Lower Thurlow Rd. TQ1: Torq 3B 24
LOWER TOWN...4C 36
Lower Union La. TQ2: Torq 4B 24
Lower Union Rd. TQ7: Kingsb......................3B 38
Lower Warberry Rd. TQ1: Torq 4C 24
Lower Warren Rd. TQ7: Kingsb 5C 38
Lower Woodfield Rd. TQ1: Torq...................6D 24
Lower Yalberton Holiday Pk. TQ4: Paig.......4A 28
Lower Yalberton Rd. TQ4: Paig 3A 28
Lowley Brook Ct. TQ2: Torq 1E 23
Loxbury Ri. TQ2: Torq.................................5G 23
Loxbury Rd. TQ2: Torq 4G 23
Lucerne TQ1: Torq......................................5E 25
Lucius St. TQ2: Torq...................................4A 24
Lulworth Cl. TQ4: Paig.................................3C 28
Lummaton Cross TQ2: Torq 5F 21
Lummaton Pl. TQ2: Torq 6G 21
Lupton House...4H 31
Luscombe Cl. TQ12: Ipp 6B 18
Luscombe Cl. TQ3: Paig 4A 26
Luscombe Cres. TQ3: Paig 5B 26
Luscombe La. TQ3: Paig 3A 26
Luscombe Rd. TQ3: Paig 4A 26
Luscombe Ter. EX7: Daw.............................4D 4
Lutyens Dr. TQ3: Paig.................................4A 26
Luxton Rd. TQ12: E Ogw 5E 15
Lydford Ho. TQ12: New A 1A 16
                                     (off Hameldown Way)
Lydwell Pk. Rd. TQ1: Torq 3E 25
Lydwell Rd. TQ1: Torq 3E 25
Lyme Bay Rd. TQ14: Teignm 2E 13
Lyme Vw. Cl. TQ1: Torq 2E 25
Lyme Vw. Rd. TQ1: Torq 2D 24
Lymington Rd. TQ1: Torq 2A 24

Lyncombe Cres. TQ1: Torq..........................6F 25
Lyncourt TQ1: Torq.....................................6E 25
Lyndale Rd. TQ12: Kingst 3C 10
Lyndhurst Av. TQ12: Kingsk.........................2H 19
Lyndhurst Cl. TQ12: Kingsk.........................2H 19
Lyn Gro. TQ12: Kingsk 1G 19
Lyngrove Ct. TQ12: Kingsk 1G 19
                                          (off Moor Pk. Rd.)
Lynmouth Av. TQ4: Paig 3C 28
Lynway Ct. TQ1: Torq..................................3C 24
Lynwood TQ12: E Ogw 4E 15
Lyte Hill Ct. TQ2: Torq 4E 21
                                             (off Lyte Hill La.)
Lyte Hill La. TQ2: Torq................................4E 21
Lyte's Rd. TQ5: Brixh 3E 33
Lytton Ho. TQ2: Torq 5B 24
                                       (off St Luke's Rd. Sth.)

M

Mabel Pl. TQ4: Paig...................................6E 27
Mcilwraith Rd. TQ8: Salc.............................2F 39
McKay Av. TQ1: Torq..................................3A 24
Mackrells Ter. TQ12: New A 3F 15
Maddacombe Rd. TQ12: Kingsk 3E 19
Maddacombe Ter. TQ12: A'well...................3D 18
Maddicks Orchard TQ9: Sto G 6A 28
Madeira Pl. TQ2: Torq 4B 24
Madrepore Pl. TQ1: Torq 4C 24
                                                   (off Pimlico)
Madrepore Rd. TQ1: Torq 5C 24
Magdalene Cl. TQ9: Tot 4F 35
Magdalene Rd. TQ1: Torq............................3A 24
Magistrates' Court Newton Abbot
                                                         .2G 15
Magistrates' Court Torquay 4B 24
MAIDENCOMBE...1H 21
Maidencombe Ho. TQ1: Torq 3H 21
Maidenfield TQ1: Maid 2G 21
Maidenway La. TQ3: Paig............................3C 26
Maidenway Rd. TQ3: Paig 3C 26
Main Av. TQ1: Torq.....................................1B 24
Main Rd. TQ8: Salc 3F 39
Malderek Av. TQ3: Pres...............................2F 27
Mallands Mdw. TQ12: A'well.......................6F 15
Mallard Cl. TQ12: Kingsk 3B 10
Mallard Cl. TQ2: Torq 4C 20
Mallock Rd. TQ2: Torq 4H 23
Malt Ho., The TQ9: Tot 4G 35
Malt Mill La. TQ9: Tot 3E 35
Malvernleigh TQ1: Torq...............................1C 24
                                      (off St Marychurch Rd.)
Manaton Tor Rd. TQ3: Pres 2C 26
Mannings Mdw. TQ13: Bov T 3C 6
Manor Av. TQ3: Pres..................................3F 27
Manor Bend TQ5: Galm 2F 31
Manor Cl. EX7: Daw....................................4D 4
Manor Cl. TQ12: A'well 6F 15
Manor Cl. TQ12: Kingsk 4H 19
Manor Cotts. TQ12: New A 2G 15
                                       (off Wolborough St.)
Manor Ct. TQ12: Kingsk 4H 19
                                                (off Torquay Rd.)
Manor Cres. TQ3: Pres 3F 27
Manor Dr. TQ12: Kingsk 4H 19
Manor Farm Camp Site TQ12: Dacc 3D 20
Manor Gdns. TQ1: Torq 6F 25
Manor Gdns. TQ12: A'well...........................1C 18
Manor Gdns. TQ12: Kingsk 4H 19
Manor Gdns. TQ3: Pres 3F 27
Manor Gdns. TQ7: Kingsb............................2C 38
Manorglade Ct. TQ1: Torq...........................4E 25
Manor Ho. TQ1: Torq 6F 25
Manor Ho., The TQ9: Tot 3F 35
Manor Ho. Apts., The TQ2: Torq..................6H 23
                                               (off Seaway La.)
Manor Orchard TQ12: E Ogw 4C 14
                                              (off Garners La.)
Manor Pk. TQ7: Kingsb...............................2C 38
Manor Rd. TQ1: Torq..................................1C 24
Manor Rd. TQ12: A'well...............................6F 15
Manor Rd. TQ12: New A 2E 15
Manor Rd. TQ14: Bi'ton 5G 13

Manor Rd. TQ3: Pres 3F 27
Manor Rd. TQ5: Brixh 2D 32
Manor Row EX7: Daw..................................4D 4
                                                 (off Brook St.)
Manor Steps TQ5: Brixh 2D 32
Manor St. TQ6: Ditt 5A 30
Manor Ter. TQ3: Paig 6D 26
Manor Ter. TQ5: Brixh 2D 32
Manor Va. Rd. TQ5: Galm............................2F 31
Manor Vw. TQ12: New A 2F 15
Manor Way TQ9: Tot...................................4F 35
Mansbridge Rd. TQ9: Tot 4H 35
Manscombe Cl. TQ2: Torq...........................6G 23
Manscombe Rd. TQ2: Torq..........................1G 27
Mansion Ho. St. TQ6: Dartm 2B 34 (4C 34)
                                        (off Newcomen Rd.)
Maple Av. TQ13: Bov T................................6B 6
Maple Cl. TQ12: Kingst 5D 10
Maple Cl. TQ13: Chud K..............................2H 7
Maple Cl. TQ5: Brixh 5B 32
Mapledene Cl. TQ9: Sto G 5A 28
Maple Gro. TQ4: Good 3E 29
Maple Rd. TQ5: Brixh 5B 32
                                             (not continuous)
Mapleton Cl. TQ12: New A 1E 15
Mapleton Pl. TQ12: New A 2H 15
Maple Wlk. TQ12: New A 1F 23
Marble Ct. TQ1: Torq..................................2A 24
Marcent Ho. TQ5: Brixh 4E 33
Marcombe Rd. TQ2: Torq 4H 23
Mardle Way TQ11: B'leigh 4B 36
Mardle Way Ind. Est. TQ11: B'leigh 4B 36
Margaret Cl. TQ12: E Ogw 4E 15
Margaret Cl. TQ12: Kingst 4D 10
Margaret Gdns. TQ12: New A 3C 16
Margaret Rd. TQ12: E Ogw 4E 15
Margaret Rd. TQ12: Kingst 4D 10
Marguerite Cl. TQ12: New A 1E 15
Marguerite Way TQ12: Kingsk 3H 19
Marina Cl. TQ5: Brixh 2F 33
Marina Ct. TQ4: Paig 6F 27
                                           (off Roundham Rd.)
Marina Dr. TQ5: Brixh 2F 33
Marina Rd. TQ5: Brixh 3F 33
Marine Ct. TQ3: Pres 3F 27
Marine Dr. TQ3: Pres 4F 27
Marine Gdns. TQ3: Pres 3F 27
Marine Mt. TQ1: Torq..................................6H 25
Marine Palms TQ2: Torq 5B 24
Marine Pde. EX7: Daw 5E 5
Marine Pde. TQ14: Shal 6D 12
Marine Pde. TQ3: Pres.................................3G 27
Marine Pk. TQ3: Pres 4F 27
Mariners Ct. TQ14: Shal 6C 12
                                          (off Commons Old Rd.)
Mariners Way TQ3: Pres..............................2C 26
Marine Ter. TQ14: Teignm 5D 12
                                             (off Foresters Ter.)
Marine Wlk. TQ5: Brixh 1D 32
Market, The TQ6: Dartm 1A 34 (4C 34)
                                                (off Market St.)
Market Cl. TQ11: B'leigh 4A 36
Market Cl. TQ13: Ashb 4F 37
Market Sq. TQ12: New A 2G 15
Market Sq. TQ6: Dartm................1A 34 (4C 34)
Market St. TQ1: Torq 4C 24
Market St. TQ11: B'leigh 4B 36
Market St. TQ12: New A 2G 15
Market St. TQ5: Brixh 2D 32
Market Steps TQ6: Dartm 1A 34 (4C 34)
Market St. TQ8: Salc 2H 39
Market Wlk. TQ12: New A 2G 15
Markham Ct. TQ4: Paig 6E 27
                                          (off Dartmouth Rd.)
Marlborough Av. TQ1: Torq 4E 25
Marlborough Pl. TQ12: New A 1F 15
Marlborough Ter. TQ13: Bov T 3A 6
MARLDON...1A 26
Marldon Av. TQ3: Paig.................................5D 26
Marldon Cross Hill TQ3: Marl.......................6A 22
Marldon Gro. TQ3: Marl...............................6A 22
Marldon Rd. TQ2: Torq 2C 22
Marldon Rd. TQ3: Paig 2B 26

Marldon Way TQ3: Marl................1B **26**
Marlowe Cl. TQ2: Torq..................2G **23**
Marnham Rd. TQ1: Torq.................2C **24**
Marsh La. TQ13: Bov T.....................4B **6**
Marsh Path TQ13: Bov T..................3B **6**
Marsh Rd. TQ12: New A...................2H **15**
Marston Cl. EX7: Daw.......................3F **5**
Martinique Gdns. TQ2: Torq.............4E **21**
Martinique Gro. TQ2: Torq...............4E **21**
Mary St. TQ13: Bov T........................2B **6**
Mashford Av. TQ6: Dartm.................3A **34**
Mathill Cl. TQ5: Brixh.......................4C **32**
Mathill Rd. TQ5: Brixh......................4C **32**
Matlock Lodge TQ2: Torq.................4B **24**
................................(off St Luke's Rd.)
Maudlin Dr. TQ14: Teignm...............1D **12**
Maudlin Rd. TQ9: Tot.......................4F **35**
Maxstoke Ct. TQ1: Torq....................4E **25**
Maxwell Ct. TQ1: Torq......................3A **24**
................................(off McKay Av.)
Maxwell Ct. TQ12: New A.................3A **16**
Mayfair Rd. TQ12: Ipp.......................5B **18**
Mayfield Cres. TQ12: New A.............2E **15**
Mayflower Av. TQ12: New A..............3C **16**
Mayflower Cl. EX7: Daw....................4E **5**
Mayflower Cl. TQ6: Dartm................3A **34**
Mayflower Dr. TQ5: Brixh..................4D **32**
Mayor's Av. TQ6: Dartm ... 1B **34** (4C **34**)
Mead Cl. TQ3: Paig..........................4E **27**
Meadfoot Cl. TQ1: Torq....................5G **25**
Meadfoot Ct. TQ1: Torq....................6D **24**
Meadfoot Cross TQ1: Torq................6D **24**
................................(off Parkhill Rd.)
Meadfoot Grange TQ1: Torq.............6D **24**
Meadfoot La. TQ1: Torq....................6D **24**
Meadfoot Rd. TQ1: Torq...................6D **24**
Meadfoot Sea Rd. TQ1: Torq............6E **25**
Mead La. TQ3: Paig..........................4E **27**
Meadow Brook TQ9: Tot...................4G **35**
Meadow Cl. TQ12: Kingsk.................1G **19**
Meadow Cl. TQ9: Tot........................4H **35**
Meadowcroft Dr. TQ12: Kingst...........2C **10**
Meadow Halt TQ12: E Ogw................3F **15**
Meadow Pk. EX7: Daw.......................3C **4**
Meadow Pk. TQ11: B'leigh................3D **36**
Meadow Pk. TQ12: Ipp......................5C **18**
Meadow Pk. TQ3: Marl......................6A **22**
Meadow Pk. TQ5: Brixh....................2C **32**
Meadow Ri. EX7: Daw........................3C **4**
Meadow Ri. TQ1: Torq......................4G **25**
Meadow Ri. TQ12: New A...................6E **9**
Meadow Rd. TQ2: Torq.....................6H **23**
Meadows, The TQ12: Kingst.............5E **11**
Meadow Side TQ12: New A................2F **15**
Meadowsweet La. TQ4: Paig.............3B **28**
Meadow Vw. TQ12: E Ogw................4E **15**
Meadow Vw. TQ14: Bi'ton..................4G **11**
Mead Rd. TQ2: Torq.........................1G **27**
Mead Way TQ12: New A....................5A **16**
Meadwood TQ1: Torq........................6E **25**
Meavy Av. TQ2: Torq........................2E **23**
Medway Rd. TQ2: Torq.....................5G **21**
Melbourne Cotts. TQ6: Dartm ... 2A **34** (4C **34**)
................................(off Crowther's Hill)
Melcot Cl. TQ12: Kingst....................4D **10**
Meldrum Cl. EX7: Daw.......................4E **5**
Mellons Cl. TQ12: New A..................1C **14**
Mellons Wlk. TQ12: New A.................1C **14**
................................(off Mellons Cl.)
Mellows Mdw. TQ12: New A..............2E **15**
Melville La. TQ2: Torq......................5C **24**
Melville Pl. TQ2: Torq.......................5C **24**
................................(off Melville St.)
Melville St. TQ2: Torq......................5C **24**
Mena Pk. Cl. TQ4: Paig....................3C **28**
Mendip Rd. TQ2: Torq......................6F **23**
Merchants Cnr. TQ12: New A............2A **16**
................................(off Quay Rd.)
Mere La. TQ14: Teignm....................4E **13**
Merivale Cl. TQ14: Teignm...............2E **13**
Merlin Way TQ2: Torq......................5C **20**
Merrifield Rd. TQ11: B'leigh.............3A **36**

Merritt Flats TQ3: Paig......................6D **26**
................................(off Merritt Rd.)
Merritt Rd. TQ3: Paig........................6D **26**
Merrivale Cl. TQ2: Torq....................3G **21**
Merryland Cl. TQ3: Pres...................1E **27**
Merryland Gdns. TQ3: Pres..............1E **27**
Merrywood TQ12: E Ogw..................4E **15**
Metherall Av. TQ5: Brixh..................4D **32**
Metherell Av. Ind. Est. TQ5: Brixh.....4D **32**
Mews, The EX7: Daw.........................4E **5**
Mews Gdns. TQ6: Dartm ... 1A **34** (4C **34**)
................................(off Northford Rd.)
Meyrick Rd. TQ1: Torq......................2D **24**
Middle Budleigh Mdw. TQ12: New A...2E **15**
Middle Lincombe Rd. TQ1: Torq.......6E **25**
Middle St. TQ14: Shal.......................6C **12**
Middle St. TQ5: Brixh.......................2D **32**
Middle Warberry Rd. TQ1: Torq.........4D **24**
Midvale Rd. TQ4: Paig......................6E **27**
Midway TQ12: Kingsk........................1G **19**
Miglo Ind. Est. TQ4: Paig..................2B **28**
MILBER................................4B **16**
Milber La. TQ12: Coff........................6D **16**
Milber La. TQ12: New A....................3D **16**
Milber La. TQ12: New A....................6D **16**
Milber Trad. Est. TQ12: New A...........4B **16**
MILE END................................6F **9**
Mile End Rd. TQ12: New A...............6F **9**
Milford Cl. TQ14: Teignm..................4C **12**
Mill, The TQ12: New A......................1H **15**
Millbrook Pk. Rd. TQ2: Torq..............4H **23**
Millbrook Rd. TQ3: Paig....................5E **27**
Mill Cl. TQ12: New A........................1D **14**
Mill Ct. EX7: Daw..............................4C **4**
Mill Cres. TQ6: Dartm.......................3A **34**
Mill End TQ12: Kingst........................1D **10**
Mill Hill TQ9: Sto G..........................6A **28**
Mill Hill Ct. TQ9: Sto G.....................6A **28**
Mill La. TQ12: E Ogw........................4C **14**
Mill La. TQ12: N Whil........................5D **18**
................................(not continuous)
Mill La. TQ13: Ashb.........................3E **37**
Mill La. TQ14: Teignm......................3B **12**
Mill La. TQ3: Comp..........................4A **24**
Mill La. TQ3: Paig............................6D **18**
Mill La. TQ3: Paig............................4E **27**
Mill La. TQ5: Brixh...........................6B **32**
Mill La. TQ5: Galm...........................3C **30**
Mill La. TQ9: Tot..............................4G **35**
Mill Leat TQ12: E Ogw......................2A **14**
Millmans Rd. TQ3: Marl....................6A **22**
Mill Mdw. TQ13: Ashb......................3E **37**
Mill Path TQ13: Ashb.......................4F **37**
................................(off St Andrews Cl.)
Mill St. TQ7: Kingsb.........................3B **38**
Mill Tail TQ9: Tot..............................4F **35**
Millwood TQ13: Bov T........................6B **6**
Millwood Bus. Pk. TQ12: New A........1B **16**
Milton Cl. TQ5: Brixh........................5C **32**
Milton Cres. TQ5: Brixh....................5C **32**
Milton Flds. TQ5: Brixh....................5B **32**
Milton Ho. TQ12: New A...................3H **15**
Milton La. TQ6: Dartm......................5A **34**
Milton Pk. TQ5: Brixh.......................5C **32**
Milton Rd. TQ12: New A...................1G **15**
Milton St. TQ5: Brixh........................6B **32**
Mimosa Way TQ4: Paig....................3B **28**
Minacre La. TQ12: N Whil..................6F **19**
Mincent Cl. TQ2: Torq......................4F **21**
Mincent Hill TQ2: Torq......................4F **21**
Minden Rd. TQ14: Teignm................4D **12**
Miners Cl. TQ13: Ashb......................3G **37**
Minerva Bus. Pk. TQ12: New A..........2A **16**
Minerva Way TQ12: New A................2B **16**
MINOR INJURIES UNIT (DAWLISH)........4D **4**
MINOR INJURIES UNIT (KINGSBRIDGE)...2B **38**
MINOR INJURIES UNIT (NEWTON ABBOT)...6A **10**
Miranda Rd. TQ3: Pres....................3C **26**
Mitre Cl. TQ14: Bi'ton.......................5F **13**
................................(not continuous)
Moat Hill TQ9: Tot...........................5F **35**
Moles La. TQ12: Kingst.....................1B **22**

Moles La. TQ12: N Whil.....................1B **22**
Moles La. TQ3: Marl.........................1B **22**
Monastery Rd. TQ3: Paig..................5D **26**
Monksbridge Rd. TQ5: Brixh............4C **32**
Monks Orchard TQ12: A'well............1B **18**
Monks Way TQ13: Bov T....................1A **6**
Monro Mead TQ12: Live....................1A **8**
Montagu Cl. TQ7: Kingsb.................2C **38**
Montagu M. TQ7: Kingsb..................2C **38**
................................(off Montagu Cl.)
Montagu Rd. TQ7: Kingsb................3B **38**
Monterey TQ4: Good.........................4F **29**
................................(off Hookhills Rd.)
Monterey Cl. TQ2: Torq.....................6H **23**
Monterey Pk. TQ12: New A...............4C **16**
Montesson Cl. TQ3: Paig..................4A **26**
Montesson Rd. TQ3: Paig.................4A **26**
Montpelier Cl. TQ3: Pres..................2E **27**
Montpelier Rd. TQ1: Torq.................5C **24**
Montpellier Rd. TQ1: Torq................5C **24**
................................(off Montpellier Rd.)
Montpellier Ter. TQ1: Torq................5C **24**
Montserrat Ri. TQ2: Torq..................4D **20**
Moorashes TQ9: Tot........................4F **35**
................................(off Grove Cl.)
Moor Cl. TQ14: Teignm.....................2E **13**
Moore Cl. TQ12: New A....................5C **16**
Moorhaven Cl. TQ1: Torq..................2H **23**
Moorhayes TQ13: Bov T....................3C **6**
Moorhen Cl. TQ12: Kingst.................4B **10**
Moorings, The TQ4: Paig..................6F **27**
................................(off Belle Vue Rd.)
Moorings, The TQ7: Kingsb...............5C **38**
Moorings Reach TQ5: Brixh..............2E **33**
Moorland Av. TQ12: Den....................6A **14**
Moorland Ga. TQ12: H'fld..................5F **7**
Moorland Pk. Cvn. Pk. TQ13: Bov T...6C **6**
Moorlands Cl. TQ12: New A..............3C **16**
Moorlands Vw. Ind. Est. TQ4: Paig....4C **28**
Moorland Vw. TQ11: B'leigh..............4A **36**
Moorland Vw. TQ12: New A...............3C **16**
Moor La. TQ13: Bov T........................5B **6**
Moor La. TQ2: Torq...........................4F **21**
Moor La. Cl. TQ2: Torq......................4F **21**
Moor Pk. TQ12: Kingsk......................1G **19**
Moor Pk. Rd. TQ12: Kingsk................1G **19**
Moors End TQ12: Kingst....................4C **10**
Moorsend TQ12: New A......................1D **14**
Moors Pk. TQ14: Bi'ton.....................6G **13**
Moorstone Leat TQ4: Good...............4F **29**
Moor Vw. TQ13: Bov T.......................5B **6**
................................(off Brimley Rd.)
Moorview TQ3: Marl..........................1A **26**
Moorview Cres. TQ3: Marl.................1A **26**
Moor Vw. Dr. TQ14: Teignm..............2B **12**
Moorview End TQ3: Marl...................1A **26**
Moretonhampstead Rd. TQ13: Bov T....1B **6**
Morgan Av. TQ3: Pres......................3E **27**
Morgans Quay TQ14: Teignm...........6D **12**
Morin Rd. TQ3: Pres.........................3F **27**
Morlaix Cl. EX7: Daw.........................2E **5**
Morningside EX7: Daw.......................6C **4**
Morningside TQ1: Torq......................4F **25**
................................(off Barrington Rd.)
Mortimer Av. TQ3: Pres.....................3E **27**
Motehole Rd. TQ12: Ipp....................5B **18**
Motherhill Ct. TQ8: Salc....................2F **39**
Moult Hill TQ8: Salc.........................5E **39**
Moult Rd. TQ8: Salc..........................5E **39**
Mount, The TQ14: Teignm.................3D **12**
Mount, The TQ2: Torq........................3E **21**
Mount, The TQ5: Brixh......................1D **32**
Mount Boone TQ6: Dartm ... 1A **34** (3B **34**)
Mount Boone Hill TQ6: Dartm..........3C **34**
Mount Boone La. TQ6: Dartm ... 1A **34** (3C **34**)
Mount Boone Way TQ6: Dartm.........3B **34**
Mount Braddons M. TQ1: Torq..........5D **24**
Mount Flagon Steps TQ6: Dartm ... 1A **34** (4C **34**)
................................(off Clarence Hill)
Mount Galpine TQ6: Dartm ... 1A **34** (3C **34**)
................................(off Clarence Hill)
Mount Hermon Rd. TQ1: Torq............3C **24**
Mount Pleasant Cl. TQ12: Kingsk......4H **19**
Mount Pleasant Cl. TQ7: Kingsb.......2C **38**

Mount Pleasant La. TQ14: Shal..................6C 12
Mount Pleasant M. TQ5: Brixh 3D 32
Mount Pleasant Rd. EX7: Daw W 1G 5
Mount Pleasant Rd. TQ1: Torq..................3C 24
Mount Pleasant Rd. TQ12: Kingsk 4H 19
Mount Pleasant Rd. TQ12: New A..............3H 15
Mount Pleasant Rd. TQ5: Brixh 3D 32
Mount Rd. TQ5: Brixh 3E 33
MOUNT STUART PRIVATE HOSPITAL 2A 24
Mount Vw. Ter. TQ9: Tot 4F 35
....(off Heath Way)
Mudstone La. TQ5: Brixh 4E 33
Mulberry Cl. TQ3: Paig 4B 26
Mulberry St. TQ14: Teignm 4D 12
Murley Cres. TQ14: Bi'ton 5F 13
Murley Grange TQ14: Bi'ton 5F 13
Museum Ct. TQ7: Kingsb 2B 38
Museum Rd. TQ1: Torq................................5D 24
Museum Way TQ1: Torq..............................5D 24
Musket Rd. TQ12: H'fld 5E 7
Myrtle Hill TQ14: Teignm 4E 13

N

Naida Va. TQ6: Dartm 2C 34
Naseby Dr. TQ12: H'fld 5E 7
Nash Gdns. EX7: Daw 6D 4
Nellies Wood Vw. TQ9: Darti 1E 35
Nelson Cl. TQ14: Teignm 3C 12
Nelson Pl. TQ12: New A................................6A 10
Nelson Rd. TQ5: Brixh 2D 32
Nelson Rd. Ind. Est. TQ6: Dartm 3A 34
....(off Nelson Rd.)
Ness Dr. TQ14: Shal......................................6D 12
Ness Vw. Rd. TQ14: Teignm 1E 13
Netherleigh Rd. TQ1: Torq..........................2C 24
Nether Mdw. TQ3: Marl 6A 22
NETHERTON 2F 17
Netley Rd. TQ12: New A 1G 15
Nettle Cl. TQ12: New A 6D 8
Neville Rd. TQ12: New A..............................1F 15
Newbury Dr. TQ13: Bov T 3D 6
Newcause TQ11: B'leigh................................4B 36
....(off Jordan St.)
New Central Cinema TQ2: Torq..................4B 24
Newcomen Engine House 1B 34 (4C 34)
Newcomen Rd. TQ6: Dartm 2B 34 (4C 34)
Newcross Pk. TQ12: Kingst 2B 10
New Esplanade Ct. TQ3: Paig......................5F 27
Newfoundland Rd. TQ14: Teignm 4B 12
Newfoundland Way TQ12: New A 2G 15
Newhay, The EX7: Daw 4C 4
Newhay Cl. EX7: Daw 4C 4
Newhayes TQ12: Ipp 6A 18
Newlands EX7: Daw 3E 5
Newlands Dr. TQ13: Bov T 6B 6
New Pk. TQ13: Bov T 6B 6
New Pk. Cl. TQ5: Brixh 3E 33
New Pk. Cres. TQ12: Kingst 3C 10
New Pk. Rd. TQ12: Kingst 3C 10
New Pk. Rd. TQ3: Paig 4C 26
Newport St. TQ6: Dartm 1A 34 (4C 34)
New Quay La. TQ5: Brixh..............................2E 33
New Quay St. TQ14: Teignm........................5D 12
New Rd. TQ11: B'leigh 4B 36
New Rd. TQ14: Teignm 4B 12
....(not continuous)
New Rd. TQ5: Brixh 3C 32
New Rd. TQ9: Sto G 6A 28
New Rd. TQ9: Tot 3G 35
New St. TQ3: Paig 5E 27
NEWTAKE 4C 16
Newtake Ho. TQ2: Torq 6E 21
Newtake Mt. TQ12: New A 3C 16
Newtake Ri. TQ12: New A 4C 16
NEWTON ABBOT 2A 16
NEWTON ABBOT COMMUNITY HOSPITAL....6A 10
Newton Abbot Leisure Cen.........................1F 15
Newton Abbot Racecourse 6C 10
Newton Abbot Rd. TQ9: Tot 4G 35
Newton Abbot Sailing Club 4H 15
Newton Abbot Station (Rail)........................2A 16
Newton Abbot Tourist Info. Cen.................2G 15

Newton Abbot Town & GWR Mus...............2G 15
Newton Hall TQ12: New A 3H 15
Newton Hill TQ12: S'head............................1E 21
Newton Rd. TQ12: H'fld 6D 6
Newton Rd. TQ12: Kingsk 2H 19
Newton Rd. TQ12: Kingst.............................1H 15
Newton Rd. TQ12: New A 1H 15
Newton Rd. TQ13: Bov T 3B 6
Newton Rd. TQ14: Bi'ton 4G 11
Newton Rd. TQ2: Torq 6B 20
Newton Rd. TQ8: Salc...................................3G 39
Newton Rd. TQ9: L'ton 3G 35
Newton Rd. TQ9: Tot 3G 35
Newton Rd. Retail Pk...................................5C 10
New Wlk. TQ1: Torq......................................4G 35
Nicholls Pl. TQ13: Bov T 1E 7
Nicholson Rd. TQ12: Torq 5C 20
Nightingale Cl. TQ2: Torq 5D 20
Nightjar Cl. TQ2: Torq..................................5D 20
Noelle Dr. TQ12: New A................................1F 15
Norden La. TQ7: Kingsb................................3A 38
Norman Cl. TQ12: New A..............................6F 9
Normandy Way TQ8: Salc.............................2H 39
Norman Rd. TQ3: Paig 4F 27
North Boundary Rd. TQ5: Brixh..................2B 32
North Emb. TQ6: Dartm 1B 34 (3C 34)
North End Cl. TQ12: Ipp................................5A 18
Northernhay TQ12: New A............................3H 15
Northfields Ind. Est. TQ5: Brixh..................2C 32
Northfields La. TQ5: Brixh 2C 32
Northford Rd. TQ6: Dartm 1A 34 (4B 34)
North Furzeham Rd. TQ5: Brixh 1D 32
Northgate TQ9: Tot 3F 35
....(off Castle St.)
North Hill Cl. TQ5: Brixh 2C 32
Northleat Av. TQ3: Paig................................6B 26
North Lodge Cl. EX7: Daw 5C 4
North Rocks Rd. TQ4: Broads......................6E 29
North St. TQ12: Ipp......................................5A 18
North St. TQ13: Ashb 3E 37
North St. TQ9: Tot..3F 35
Northumberland Pl. TQ14: Teignm 5D 12
North Vw. TQ14: Shal 6C 12
....(off Commons Old Rd.)
North Vw. Rd. TQ5: Brixh 2E 33
Northville Pk. TQ7: Kingsb 2B 38
Northville Rd. TQ7: Kingsb 2B 38
NORTH WHILBOROUGH 6F 19
Northwood La. TQ11: Buck 1B 36
Northwoods TQ13: Bov T 6B 6
Nursery Cl. TQ3: Paig 6D 26
Nursery Rd. TQ12: Kingst 4D 10
Nut Bush La. TQ2: Torq 2E 23
Nuthatch Dr. TQ2: Torq................................5D 20
Nut Tree Ct. TQ5: Brixh................................5C 32
Nut Tree Orchard TQ5: Brixh......................5C 32

O

Oakbank TQ13: Bov T 6B 6
Oakcliff Holiday Pk. EX7: Daw W................1H 5
....(not continuous)
Oak Cl. TQ12: Kingst 5E 11
Oak End Ct. TQ3: Marl 1A 26
Oakford TQ12: Kingst 4C 10
Oak Hill EX7: Daw 6C 4
Oak Hill Cross Rd. EX7: Holc........................6C 4
Oak Hill Cross Rd. TQ14: Teignm 2F 13
Oak Hill Rd. TQ1: Torq 3A 24
Oakland Dr. EX7: Daw 5D 4
Oakland Rd. TQ12: New A 3B 16
Oaklands Cl. TQ11: B'leigh 4A 36
Oaklands Pk. TQ11: B'leigh 3A 36
Oaklands Rd. TQ11: B'leigh 2A 36
Oakland Wlk. EX7: Daw 5D 4
Oak Lawn TQ12: New A................................3H 15
Oaklawn Ct. TQ1: Torq 2A 24
....(off Barton Rd.)
Oaklawn Ter. TQ1: Torq 2A 24
....(off St Vincent's Rd.)
Oaklea Cl. TQ7: Kingsb 4B 38
Oaklea Pk. TQ12: Live 1B 8
Oakley Cl. TQ14: Teignm 2D 12

Oak Pk. Av. TQ2: Torq 1G 23
Oak Pk. Cl. TQ2: Torq 1G 23
Oak Pk. Rd. TQ12: New A 1E 15
Oak Pk. Vs. EX7: Daw....................................3E 5
Oak Pl. TQ12: New A 2H 15
....(not continuous)
Oaks, The TQ12: New A................................5C 16
Oaks, The TQ13: Bov T 3D 6
Oak Tree Dr. TQ12: New A 5C 16
Oak Tree Gro. TQ14: Shal............................6C 12
Oak Vw. Cl. TQ2: Torq 6A 20
Oakymead Pk. TQ12: Kingst 5C 10
Oathills Cres. TQ4: Paig...............................4C 28
Oathills Pl. TQ4: Paig 4C 28
Oatlands Dr. TQ4: Paig 1D 28
Occombe Farm..6B 22
Occombe Valley Rd. TQ3: Pres 1D 26
Ocean Vw. Cres. TQ5: Brixh 6B 32
Ocean Vw. Dr. TQ5: Brixh 6B 32
Ochre Ct. TQ5: Brixh 3E 33
Octon Gro. TQ1: Torq..................................2H 23
Oddicombe Beach Hill TQ1: Torq................1D 24
Odle Hill TQ12: A'well 6F 15
Odlehill Gro. TQ12: A'well............................1B 18
Ogwell End Dr. TQ12: E Ogw 3E 15
Ogwell Grn. TQ12: E Ogw............................4D 14
Ogwell Mill Rd. TQ12: New A 3D 14
Ogwell Rd. TQ12: E Ogw 4D 14
Oke Tor Cl. TQ3: Pres 1D 26
Old Brewery, The TQ2: Torq........................6G 21
....(off Lummaton Pl.)
Old Cider Press, The TQ4: Paig 6E 27
....(off Fisher St.)
Old Cider Works La. TQ12: A'well 6F 15
Old Cockington School M., The TQ2: Torq
....4H 23
Oldenburg Pk. TQ3: Paig 4F 27
Old Exeter Rd. TQ12: New A........................1G 15
Old Exeter Rd. TQ13: Ashb 2H 37
Old Farm Way EX7: Daw 6D 4
Old Gatehouse Rd. EX7: Daw 3E 5
Old Mkt., The TQ6: Dartm 1A 34 (4C 34)
....(off Market St.)
Old Mill Rd. TQ2: Torq 1H 27
....(not continuous)
Old Newton Rd. TQ12: H'fld 6D 6
Old Newton Rd. TQ12: Kingsk 1F 19
Old Newton Rd. TQ13: Bov T 5C 6
Old Orchard TQ13: Bov T 3C 6
Old Paignton Rd. TQ2: Torq Roundhill Rd. 1G 27
Old Paignton Rd. TQ2: Torq Stoneleigh Dr....6G 23
Old Plymouth Rd. TQ7: Kingsb 2B 38
Old Quay TQ14: Teignm..............................5D 12
Old Quay St. TQ14: Teignm 5D 12
Old Rd. TQ5: Galm 2E 31
Old School M. EX7: Daw 4D 4
....(off School Hill)
Old Station Yd. TQ7: Kingsb........................3B 38
Old Teignmouth Rd. EX7: Daw......................6D 4
Old Torquay Rd. TQ3: Pres 3F 27
Old Torwood Rd. TQ1: Torq 5D 24
Old Totnes Rd. TQ11: B'leigh 4C 36
Old Totnes Rd. TQ12: New A 3F 15
....(not continuous)
Old Totnes Rd. TQ13: Ashb 5E 37
Old Town Hall, The TQ1: Torq 1D 24
Old Town St. EX7: Daw 4C 4
OLDWAY 4E 27
Oldway Mansion 3E 27
Oldway Oaks TQ3: Paig 4D 26
Oldway Rd. TQ3: Paig 4E 27
Oldway Rd. TQ3: Pres 4E 27
Old Widdicombe La. TQ3: Paig....................4A 26
Old Woods Hill TQ2: Torq............................2H 23
Old Woods Trad. Est. TQ2: Torq 1H 23
Oliver Pl. TQ12: H'fld 5F 7
Onslow Rd. TQ8: Salc..................................2F 39
Orange Gro. TQ2: Torq................................5F 21
Orbec Av. TQ12: New A................................4E 11
Orchard, The EX7: Holc 1G 13
Orchard, The TQ11: B'leigh 4C 36
Orchard, The TQ12: A'well 1C 18
Orchard, The TQ14: Bi'ton 5G 13

Orchard, The TQ9: Tot 4G 35
....(off Shute Rd.)
Orchard Cl. TQ12: Kingst Ware Cl. 4E 11
Orchard Cl. TQ12: Kingst Woodlands Cops
....1C 10
Orchard Cl. EX7: Daw 4D 4
Orchard Cl. TQ12: E Ogw..............................4C 14
Orchard Cl. TQ14: Shal 6B 12
Orchard Cl. TQ5: Brixh..................................4D 32
Orchard Cl. TQ5: Galm....................................2F 31
Orchard Cl. TQ9: Sto G..................................6A 28
....(off Paignton Rd.)
Orchard Ct. TQ12: New A................................2G 15
....(off Bradley La.)
Orchard Ct. TQ8: Salc....................................2G 39
....(off Island St.)
Orchard Dr. TQ12: Ipp 5B 18
Orchard Dr. TQ12: Kingsk..............................3G 19
Orchard Dr. TQ8: Salc....................................2F 39
Orchard Gdns. EX7: Daw..................................4D 4
Orchard Gdns. TQ12: Kingst 4D 10
....(off Crossley Moor Rd.)
Orchard Gdns. TQ14: Teignm 5E 13
Orchard Gdns. TQ6: Dartm 4B 34
Orchard Gro. TQ12: New A 1C 14
Orchard Gro. TQ5: Brixh................................5D 32
Orchard Ind. Est. (North) TQ7: Kingsb 3B 38
Orchard Ind. Est. (South) TQ7: Kingsb........3B 38
Orchard Pl. TQ1: Torq......................................6E 25
Orchard Rd. TQ13: Ashb..................................4F 37
Orchard Rd. TQ2: Torq....................................6E 21
Orchards, The TQ5: Galm 2E 31
Orchard Ter. TQ11: B'leigh 4B 36
Orchard Ter. TQ12: A'well 6G 15
Orchard Ter. TQ12: Kingsk..............................2G 19
Orchard Ter. TQ13: Bov T..................................2C 6
Orchard Ter. TQ9: Tot 4F 35
Orchard Vw. TQ14: Bi'ton..............................4H 11
Orchard Way TQ13: Bov T..................................2C 6
Orchard Way TQ2: Torq..................................6A 20
Orchard Way TQ9: Sto G..................................5A 28
Orchard Waye TQ9: Tot 4E 35
Orchid Av. TQ12: Kingst................................4D 10
Orchid Paradise 4F 9
Orchid Va. TQ12: Kingst..................................2D 10
Orchid Way TQ2: Torq......................................5E 21
Orestone Dr. TQ1: Maid..................................2H 21
Orestone La. TQ12: Dacc................................4C 20
Orient Rd. TQ3: Pres......................................2G 27
Orkney Cl. TQ2: Torq......................................5D 20
Orleigh Av. TQ12: New A 6A 10
Orleigh Cross TQ12: New A 6A 10
Orleigh Pk. TQ12: New A 6A 10
Ormond Lodge TQ4: Paig................................6F 27
Osborn Cl. TQ3: Pres......................................1D 26
Osborn Cl. TQ12: Ipp 5B 18
Osborne St. TQ12: New A 2A 16
Osmonds La. TQ14: Teignm 5D 12
Osney Av. TQ4: Good......................................1E 29
Osney Cres. TQ4: Good..................................6E 27
Osney Gdns. TQ4: Good..................................1E 29
Osprey Dr. TQ2: Torq......................................4C 20
Osprey Ho. TQ1: Torq......................................2E 25
....(off Babbacombe Rd.)
Otter Cl. TQ2: Torq..2F 23
Otter Rd. TQ2: Torq..2F 23
Outlook Ct. EX7: Daw..4E 5
....(off E. Cliff Rd.)
Overbeck's 6E 39
Overbrook EX7: Daw..4C 4
Overcliff Ct. EX7: Daw......................................3E 5
Overclose TQ3: Paig..3B 26
Overdale Cl. TQ2: Torq....................................3E 21
Overgang TQ5: Brixh..2E 33
Overgang Rd. TQ5: Brixh................................1D 32
Oxenham Grn. TQ2: Torq................................3G 23
Oxford Ct. TQ2: Torq......................................6E 21
Oxford La. TQ5: Brixh....................................3B 32
Oxford St. TQ6: Dartm............2B 34 (4C 34)
Oxlea Cl. TQ1: Torq..5F 25
Oxlea Rd. TQ1: Torq..5F 25
Oyster Bend TQ4: Good..................................3F 29

Oystercatcher Ct. TQ14: Shal......................6B 12
Oyster Cl. TQ4: Good......................................3F 29

P

Packhall La. TQ5: Brixh..................................5B 32
....(not continuous)
Padacre Rd. TQ2: Torq....................................3F 21
Paddock, The EX7: Daw....................................3D 4
Paddocks, The TQ12: A'well 6G 15
Paddocks, The TQ9: Tot 3G 35
Paddons Coombe TQ12: Kingst....................2D 10
Paddons La. TQ14: Teignm 2C 12
Pafford Av. TQ2: Torq....................................5G 21
Pafford Cl. TQ2: Torq......................................5F 21
Paige Adams Rd. TQ9: Tot 3E 35
PAIGNTON 5E 27
Paignton Bus Station 5E 27
Paignton Fernacombe Towermill 2C 26
PAIGNTON HOSPITAL 5E 27
Paignton Pier 5G 27
Paignton Rd. TQ9: Sto G................................5A 28
Paignton Sailing Club................................6G 27
....(off South Quay)
Paignton Station Dartmouth Steam Railway
....6E 27
Paignton Station (Rail) 5E 27
Paignton Tourist Info. Cen. 6E 27
Paignton Zoo..1C 28
Palace Av. TQ3: Paig......................................5E 27
Palace Gdns. TQ1: Torq..................................3F 25
Palace Pl. TQ3: Paig......................................5E 27
Palace Theatre Paignton 5E 27
Palatine Cl. TQ1: Torq....................................4C 24
Palermo TQ1: Torq..5E 25
Palermo Rd. TQ1: Torq....................................2D 24
Palk Cl. TQ14: Shal..6B 12
Palk Pl. TQ1: Torq..6G 21
....(off Teignmouth Rd.)
Palk St. TQ2: Torq..5C 24
Palm Rd. TQ2: Torq..4B 24
Palms, The TQ1: Torq......................................5E 25
Palm Tree Vw. TQ4: Good................................3E 29
Panorama TQ2: Torq..1H 27
....(off Livermead Hill)
Paradise Glen TQ14: Teignm 3D 12
Paradise Pl. TQ5: Brixh..................................2D 32
Paradise Rd. TQ14: Teignm 3D 12
Paradise Wlk. TQ4: Good................................1F 29
Paradise Wlk. TQ9: Tot 5H 35
Paris Rd. TQ3: Pres..3F 27
Park & Ride Brixham 2G 31
Park & Ride Salcombe..................................2F 39
Park Av. TQ5: Brixh..4C 32
Parkbay Av. TQ4: Paig....................................3B 28
Park Ct. TQ5: Brixh..2F 33
Park Cres. TQ1: Torq......................................6G 21
Parkelands TQ13: Bov T....................................3B 6
Parkers Cl. TQ9: Tot 5G 35
Parkers Way TQ9: Tot......................................5G 35
Parkfield 4F 27
Parkfield Cl. TQ3: Marl..................................6A 22
Parkfield Rd. TQ9: Tot 4H 35
Parkfield Rd. TQ1: Torq..................................2A 24
Park Hall TQ1: Torq..6D 24
Parkham Field..3D 32
Parkham Glade TQ5: Brixh............................3D 32
Parkham La. TQ5: Brixh..................................3D 32
Parkham Rd. TQ5: Brixh................................5B 26
Parkham Towers TQ5: Brixh..........................3D 32
....(off Wren Hill)
Park Hill TQ14: Teignm..................................5D 12
Parkhill Rd. TQ1: Torq....................................6C 24
Parkhurst Rd. TQ1: Torq................................2A 24
Parklands TQ9: Tot..3F 35
Parklands Way TQ13: Bov T..............................6B 6
Park La. TQ1: Torq..6C 24
Park La. Steps TQ1: Torq................................6D 24
....(off Park La.)
Park M. TQ5: Brixh..2F 33
Park Ri. EX7: Daw..5D 4
Park Ri. TQ8: Salc..3F 39
Park Rd. EX7: Daw..4D 4

Park Rd. TQ1: Torq..6G 21
Park Rd. TQ12: Kingsk....................................2G 19
Parkside TQ8: Salc..2G 39
Parkside Rd. TQ4: Paig....................................5F 27
Parkside Vs. TQ1: Torq....................................2D 24
....(off Palermo Rd.)
Park Vw. TQ12: New A....................................5C 16
Parson St. TQ14: Teignm 4D 12
Paternoster La. TQ12: Ipp 5A 18
Pathfields TQ9: Tot..4G 35
Pathfields Cl. TQ9: Tot 4G 35
Pavilions 5E 13
Pavilions Cl. TQ5: Brixh..................................2C 32
Pavor Rd. TQ2: Torq..5G 21
Paynsford M. TQ12: New A 1G 15
Paynsford Rd. TQ12: New A............................1G 15
Peak Tor Av. TQ1: Torq....................................6D 24
Peaseditch TQ5: Brixh....................................4E 33
Peasland Rd. TQ2: Torq..................................3F 21
Pebble Cl. TQ4: Good......................................1E 29
Pegasus Ct. TQ3: Paig....................................3E 27
Pellew Arc. TQ14: Teignm 5D 12
....(off Teign St.)
Pellew Ho. TQ14: Teignm 5D 12
....(off Teign St.)
Pellew Way TQ14: Teignm..............................2C 12
Pembroke Pk. TQ3: Marl..................................6B 22
Pembroke Rd. TQ1: Torq................................4C 24
Pembroke Rd. TQ3: Marl..................................4B 26
Pencarrow Rd. TQ3: Paig................................4A 26
Pencorse Rd. TQ2: Torq..................................1A 24
Pendennis Rd. TQ2: Torq................................1A 24
Penfield Gdns. EX7: Daw..................................4D 4
Pengelly Cl. TQ12: Kingst..............................4E 11
Pengelly Way TQ2: Torq..................................4D 20
Penn Ct. TQ5: Brixh..4E 33
Pennine Dr. TQ4: Coll M..................................1A 28
PENNINN..4A 16
Penn Inn Cl. TQ12: New A 3B 16
Penn La. TQ5: Brixh..4D 32
Penn Mdws. TQ5: Brixh..................................4E 33
Penn Mdws. Cl. TQ5: Brixh............................4E 33
Penns Way TQ12: Kingst................................5E 11
Pennsylvania Rd. TQ1: Torq..........................4C 24
Pennyacre Rd. TQ14: Teignm 3E 13
Penny's Hill TQ1: Torq....................................2A 24
Penpethy Cl. TQ5: Brixh..................................3C 32
Penpethy Ct. TQ5: Brixh..................................3C 32
Penpethy Rd. TQ5: Brixh................................2C 32
Penrhyn Pl. TQ14: Shal..................................6C 12
Penshurst Rd. TQ12: New A 4G 15
Pensilva Pk. TQ5: Brixh..................................4D 32
Pentridge Av. TQ2: Torq..................................1F 27
Penwill Way TQ4: Good....................................1C 28
Penwill Way TQ4: Paig....................................1C 28
Peppery La. TQ14: Shal..................................6B 12
Peregrine Cl. TQ2: Torq..................................4C 20
Perinville Cl. TQ1: Torq....................................3F 25
Perinville Rd. TQ1: Torq..................................2E 25
Perros Cl. TQ14: Teignm................................3B 12
Perry La. TQ12: New A......................................5D 8
Peters Cl. TQ4: Paig..4C 24
Peters Cres. TQ3: Marl....................................6A 22
Petitor M. TQ1: Torq..6G 21
Petitor Rd. TQ1: Torq......................................6G 21
Petitwell La. TQ1: Torq....................................6G 21
Petrel Cl. TQ2: Torq..4B 20
Petroc Dr. TQ12: New A..................................1H 15
Phoenix Pl. TQ7: W Alv....................................4A 38
Pidgley Rd. EX7: Daw..1F 5
Piermont Pl. EX7: Daw......................................4E 5
Pilgrim Cl. TQ5: Brixh......................................2F 33
Pillar Av. TQ5: Brixh..2C 32
Pillar Cl. TQ5: Brixh..2C 32
Pillar Cres. TQ5: Brixh....................................2C 32
Pilmuir Av. TQ2: Torq......................................4H 23
Pimlico TQ1: Torq..4C 24
Pimm Rd. TQ3: Paig..4B 26
Pine Cl. TQ14: Teignm......................................2F 13
Pine Cl. TQ5: Brixh..2C 32
Pine Ct. TQ1: Torq..4E 25
Pines Rd. TQ3: Paig..3B 26
Pine Vw. Av. TQ1: Torq....................................3D 24

Pine Vw. Gdns. – Reddenhill Rd.

Pine Vw. Gdns. TQ1: Torq 3D **24**
Pine Vw. Rd. TQ1: Torq 3D **24**
Pinewood Cl. EX7: Daw 2G **5**
Pinewood Rd. TQ12: New A 3B **16**
Pioneer Ter. TQ11: B'leigh 4A **36**
Pipehouse La. TQ13: Chud K 2H **7**
Pipistrelle Way TQ12: Kingst 3B **10**
Pippins M. TQ13: Ashb 3G **37**
....*(off Eastern Rd.)*
Pitcairn Cres. TQ2: Torq 4D **20**
Pitland La. TQ12: Dacc 1D **20**
Pitley Rd. TQ13: Ashb 3H **37**
Pitt Hill Rd. TQ12: New A 6G **9**
Pitt La. EX7: Daw 3B **4**
Place La. TQ13: Ashb 2G **37**
PLAINMOOR 2C **24**
Plainmoor **2C 24**
Plainmoor Community Swimming Pool
....**2C 24**
Plainmoor Rd. TQ1: Torq 2C **24**
Plains, The TQ9: Tot 4G **35**
Plantation Cl. TQ12: New A 4C **16**
Plantation Ter. EX7: Daw 4D **4**
Plantation Way TQ2: Torq 6B **20**
Plant World Gdns. **6F 17**
Platt Cl. TQ8: Salc 3E **39**
Platway La. TQ14: Shal 6B **12**
Pleasant Ter. TQ3: Paig 5D **26**
Plym Cl. TQ2: Torq 2E **23**
Plymouth Rd. TQ11: B'leigh 6A **36**
....(not continuous)
Plymouth Rd. TQ11: Lwr D 6A **36**
....(not continuous)
Plymouth Rd. TQ13: Chud K 2H **7**
Polhearne La. TQ5: Brixh 4C **32**
Polhearne Way TQ5: Brixh 4C **32**
Pollyblank Rd. TQ12: New A 2G **15**
Polperro Cl. TQ3: Paig 4A **26**
Polsham Pk. TQ3: Paig 4E **27**
Pomeroy Av. TQ5: Brixh 2B **32**
Pomeroy Pl. TQ12: Live 1A **8**
Pomeroy Rd. TQ12: New A 2G **15**
Pomeroy Vs. TQ9: Tot 3G **35**
Pook La. TQ13: Ashb 3F **37**
Poplar Cl. TQ12: New A 5D **16**
Poplar Cl. TQ5: Brixh 6A **32**
Poplar Dr. TQ7: Kingsb 3B **38**
Poplars, The TQ13: Chud K 1H **7**
Poplars Dr. TQ3: Marl 1A **26**
Poplar Ter. TQ12: Ipp 5B **18**
Porlock Way TQ4: Paig 3C **28**
Portland Av. TQ14: Teignm 2E **13**
Portland Ct. TQ1: Torq 2E **25**
....*(off Portland Rd.)*
Portland Rd. TQ1: Torq 2E **25**
Potters Hill TQ1: Torq 4C **24**
Potters Lea Development TQ12: Kingst
....3B **10**
Pottery, The TQ6: Dartm 6D **34**
....*(off Warfleet Creek Rd.)*
Pottery Cl. TQ13: Bov T 5B **6**
Pottery Cotts. TQ6: Dartm 6D **34**
....*(off Warfleet Creek Rd.)*
Pottery Ct. TQ6: Dartm 4A **34**
Pottery Rd. TQ12: Kingst 5C **10**
Pottery Rd. TQ13: Bov T 5B **6**
Pound Fld. TQ9: Sto G 5A **28**
Pound La. TQ12: Kingsk 3G **19**
Pound La. TQ14: Shal 6A **12**
Pound La. TQ14: Teignm 5E **13**
Pound Pl. TQ12: New A 2G **15**
....*(off Jubilee Rd.)*
Pound Pl. TQ13: Bov T 2C **6**
Poundsgate Cl. TQ5: Brixh 3F **33**
Poundstone Ct. TQ8: Salc 3G **39**
Powderham Cl. TQ12: New A 3G **15**
Powderham Ct. TQ12: New A 2G **15**
....*(off Powderham Rd.)*
Powderham Rd. TQ12: New A 2G **15**
Powderham Rd. TQ2: Torq 6E **21**
Powderham Ter. TQ12: New A 3G **15**
Powderham Ter. TQ14: Teignm 5E **13**
Precinct, The TQ7: Kingsb 2C **38**
Prestbury Pk. TQ2: Torq 3A **24**
....*(off Vansittart Rd.)*
PRESTON 1A **10**
PRESTON 2F **27**
Preston Down Av. TQ3: Pres 1E **27**
Preston Down Rd. TQ3: Pres 6B **22**
Prigg Mdw. TQ13: Ashb 4F **37**
Primley Ct. TQ3: Paig 6B **26**
PRIMLEY CROSS 6C **26**
Primley Pk. TQ3: Paig 6C **26**
Primley Pk. E. TQ3: Paig 6D **26**
Primrose Cl. TQ12: Kingst 4D **10**
Primrose Dr. TQ12: New A 6E **9**
Primrose Ter. TQ9: Tot 4H **35**
Primrose Way TQ12: Kingsk 1G **19**
Prince Albert Pl. EX7: Daw 4D **4**
....*(off Brook St.)*
Prince Charles Ct. TQ2: Torq 4F **21**
Prince of Wales Dr. TQ6: Dartm 3C **34**
Prince of Wales Rd. TQ7: Kingsb 3B **38**
Prince Rupert Way TQ12: H'fld 5F **7**
Prince's Point TQ1: Torq 6D **24**
Princes Rd. TQ1: Torq 4C **24**
Princes Rd. E. TQ1: Torq 4D **24**
Princes Rd. W. TQ1: Torq 4C **24**
Princess Gdns. **6C 24**
....*(off Princess Pde.)*
Princess Pde. TQ2: Torq 6C **24**
Princess Rd. TQ12: Kingsk 3H **19**
Princess Rd. TQ12: Kingst 3C **10**
Princess Theatre Torquay **6B 24**
Princes St. EX7: Daw 4D **4**
Princes St. TQ1: Torq 2E **25**
Princes St. TQ3: Paig 5E **27**
Prince St. TQ12: New A 2H **15**
Prince William Ct. TQ5: Brixh 3D **32**
Prings Ct. TQ5: Brixh 2D **32**
....*(off Market St.)*
Priory TQ13: Bov T 2B **6**
Priory, The TQ12: A'well 6H **15**
Priory Av. TQ12: Kingsk 2H **19**
Priory Av. TQ9: Tot 3F **35**
Priory Ct. TQ9: Tot 4F **35**
Priory Dr. TQ9: Tot 3F **35**
Priory Gdns. EX7: Daw 4E **5**
Priory Gdns. TQ9: Tot 3F **35**
Priory Ga. TQ9: Tot 3F **35**
Priory Hill EX7: Daw 4E **5**
Priory Hill TQ9: Tot 3F **35**
Priory Pk. Rd. EX7: Daw 4D **4**
Priory Rd. EX7: Daw 4E **5**
Priory Rd. TQ1: Torq 1C **24**
Priory Rd. TQ12: A'well 6G **15**
Priory St. TQ6: Kingsw 5D **34**
Priory Ter. TQ9: Tot 3F **35**
....*(off Priory Hill)*
Priscott Way TQ12: Kingst 5D **10**
Promenade TQ14: Teignm 5E **13**
Promenade TQ3: Pres 3G **27**
Promenade TQ4: Broads 6G **29**
Promenade TQ4: Good 1F **29**
....(not continuous)
Promenade TQ7: Kingsb 3C **38**
Promenade, The TQ7: Kingsb 3C **38**
....*(off Bridge St.)*
Prospect Rd. TQ5: Brixh 2D **32**
Prospect Steps TQ5: Brixh 2D **32**
....*(off Sth. Furzeham Rd.)*
Prospect Ter. TQ12: New A 2H **15**
Provident Cl. TQ5: Brixh 2F **33**
Puddavine Ter. TQ9: Darti 1E **35**
Puffin Cl. TQ2: Torq 5B **20**
Pump St. TQ5: Brixh 2E **33**
Purbeck Av. TQ2: Torq 1F **27**

Q

Quantocks Rd. TQ2: Torq 6F **23**
Quarry Gdns. TQ3: Paig 4D **26**
Quarry Wood Cl. TQ4: Paig 4C **28**
Quarry Wood Ct. TQ4: Paig 4C **28**
Quay, The TQ5: Brixh 2E **33**
Quay, The TQ6: Dartm 1B **34** (4C **34**)
Quay, The TQ6: Ditt 5A **30**
Quay, The TQ7: Kingsb 3B **38**
....*(off Prince of Wales Rd.)*
Quay, The TQ8: Bat 1F **39**
Quay La. TQ7: Kingsb 3C **38**
Quay Rd. TQ12: New A 2A **16**
....(not continuous)
Quay Rd. TQ14: Teignm 5D **12**
Quayside TQ9: Tot 5G **35**
Quayside Leisure Cen. **4C 38**
Quay Ter. TQ12: New A 2A **16**
Queen Annes Copse TQ12: E Ogw 4E **15**
Queen Elizabeth Av. TQ6: Dartm 3B **34**
Queen Elizabeth Dr. TQ3: Paig 5B **26**
Queen La. EX7: Daw 4D **4**
Queens Cl. TQ12: Kingst 3E **11**
Queen's Cres. TQ5: Brixh 4E **33**
Queen's Pk. Rd. TQ4: Paig 5F **27**
Queen's Rd. TQ4: Paig 5F **27**
Queen's Rd. TQ5: Brixh 1D **32**
Queens Steps TQ5: Brixh 2E **33**
....*(off King St.)*
Queen's Ter. TQ9: Tot 3F **35**
Queen St. EX7: Daw 4D **4**
Queen St. TQ1: Torq 4C **24**
Queen St. TQ12: New A 2H **15**
Queen St. TQ14: Teignm 5D **12**
Queensway TQ12: New A 3B **16**
Queensway TQ2: Torq 3G **23**
Queensway Cl. TQ2: Torq 2H **23**
Queensway Cres. TQ2: Torq 2H **23**
Queensway Ho. TQ12: New A 3B **16**
Quentin Av. TQ5: Brixh 5C **32**
Quinnell Ho. TQ14: Teignm 4C **12**
....*(off Coombe Va. Rd.)*
Quinta Cl. TQ1: Torq 3D **24**
Quinta Ct. TQ1: Torq 2D **24**
Quinta Rd. TQ1: Torq 3D **24**

R

Rack Pk. Rd. TQ7: Kingsb 3C **38**
Radford Grange EX7: Daw 3A **4**
Radnor Ter. TQ9: Tot 3F **35**
Radway Ct. TQ14: Bi'ton 5H **13**
Radway Gdns. TQ14: Bi'ton 5H **13**
Radway Hill TQ14: Bi'ton 5H **13**
Radway St. TQ14: Bi'ton 5H **13**
Rainbow Ct. TQ2: Torq 2H **23**
Raleigh Av. TQ2: Torq 3G **23**
Raleigh Cl. TQ2: Torq 3G **23**
Raleigh Dr. TQ4: Good 3E **29**
Raleigh Rd. TQ12: New A 2C **16**
Raleigh Rd. TQ14: Teignm 2C **12**
Raleigh Rd. TQ6: Dartm 3B **34**
Raleigh Rd. TQ8: Salc 3F **39**
Raleigh St. TQ6: Dartm 1B **34** (4C **34**)
Ramparts Wlk. TQ9: Tot 4F **35**
....*(off High St.)*
Ramshill Rd. TQ3: Paig 3B **26**
Randolph Ct. TQ12: New A 1F **15**
Rangers Cl. TQ11: B'leigh 5B **36**
Ranscombe Cl. TQ5: Brixh 2F **33**
Ranscombe Rd. TQ5: Brixh 2E **33**
Rathlin TQ1: Torq 2D **24**
....*(off Palermo Rd.)*
Rathmore Rd. TQ2: Torq 5H **23**
....(not continuous)
Ravensbury Dr. TQ6: Dartm 5D **34**
Rawlyn Rd. TQ2: Torq 5G **23**
Rea Barn Cl. TQ5: Brixh 3E **33**
Rea Barn Rd. TQ5: Brixh 3E **33**
Rea Dr. TQ5: Brixh 2E **33**
Rear Dunmere Rd. TQ1: Torq 3C **24**
....*(off Dunmere Rd.)*
Rectory Rd. TQ12: E Ogw 4D **14**
Redavon Ri. TQ2: Torq 1E **23**
Red Brook Cl. TQ4: Good 4F **29**
Redburn Cl. TQ3: Paig 4D **26**
Redburn Rd. TQ3: Paig 4D **26**
Redcliffe Ct. TQ3: Pres 4G **27**
Redcliffe Rd. TQ1: Torq 6H **21**
Reddenhill Rd. TQ1: Torq 3D **24**

Redford Mdw. TQ7: Kingsb............3B 38
Redford Way TQ7: Kingsb............3B 38
Redgate Cl. TQ1: Torq............3E 25
Red Ho. Cl. TQ13: Chud K............2H 7
Redlands Ct. TQ3: Paig............4C 26
Redoubt Hill TQ6: Kingsw............4D 34
Redstart Cl. TQ12: E Ogw............4E 15
Redwalls Mdw. TQ6: Dartm............3B 34
Redwell La. TQ3: Paig............3C 26
Redwell Rd. TQ3: Paig............3C 26
Redwood Cl. TQ13: Bov T............6B 6
Redwood Ct. EX7: Daw............4E 5
Redwoods TQ13: Bov T............5B 6
Redworth Ct. TQ9: Tot............3E 35
............(off Station Rd.)
Redworth Ter. TQ9: Tot............3F 35
Reed Va. TQ14: Teignm............4C 12
Reeves Cl. TQ9: Tot............4G 35
............(off New Wlk.)
Reeves Rd., The TQ2: Torq............4G 23
Regard Cl. TQ5: Brixh............2F 33
Regent Cl. TQ2: Torq............1H 23
Regent Gdns. TQ14: Teignm............5E 13
............(off Regent St.)
Regents Ct. TQ4: Paig............6F 27
Regent St. EX7: Daw............4D 4
Regent St. TQ14: Teignm............5E 13
Rendells Mdw. TQ13: Bov T............3D 6
Retreat Cl. TQ7: Kingsb............3B 38
REW............2F 37
Rewlea Cotts. TQ13: Ashb............2F 37
Rew Rd. TQ13: Ashb............1F 37
Reynell Av. TQ12: New A............2C 16
Reynell Rd. TQ12: E Ogw............5E 15
Rhine Vs. TQ9: Tot............4G 35
Rhodanthe Rd. TQ3: Pres............2E 27
Richards Cl. EX7: Daw............5D 4
Richardson Wlk. TQ1: Torq............3A 24
............(off Barton Rd.)
Richmond Cl. TQ1: Torq............4H 25
Richmond Ct. EX7: Daw............4E 5
............(off Richmond Pl.)
Richmond Ct. TQ3: Paig............4E 27
Richmond Hill TQ12: Kingsk............2H 19
Richmond Pl. EX7: Daw............4E 5
Richmond Pl. TQ14: Shal............6B 12
Ridge Hill TQ6: Dartm............3C 34
Ridge La. TQ3: Marl............1C 22
Ridgemark Cl. TQ5: Brixh............2F 33
Ridge Rd. TQ1: Maid............1G 21
Ridge Rd. TQ12: Coff............2G 17
Ridge Rd. TQ12: Hacc............2G 17
Ridge Rd. TQ12: N'ton............2G 17
Ridges, The TQ6: Dartm............5A 34
Ridgeway Cl. TQ12: New A............4C 16
Ridgeway Hgts. TQ1: Torq............5E 25
Ridgeway Hill TQ3: Comp............3A 22
Ridgeway La. TQ12: Coff............1B 20
Ridgeway Rd. TQ1: Torq............6E 25
Ridgeway Rd. TQ12: New A............4C 16
Ridley Hill TQ6: Kingsw............5D 34
Rillage La. TQ2: Torq............3A 24
RINGMORE............6B 12
Ringmore Cl. TQ14: Shal............6B 12
Ringmore Rd. TQ14: Shal............6A 12
Ringrone TQ8: Salc............5E 39
Ringslade Cl. TQ12: New A............6G 9
Ringslade Rd. TQ12: New A............5G 9
Rippon Cl. TQ5: Brixh............5A 32
River Cl. TQ12: Kingst............6E 11
Riverside TQ14: Shal............6C 12
Riverside TQ9: Tot............2E 35
Riverside 4 TQ12: New A............1A 16
Riverside Ct. TQ12: New A............1A 16
Riverside Ct. TQ6: Dartm............1B 34 (4C 34)
............(off South Embankment)
Riverview TQ12: New A............3C 16
Riverview Pl. TQ7: Kingsb............3B 38
............(off Fore St.)
Riviera, The TQ1: Torq............6C 24
............(off Parkhill Rd.)
Riviera, The TQ4: Paig............6E 27
Riviera Bay Holiday Pk. TQ5: Brixh............4F 33

Riviera Ct. TQ1: Torq............5D 24
Riviera International Cen.............5A 24
Riviera Ter. EX7: Daw............3F 5
Riviera Way TQ2: Torq............6A 20
Robers Rd. TQ12: Kingst............3C 10
Roberts Cl. TQ2: Torq............5G 21
Roberts Way TQ12: New A............1E 15
Robinsons Row TQ8: Salc............3H 39
............(off Fore St.)
Robin Way TQ12: Kingst............3B 10
Roborough Gdns. TQ13: Ashb............2G 37
Roborough La. TQ13: Ashb............3F 37
Roborough Ter. TQ13: Ashb............3F 37
Rock Cl. TQ4: Broads............6F 29
Rock End Av. TQ1: Torq............6D 24
Rockfield Cl. TQ14: Teignm............2F 13
Rock Ho. La. TQ1: Maid............3H 21
Rock Pk. TQ13: Ashb............2G 37
Rock Pk. TQ6: Dartm............3A 34
Rock Rd. TQ2: Torq............5C 24
Rockstone, The EX7: Daw............3G 5
Rock Wlk. TQ2: Torq............5B 24
Rocky La. TQ11: B'leigh............6A 36
Rocky La. TQ14: Teignm............3C 12
............(not continuous)
Rocombe Cl. TQ2: Torq............3E 21
Rocombe Hill TQ12: Coff............6H 17
Rodgers Ind. Est. TQ4: Paig............2A 28
Rodney Cl. TQ6: Dartm............4A 34
Rogada Ct. TQ5: Brixh............5E 33
Romaleyn Gdns. TQ4: Good............1E 29
Rookery Cotts. TQ3: Marl............5A 22
Rooklands Av. TQ1: Torq............2A 24
Rope Wlk. TQ14: Teignm............4D 12
Ropewalk TQ7: Kingsb............4B 38
Ropewalk Hill TQ5: Brixh............2D 32
Roscoff Rd. EX7: Daw............2E 5
Rose Acre Ter. TQ5: Brixh............3E 33
Rose Dene TQ2: Torq............5E 21
Rose Gdns. TQ12: Ipp............5C 18
Rose Hill TQ12: Kingsk............3G 19
Rose Hill Cl. TQ12: Kingsk............3G 19
Rosehill Cl. TQ1: Torq............4D 24
Rosehill Rd. TQ1: Torq............4C 24
Roselands Dr. TQ4: Paig............2B 28
Roseland Sq. TQ12: Kingst............4D 10
Roselands Rd. TQ4: Good............2C 28
Roselands Rd. TQ4: Paig............2B 28
Roselands Rd. TQ4: Paig............2C 28
Rosemary Av. TQ12: New A............1E 15
Rosemary Ct. TQ3: Pres............3E 27
Rosemary Gdns. TQ3: Paig............3C 26
Rosemont TQ1: Torq............5E 25
Rosemount TQ4: Good............1F 29
............(off Roundham Rd.)
Rosemount Ct. TQ8: Salc............2G 39
............(off Church St.)
Rosery Rd. TQ2: Torq............4H 23
Roseville St. TQ6: Dartm............1A 34 (4C 34)
Rosewarne Av. TQ12: New A............3C 16
Rossall Dr. TQ3: Paig............6D 26
Ross Pk. Cvn. Pk. TQ12: Ipp............4A 18
Rosyl Av. EX7: Holc............1G 13
Rotherfold TQ9: Tot............4E 35
Rougemont TQ14: Shal............6D 12
Rougemont Av. TQ2: Torq............6B 20
Round Berry Dr. TQ8: Salc............3F 39
Roundham Av. TQ4: Good............1G 29
Roundham Cres. TQ4: Good............6G 27
Roundham Gdns. TQ4: Good............1F 29
Roundham Ho. TQ4: Paig............6F 27
............(off Belle Vue Rd.)
Roundham Rd. TQ4: Paig............6F 27
Roundhead Rd. TQ12: H'fld............4E 7
ROUND HILL............1F 27
Roundhill Rd. TQ2: Torq............1G 27
Roundings, The TQ5: Galm............2E 31
Roundmoors Cl. TQ12: Kingsk............4H 19
Roundway, The TQ12: Kingsk............1G 19
Rousdown Rd. TQ2: Torq............5H 23
Rowan Cl. TQ12: E Ogw............4E 15
Rowan Rd. TQ4: Paig............3B 28

Rowantree Rd. TQ12: New A............4B 16
Rowan Way TQ5: Brixh............5A 32
Rowbrook Cl. TQ4: Paig............2B 28
ROWCROFT HOSPICE............3H 23
Rowcroft Rd. TQ3: Pres............3F 27
Rowdens, The TQ14: Teignm............3F 13
Rowdens, The TQ2: Torq............4A 24
............(off Belgrave Rd.)
Rowdens Rd. TQ2: Torq............4A 24
Rowells Mead TQ12: Live............1A 8
Rowes Farm Barns TQ9: Sto G............5A 28
Rowley Rd. TQ2: Torq............1D 24
Rowsell's La. TQ9: Tot............4G 35
Royal Ct. TQ1: Torq............2E 25
............(off Bedford Rd.)
Royal Ct. TQ12: New A............2H 15
Royal Ct. TQ14: Teignm............5E 13
............(off Den Cres.)
Royal Dart Yacht Club............5D 34
Royal Pines TQ1: Torq............6E 25
Royal Terrace Gdns.............5B 24
Royal Torbay Yacht Club............6C 24
Rozel TQ1: Torq............6E 25
Ruckamore Rd. TQ2: Torq............4H 23
Rundle Rd. TQ12: New A............1H 15
Rushlade Cl. TQ4: Paig............3C 28
Rush Way TQ9: Tot............4H 35
Russell Ct. TQ8: Salc............2H 39
............(off Fore St.)
Russell Ct. TQ9: Tot............4F 35
Russets La. TQ11: B'leigh............4C 36
Ryde Cl. TQ2: Torq............5F 21
Ryders Bank TQ11: B'leigh............5A 36
RYDON............3D 10
Rydon Acres TQ12: Kingst............3D 10
Rydon Acres TQ9: Sto G............5A 28
Rydon Av. TQ12: Kingst............3D 10
Rydon Est. TQ12: Kingst............3D 10
Rydon Ind. Est. TQ12: Kingst............5C 10
Rydon La. TQ12: A'well............1D 18
Rydon Path TQ12: Kingst............2D 10
Rydon Rd. TQ12: Kingst............2D 10
Rydons TQ5: Brixh............3B 32

S

Sackery TQ12: C'head............1G 17
Saddle, The TQ4: Good............3F 29
Saddleback Cl. TQ12: E Ogw............5E 15
Sadler Grn. TQ13: Bov T............4B 6
Saffron Cl. TQ7: Kingsb............3C 38
Saffron Pk. TQ7: Kingsb............3C 38
St Agnes La. TQ2: Torq............6H 23
St Albans La. TQ1: Torq............2D 24
St Albans Rd. TQ1: Torq............2D 24
St Andrews Cl. TQ13: Ashb............4F 37
St Andrews Rd. TQ4: Paig............6F 27
St Anne's Ct. TQ12: New A............2F 15
St Anne's Rd. TQ1: Torq............2D 24
St Augustine's Cl. TQ2: Torq............4F 21
St Bartholomews Rd. TQ2: E Ogw............5E 15
St Bartholomew Way TQ12: E Ogw............5C 14
St Bernard's Cl. TQ11: Buck............2B 36
............(not continuous)
St Catherine's Rd. TQ1: Torq............1C 24
St Clements Ct. TQ6: Dartm............3B 34
............(off Church Rd.)
St Columba Cl. TQ12: Kingst............3D 10
St Davids Rd. TQ14: Teignm............1D 12
St Dominics Cl. TQ1: Torq............1C 24
St Dunstans Rd. TQ8: Salc............3F 39
St Edmunds TQ7: Kingsb............2B 38
St Edmund's Rd. TQ2: Torq............2C 24
............(not continuous)
St Edmunds Wlk. TQ7: Kingsb............3B 38
St Efride's Rd. TQ2: Torq............4A 24
St Elmo Ct. TQ8: Salc............4E 39
St George's Ct. TQ2: Torq............4G 21
St Georges Cres. TQ1: Torq............2D 24
St George's Rd. TQ1: Torq............2D 24
St Georges Sq. TQ6: Dartm............2B 34 (4C 34)
............(off Fairfax Pl.)
St Ive's Ct. TQ1: Torq............3B 24

St James Pl. TQ1: Torq.................................2E **25**
St James Rd. TQ1: Torq................................2B **24**
St James's Ho. TQ14: Teignm....................4D **12**
....(off Fore St.)
St James's Pct. TQ14: Teignm......................4D **12**
....(off Bitton Pk. Rd.)
St John's Cl. TQ13: Bov T...............................4B **6**
St John's Cl. TQ14: Bi'ton.............................6C **13**
St John's Ct. TQ3: Paig.................................5E **27**
....(off Littlegate Rd.)
St John's Ct. TQ9: Tot..................................4G **35**
....(off Weston Rd.)
St Johns La. TQ13: Bov T...............................3B **6**
St Johns Pl. TQ1: Torq.................................5C **24**
....(off Braddons Hill Rd. W.)
St Johns St. TQ12: New A..............................1H **15**
St John's Ter. TQ9: Tot.................................3E **35**
St Josephs Ct. TQ14: Teignm........................5E **13**
....(off Carlton Pl.)
St Katherine's M. TQ9: Tot............................4F **35**
....(off St Katherine's Way)
St Katherine's Rd. TQ1: Torq........................3H **23**
St Katherine's Way TQ9: Tot........................4F **35**
St Kitts Cl. TQ2: Torq...................................5E **21**
St Lawrence La. TQ13: Ashb..........................4F **37**
St Leonard's Cl. TQ12: New A.......................3G **15**
St Leonard's Rd. TQ12: New A......................3G **15**
St Leonard's Tower Newton Abbot.............2G **15**
St Luke's Cl. TQ12: New A.............................4C **16**
St Lukes Dr. TQ14: Teignm...........................3C **12**
St Luke's Pk. TQ2: Torq................................5B **24**
St Luke's Rd. TQ12: New A...........................4B **16**
St Luke's Rd. TQ2: Torq................................4B **24**
St Luke's Rd. Nth. TQ2: Torq........................5B **24**
St Luke's Rd. Sth. TQ2: Torq.........................5B **24**
St Marco Gdns. TQ7: Kingsb........................2C **38**
St Margaret's Av. TQ1: Torq........................2C **24**
St Margaret's Cl. TQ1: Torq..........................1C **24**
St Margaret's Ct. TQ1: Torq..........................1C **24**
....(off St Margaret's M.)
St Margaret's M. TQ1: Torq..........................1C **24**
St Margaret's Rd. TQ1: Torq........................1C **24**
St Mark's Dr. TQ1: Torq................................6E **25**
....(off St Mark's Rd.)
St Mark's Rd. TQ1: Torq...............................6E **25**
St Martins Ct. TQ2: Torq...............................6E **21**
St Martin's M. TQ1: Torq..............................1D **24**
....(off Fore St.)
ST MARYCHURCH...6H **21**
St Marychurch Rd. TQ1: Torq......................6G **21**
....(not continuous)
St Marychurch Rd. TQ12: Coff.....................3B **16**
St Marychurch Rd. TQ12: Dacc....................3B **16**
St Marychurch Rd. TQ12: New A..................3B **16**
St Marychurch Rd. TQ12: S'head..................3B **16**
St Mary Magdalen Cl. TQ14: Bi'ton............6G **13**
St Mary's Cl. TQ5: Brixh...............................5C **32**
St Marys Cl. TQ12: A'well.............................1B **18**
St Mary's Ct. TQ3: Paig................................5D **26**
St Marys Ct. TQ12: New A.............................2G **15**
....(off Highweek St.)
St Mary's Dr. TQ5: Brixh...............................4E **33**
St Mary's Hill TQ5: Brixh..............................4E **33**
St Mary's Pk..5D **32**
St Mary's Pl. TQ12: Ipp................................5B **18**
....(off Caunters Cl.)
St Mary's Rd. TQ12: New A...........................3G **15**
St Mary's Rd. TQ14: Teignm.........................2C **12**
St Mary's Rd. TQ5: Brixh..............................5D **32**
St Mary's Sq. TQ5: Brixh..............................4C **32**
St Matthew's Rd. TQ2: Torq........................5G **23**
St Matthias Chu. Rd. TQ1: Torq...................4F **25**
St Mawes Dr. TQ4: Good..............................5E **29**
ST MICHAELS..6E **27**
St Michael's Cl. TQ1: Torq............................3H **23**
St Michael's Ct. TQ4: Paig...........................1D **28**
....(off Derrell Rd.)
St Michael's Rd. TQ1: Torq..........................2H **23**
St Michael's Rd. TQ12: Kingst......................5C **10**
St Michael's Rd. TQ12: New A.......................4A **16**
St Michael's Rd. TQ14: Teignm....................2E **13**
St Michael's Rd. TQ4: Paig...........................6D **26**
St Michael's Ter. TQ1: Torq.........................4C **24**

St Patricks Cl. TQ14: Teignm......................3C **12**
St Pauls Cl. TQ13: Bov T................................3C **6**
St Pauls Ct. TQ1: Torq..................................2C **24**
....(off St Edmunds Rd.)
St Paul's Cres. TQ1: Torq.............................2C **24**
St Paul's Rd. TQ1: Torq................................2C **24**
St Paul's Rd. TQ12: New A............................2H **15**
St Paul's Rd. TQ3: Pres................................2G **27**
St Peter's Cl. TQ13: Bov T.............................2D **6**
St Peters Cl. TQ2: Torq.................................3G **23**
St Peter's Hill TQ5: Brixh..............................2E **33**
St Peter's Quay TQ9: Tot.............................5G **35**
St Peters Ter. TQ5: Brixh..............................2E **33**
....(off Elkins Hill)
St Scholasticas TQ14: Teignm......................2F **13**
St Thomas Cl. TQ13: Bov T...........................3D **6**
St Vincent's Cl. TQ1: Torq...........................3A **24**
St Vincent's Rd. TQ1: Torq..........................2A **24**
SALCOMBE...2H **39**
Salcombe Hgts. Cl. TQ8: Salc......................2F **39**
Salcombe Maritime Mus...........................2H **39**
Salcombe Park & Ride Summer only...........2F **39**
Salcombe RNLI Mus....................................2H **39**
Salcombe Tourist Info. Cen........................2H **39**
Salcombe Yacht Club.................................3G **39**
Salem Pl. TQ12: New A.................................2G **15**
Salisbury Av. TQ2: Torq...............................5E **21**
Salisbury Rd. TQ12: New A...........................1A **16**
Salisbury Ter. TQ14: Teignm.......................4E **13**
Salmon Leap Cl. TQ11: B'leigh....................4C **36**
Salmons Leap TQ9: Darti.............................2E **35**
Saltern Rd. TQ4: Good.................................4F **29**
Saltings, The TQ14: Shal.............................6B **12**
Salt Quay Moorings TQ7: Kingsb.................4C **38**
....(off Embankment Rd.)
Salty La. TQ14: Shal.....................................6B **12**
Samara Bus. Pk. TQ12: H'fld.........................4E **7**
Sanders Rd. TQ5: Brixh................................2B **32**
Sandford Orleigh TQ12: New A....................6A **10**
Sandford Vw. TQ12: New A...........................1G **15**
Sandhills Rd. TQ8: Salc................................4F **39**
Sandown Rd. TQ4: Paig...............................3C **28**
Sandpath Rd. TQ12: Kingst.........................5D **10**
Sandpiper EX7: Daw W................................1G **5**
Sandpiper Way TQ2: Torq...........................5B **20**
Sandquay Rd. TQ6: Dartm...........................2C **34**
Sandquay Way TQ6: Dartm.........................2C **34**
Sandringham Dr. TQ3: Pres.........................1D **26**
Sandringham Gdns. TQ3: Pres....................1E **27**
Sandringham Rd. TQ12: New A...................2B **16**
Sands Ct. TQ4: Paig.....................................6E **27**
Sands Rd. TQ4: Paig.....................................6E **27**
Sandygate TQ12: Kingst..............................2B **10**
SANDYGATE..2C **10**
Sandygate Bus. Pk. TQ12: Kingst................2B **10**
Sandygate M. TQ12: Kingst.........................1C **10**
....(off Lower Sandygate)
Sandygate Mill TQ12: Kingst.......................1C **10**
Sandy La. EX7: Daw.......................................2F **5**
Sanford Rd. TQ2: Torq..................................4H **23**
San Remo Ter. EX7: Daw...............................4F **5**
Saturday's La. TQ12: N Whil.........................6G **19**
Sawmill Ct. TQ9: Tot....................................5G **35**
Sawyer Dr. TQ14: Teignm............................2B **12**
Saxon Hgts. TQ5: Brixh................................3D **32**
Saxon Mdw. TQ4: Coll M.............................6A **26**
Saxon Way TQ12: Kingst...............................5E **11**
Scarborough Pl. TQ2: Torq.........................4A **24**
Scarborough Rd. TQ2: Torq........................4A **24**
Scholars Wlk. TQ7: Kingsb...........................2C **38**
School Cotts. TQ12: Teigng..........................3H **9**
School Ct. TQ6: Dartm.................................4A **34**
School Hill EX7: Daw.....................................4D **4**
School Hill TQ9: Sto G..................................6A **28**
School Hill Cotts. TQ9: Sto G.......................6A **28**
....(off School Hill)
School La. TQ14: Shal..................................6C **12**
School Rd. TQ12: Kingsk..............................2G **19**
School Rd. TQ12: New A...............................2H **15**
School Rd. TQ12: Teigng...............................3G **9**

School Steps TQ6: Dartm............... 2A **34** (4C **34**)
....(off Higher St.)
School Ter. EX7: Daw....................................4D **4**
....(off School Hill)
Scoresby Cl. TQ2: Torq.................................3G **21**
Scott Cinemas The Alexandra Cinema.....2G **15**
Scott Cl. TQ12: New A..................................2H **15**
Scratton Path TQ12: E Ogw.........................5E **15**
....(off Reynell Rd.)
Screechers Hill TQ13: Ashb.........................3E **37**
Seabourne Ct. TQ4: Good............................1F **29**
....(off Alta Vista Rd.)
Seacliff TQ14: Teignm..................................3F **13**
Seafields TQ4: Good.....................................3F **29**
Sea Front TQ1: Torq.....................................1H **27**
Sea La. TQ5: Brixh..3F **33**
Sea Lawn Ter. EX7: Daw...............................3F **5**
Seale Cl. TQ6: Dartm...................................3A **34**
Seapoint TQ14: Teignm................................5D **12**
....(off Strand)
Seascape TQ2: Torq.....................................6A **24**
Seaton Cl. TQ1: Torq....................................2E **25**
Seaview Cres. TQ5: Pres...............................2F **27**
Sea Vw. Ter. TQ5: Brixh...............................1D **33**
....(off Overgang Rd.)
Seaway Cl. TQ2: Torq...................................6H **23**
Seaway Ct. TQ2: Torq...................................6A **24**
Seaway Ct. TQ5: Brixh..................................3C **32**
Seaway Cres. TQ3: Pres...............................3G **27**
Seaway Gdns. TQ3: Pres..............................3G **27**
Seaway La. TQ2: Torq...................................5G **23**
Seaway Rd. TQ3: Pres..................................3F **27**
Secmaton La. EX7: Daw................................2E **5**
Secmaton Ri. EX7: Daw.................................1E **5**
Second Av. EX7: Daw.....................................5C **4**
Second Av. TQ1: Torq...................................1B **24**
Second Av. TQ14: Teignm.............................4C **12**
Second Dr. TQ14: Teignm Burwood Pl..........3F **13**
Second Dr. TQ14: Teignm Third Dr................4D **12**
Sefton Ct. EX7: Daw......................................4D **4**
Sefton Ct. TQ1: Torq.....................................2E **25**
Sellick Av. TQ5: Brixh...................................4E **33**
Sett Cl. TQ13: Bov T......................................3C **6**
Seven Hills Ho. TQ2: Torq............................4B **24**
....(off Burridge La.)
Severn Rd. TQ2: Torq....................................2E **23**
Seymour Cvn. Pk. TQ12: Live........................1B **8**
....(off Old Liverton Rd.)
Seymour Ct. TQ9: Tot...................................4G **35**
....(off Seymour Rd.)
Seymour Dr. TQ2: Torq.................................3F **21**
Seymour Pl. TQ9: Tot....................................4G **35**
Seymour Rd. TQ12: New A............................1G **15**
Seymour Rd. TQ9: Tot...................................4G **35**
Seymour Ter. TQ9: Tot..................................4G **35**
....(off Bridgetown)
Shackleton Cl. TQ1: Torq.............................4G **25**
Shackleton Wlk. TQ14: Teignm...................1C **12**
SHADYCOMBE..2G **39**
Shadycombe Ct. TQ8: Salc...........................2G **39**
Shadycombe Rd. TQ8: Salc..........................1F **39**
Shady Nook Cvn. Site TQ12: Kingst.............4D **10**
Shaftesbury Cl. EX7: Daw.............................4E **5**
....(off Plantation Ter.)
Shaftesbury Pl. TQ9: Tot..............................4F **35**
....(off Maudlin Rd.)
Shaftesbury Theatre Dawlish...................4D **4**
Shakespeare Cl. TQ2: Torq..........................3G **23**
SHALDON..6C **12**
Shaldon Bri. TQ14: Shal...............................5C **12**
Shaldon Rd. TQ12: C'head...........................1H **17**
Shaldon Rd. TQ12: New A.............................3B **16**
Shaldon Tourist Info. Cen............................6D **12**
Shaldon Zoo..6D **12**
Shapley Tor Cl. TQ5: Brixh...........................5B **32**
Shapley Way TQ12: Live................................1A **8**
Shaptor Vw. TQ13: Bov T...............................5A **6**
Sharkham Ct. TQ5: Brixh..............................4E **33**
Sharkham Dr. TQ5: Brixh..............................4E **33**
Sharkham Ho. TQ5: Brixh.............................4E **33**
Sharpham Dr. TQ9: Tot.................................5G **35**
Sharpitor TQ8: Salc......................................6E **39**
Sharpitor Cl. TQ3: Pres................................2C **26**

Sharp's Cl. TQ12: H'fld 5F 7
Sharp's Crest TQ12: H'fld.............................5F 7
Shearwater Dr. TQ2: Torq 4C 20
Shedden Hill TQ2: Torq 5B 24
Shelley Av. TQ1: Torq...................................1B 24
Shelston Tor Dr. TQ4: Paig 2C 28
Shepherd Cl. TQ3: Paig 6B 26
Shepherd's La. TQ14: Teignm 1A 12
Sherborne Rd. TQ12: New A.........................2G 15
Sherwell Hill TQ2: Torq 4G 23
Sherwell La. TQ2: Torq 4G 23
Sherwell Pk. Rd. TQ2: Torq 4G 23
Sherwell Ri. Sth. TQ2: Torq.........................4G 23
Sherwell Valley Rd. TQ2: Torq 3F 23
Shetland Cl. TQ2: Torq 5D 20
Shillingate Cl. EX7: Daw...............................6C 4
SHIPHAY 2F 23
Shiphay Av. TQ2: Torq..................................2F 23
Shiphay La. TQ2: Torq 1F 23
Shiphay Mnr. Dr. TQ2: Torq.........................2G 23
Shiphay Pk. Rd. TQ2: Torq 2G 23
Shirburn Rd. TQ1: Torq 2B 24
Shire Cl. TQ4: Good 5D 28
Shirley Ct. TQ1: Torq....................................5E 25
....(off Torwood Gdns. Rd.)
Shirley Towers TQ1: Torq.............................6C 24
Shoalstone Pool 1G 33
Shobbrook Hill TQ12: New A........................1D 14
Shoreside TQ14: Shal 6C 12
Shorland Cl. EX7: Daw 2F 5
SHORTON 2D 26
Shorton Rd. TQ3: Paig 3D 26
Shorton Rd. TQ3: Pres 2D 26
Shorton Rd. TQ3: Pres 3D 26
Shorton Valley Rd. TQ3: Pres......................2D 26
Shrewsbury Av. TQ2: Torq 6F 21
Shute Ct. TQ14: Bi'ton 5H 13
Shute Hill TQ14: Bi'ton 5H 13
Shute Hill TQ14: Teignm 4E 13
Shute Hill Cres. TQ14: Teignm 4E 13
Shute Rd. TQ9: Tot 4G 35
Sidney Ct. EX7: Daw......................................4D 4
....(off Old Town St.)
Sidney Wlk. TQ4: Good 4E 29
Silver Bri. Cl. TQ4: Good...............................5F 29
Silverhills Rd. TQ12: New A 5A 16
Silver St. TQ11: B'leigh 4B 36
Silver St. TQ12: Ipp 6A 18
Silverwood Av. TQ12: New A 4B 16
Singer Cl. TQ3: Paig......................................6D 26
Singmore Rd. TQ3: Marl 1B 26
Skelmersdale Cl. TQ7: Kingsw 3C 38
Skye Cl. TQ2: Torq 5D 20
Skylark EX7: Daw W......................................1G 5
Slade La. TQ12: A'well...................................1B 18
....(not continuous)
Slade La. TQ5: Galm 2E 31
Sladnor Pk. Rd. TQ1: Maid 2G 21
Slanns Mdw. TQ12: Kingst 5C 10
Sleepy La. TQ3: Pres 2D 26
Sloe Berry Wlk. TQ4: Paig 3A 28
Smallcombe Rd. TQ3: Paig 3B 26
Smalldon La. TQ1: Torq 4G 21
Smardon Av. TQ5: Brixh 2B 32
Smardon Cl. TQ5: Brixh 2B 32
Smith Ct. TQ1: Torq 3A 24
Smith Hill TQ14: Bi'ton..................................5G 13
Smith St. TQ6: Dartm......................1B 34 (4C 34)
Smokey Ho. Caravans TQ3: Marl 1B 26
Smugglers La. EX7: Holc...............................1H 13
Snowberry Cl. TQ1: Torq..............................2A 24
Snowdonia Cl. TQ4: Coll M...........................1A 28
Soby M. TQ13: Bov T.....................................5B 6
Solsbro M. TQ2: Torq....................................5H 23
Solsbro Rd. TQ2: Torq 5H 23
Somerset Ct. TQ5: Brixh 2E 33
....(off Mt. Pleasant Rd.)
Somerset Pl. TQ14: Teignm 5D 12
Somerset Pl. TQ9: Tot 4G 35
Soper Rd. TQ14: Teignm 2C 12
Soper Wlk. TQ14: Teignm 2C 12
Sophia Way TQ12: New A 3F 15
Sorrell Ct. TQ12: Kingst 4C 10

Sorrel Pl. TQ12: New A 6E 9
Sorrento TQ1: Torq 4D 24
South Bay Holiday Pk. TQ5: Brixh...............5E 33
SOUTHBROOK 1A 6
Southbrook Cl. TQ13: Bov T.........................2B 6
Southbrook La. TQ13: Bov T 2A 6
....(not continuous)
Southbrook Rd. TQ13: Bov T........................2B 6
Southcote Orchard TQ9: Tot 4H 35
South Devon Coast Path TQ14: Shal...........6D 12
South Devon M. TQ12: New A 2A 16
South Devon Miniature Railway...................4D 36
South Devon Railway Buckfastleigh Station
....4D 36
South Devon Railway Totnes Riverside Station
....2F 35
South Devon Railway Mus..............................4D 36
Southdown Av. TQ5: Brixh 5C 32
Southdown Cl. TQ5: Brixh 5C 32
Southdown Hill TQ5: Brixh 5C 32
Southdown Rd. TQ5: Brixh 6C 32
Southdowns Rd. EX7: Daw............................6D 4
South Emb. TQ6: Dartm 2B 34 (4C 34)
Southern Cl. TQ2: Torq 3F 21
Southernhay TQ12: New A 3H 15
Southey Cres. TQ12: Kingsk........................4H 19
Southey Dr. TQ12: Kingsk 4H 19
Southey La. TQ12: Kingsk............................4H 19
Southfield TQ7: W Alv 4A 38
....(off Longfields)
Southfield Av. TQ3: Pres 2C 26
Southfield Cl. TQ3: Pres 3C 26
Southfield Ri. TQ3: Paig 4D 26
Southfield Rd. TQ3: Paig 4D 26
South Ford Rd. TQ6: Dartm 1A 34 (4B 34)
South Furzeham Rd. TQ5: Brixh..................2D 32
SOUTH HAMS HOSPITAL 2B 38
South Hill Rd. TQ1: Torq 5D 24
Southlands Rd. TQ2: Torq 4A 24
South Parks Rd. TQ2: Torq 5E 21
South Pl. TQ7: Kingsb 3C 38
....(off Promenade)
South Quay TQ4: Paig...................................6F 27
South Rd. TQ12: New A 3G 15
SOUTH SANDS 5E 39
South Sands TQ4: Good 3F 29
South Sands Sailing 5E 39
South St. TQ2: Torq 4A 24
South St. TQ9: Tot 4F 35
South Town TQ6: Dartm 5C 34
South Vw. TQ12: A'well 1C 18
South Vw. TQ13: Bov T..................................3C 6
....(off Old Orchard)
South Vw. TQ14: Teignm 5D 12
Southview Rd. TQ3: Paig...............................4D 26
Southville Gdns. TQ7: Kingsb 5C 38
Southwater Ct. TQ7: Kingsb 4C 38
Southway Av. TQ2: Torq...............................6E 21
Southwood Ct. TQ1: Torq.............................4D 24
Sovereign Ho. TQ1: Torq..............................5C 24
....(off The Terrace)
Sovereign M. TQ1: Torq................................5G 21
Spa Ct. TQ1: Torq 5D 24
Sparkhays Dr. TQ9: Tot 5G 35
Sparks Barn Rd. TQ4: Paig..........................1E 29
Sparrow Rd. TQ9: Tot 4E 35
Speedwell Cl. TQ12: New A 6E 9
Speedwell Cl. TQ5: Brixh..............................4D 32
Spencer Rd. TQ12: New A 3H 15
Spencer Rd. TQ3: Paig 5B 26
Speranza Gro. TQ14: Teignm 4D 12
Spion Kop Steps TQ8: Salc 3G 39
....(off Bennett Rd.)
Spithead TQ6: Dartm 1B 34 (4C 34)
Splashdown Quaywest Waterpark..............2F 29
Spring Cl. TQ12: New A 1D 14
Spring Cotts. TQ9: Tot 4G 35
....(off Weston La.)
Springdale Cl. TQ5: Brixh.............................5D 32
Springfield TQ12: Ipp 6B 18
Springfield Dr. TQ7: Kingsb 4B 38
Springfield Gdns. EX7: Daw..........................1F 5
Springfield Pk. TQ11: B'leigh 4D 36

Springfield Rd. TQ1: Torq.............................2C 24
Spring Hill Rd. TQ9: Tot................................4H 35
Spruce Way TQ3: Paig 3B 26
Spurge Rd. TQ12: New A 6D 8
Square, The TQ6: Kingsw.............................4D 34
Square's Quay TQ7: Kingsb 4C 38
Stabb Cl. TQ4: Good......................................4D 28
Stabb Dr. TQ4: Good 4D 28
Stable La. TQ1: Torq 6G 21
....(off Havelock Rd.)
Stables, The TQ9: Tot 3G 35
Staddon Gdns. TQ2: Torq.............................5G 21
Staddons Lea La. TQ2: Torq 3F 23
Staddons Vw. TQ13: Bov T...........................2B 6
Stadium Dr. TQ12: Kingsk 5H 19
Stafford Ct. TQ9: Tot 4H 35
Stafford Rd. TQ4: Paig 6F 27
Stanbury Rd. TQ2: Torq 2F 23
Stanfield TQ1: Torq 4F 25
....(off Barrington Rd.)
Stanley Ct. TQ1: Torq 1D 24
Stanley Gdns. TQ3: Paig 4C 26
Stanley Rd. TQ1: Torq 1D 24
Stanley St. TQ14: Teignm 5D 12
Stanmore Ri. EX7: Daw 3E 5
Stanmore Tor TQ1: Torq 6D 26
Stansfeld Av. TQ3: Paig.................................5D 26
Stantaway Hill TQ1: Torq..............................2A 24
....(off Stantaway Pk.)
Stantaway Pk. TQ1: Torq..............................2A 24
Stantor La. TQ3: Marl 3C 22
Stapledon La. TQ13: Ashb 3F 37
Stapleford Dr. TQ14: Teignm 2D 12
Stapleton Cl. TQ4: Paig.................................2B 28
Starpitten Gro. TQ2: Torq 4G 21
Starpitten La. W. TQ2: Torq.........................5F 21
Start Av. TQ14: Teignm 2E 13
Station Bus. Pk. TQ14: Teignm 4E 13
....(off Lwr. Brimley Rd.)
Station Ct. TQ13: Bov T.................................3B 6
Station Hill TQ5: Brixh 2D 32
Station La. TQ4: Paig.....................................6E 27
Station Rd. EX7: Daw.....................................4E 5
Station Rd. TQ11: B'leigh 4C 36
Station Rd. TQ12: New A 2A 16
Station Rd. TQ13: Bov T................................3B 6
Station Rd. TQ14: Teignm 5E 13
Station Rd. TQ9: Tot 3F 35
Station Yd. TQ13: Ashb 4F 37
....(off Prigg Mdw.)
Station Yd. Ind. Est. TQ7: Kingsb 3B 38
Steamer Quay Cvn. Club Site TQ9: Tot.......4G 35
Steamer Quay Rd. TQ9: Tot.........................4G 35
Steartfield Rd. TQ3: Paig..............................4F 27
Steed Cl. TQ4: Good 5D 28
Steep Hill TQ1: Maid......................................1H 21
Stella Rd. TQ3: Pres......................................2D 26
Stentiford Hill TQ7: Kingsb 1B 38
Stentiford Hill Rd. TQ1: Torq.......................4C 24
Steppes Mdw. TQ12: New A 3F 15
Steps La. TQ2: Torq 4G 21
....(not continuous)
Stewart Gdns. EX7: Daw 3E 5
Stewart Ho. EX7: Daw 3E 5
....(off Old Gatehouse Rd.)
Stitchill Rd. TQ1: Torq...................................5D 24
Stockmeadow Gdns. TQ14: Bi'ton 6H 13
Stockton Av. EX7: Daw 4D 4
Stockton Hill EX7: Daw..................................4D 4
Stockton La. EX7: Daw 4D 4
....(off Stockton Rd.)
Stockton Rd. EX7: Daw..................................4D 4
STOKE GABRIEL 6A 28
Stoke Gabriel Rd. TQ5: Galm 1B 30
Stoke Gabriel Rd. TQ5: Wadd......................1B 30
Stoke Hill TQ9: Sto G 6A 28
Stokes Cl. TQ13: Bov T.................................1E 7
Stoneacre Cl. TQ5: Brixh 4D 32
Stone Ct. TQ2: Torq 6C 20
Stonelands Bri. EX7: Daw 4B 4
Stonelands Ct. EX7: Daw 4B 4
Stonelands M. EX7: Daw 4C 4
Stonelands Pk. EX7: Daw 4C 4

Stonelands Ter. EX7: Daw............................4C **4**
....(off Stonelands Pk.)
Stoneleigh Cl. TQ12: New A 1E **15**
Stoneleigh Dr. TQ2: Torq........................6G **23**
Stoneman's Hill TQ12: A'well...................5G **15**
Stone Pk. TQ4: Broads.............................1G **31**
Stonepark TQ13: Ashb.............................5E **37**
Stonepark Cres. TQ13: Ashb 5E **37**
Stonepark Ter. TQ13: Ashb 5E **37**
Stones Cl. TQ12: Kingst...........................2D **15**
STONEYCOMBE...4D **18**
Stoneyhill TQ12: A'well 4B **18**
Storrs Cl. TQ13: Bov T.............................2B **6**
Stover Country Pk.......................................6F **7**
Stover Country Pk. Interpretation Cen.....6F **7**
Stover Ct. TQ12: New A............................2H **15**
Stover Golf Course 1D **8**
Strand TQ1: Torq 5C **24**
Strand TQ14: Shal 6C **12**
Strand TQ14: Teignm...............................6D **12**
Strand, The EX7: Daw..............................4E **5**
Strand, The TQ14: Shal 6A **12**
Strand, The TQ5: Brixh 2E **33**
Strand Hill EX7: Daw 4E **5**
Strap La. TQ12: Kingst.............................1C **10**
Stratheden Ct. TQ1: Torq.........................4C **24**
....(off Market St.)
Strawberry Mdws. TQ4: Paig 3A **28**
Strawberry Ter. TQ12: Kingst 3D **10**
Stringland La. TQ3: Marl 4A **22**
Strode Rd. TQ11: B'leigh 5B **36**
Stuart Ct. EX7: Daw.................................6D **4**
Studley Rd. TQ1: Torq 2B **24**
Sturcombe Av. TQ4: Paig 2B **28**
Sugar Loaf Hill & Saltern Cove Nature Reserve
....4F **29**
Summercourt Way TQ5: Brixh...................5A **32**
Summerfield Rd. TQ2: Torq......................1H **23**
Summerhayes EX7: Daw 6C **4**
Summerhill TQ12: Live 1A **8**
Summerhill Cl. TQ12: Live 1A **8**
Summerhill Cres. TQ12: Live 1A **8**
Summerhill Rd. TQ12: Live 1A **8**
Summerland EX7: Daw 3D **4**
Summerland Cl. EX7: Daw 4D **4**
Summerland Cotts. TQ12: New A 2H **15**
....(off Carlisle St.)
Summerland Ct. TQ12: New A 2H **15**
Summerlands Cl. TQ5: Brixh......................5B **32**
Summerlands Ct. TQ12: Live 1B **8**
Summerlands Ct. TQ5: Brixh 5B **32**
Summer La. TQ12: Teigng.........................1F **9**
Summer La. TQ5: Brixh 4B **32**
Summersfield Ct. TQ4: Paig 6F **27**
Sunbury Hill TQ1: Torq.............................3B **24**
Sunbury Rd. TQ4: Paig 6E **27**
Sun Ct. TQ12: New A 2G **15**
Suncrest Cvn. Site TQ2: Torq....................4E **21**
Suncrest Cl. TQ2: Torq 5E **21**
Sun La. TQ14: Teignm 5D **12**
....(off Teign St.)
Sunnybank TQ12: A'well 1C **18**
Sunnybank TQ12: New A...........................6A **10**
Sunny Cl. TQ12: New A 2C **16**
Sunny Hollow TQ12: E Ogw.......................5C **14**
Sunny Lands Way EX7: Holc......................1H **13**
Sunnymead Ter. TQ9: Tot 4F **35**
....(off Maudlin Rd.)
Sunnyside Rd. TQ12: Kingsk 4H **19**
Sun Valley Cl. TQ5: Brixh..........................2D **32**
Sussex Cl. TQ2: Torq................................4F **21**
Sutherland Cl. TQ12: New A......................5C **16**
Sutherland Dr. TQ2: Torq 5G **21**
Sutherland Rd. TQ1: Torq.........................4D **24**
Sutton Cl. EX7: Daw 3D **4**
Sutton Cl. TQ2: Torq 3E **21**
Sutton M. TQ2: Torq 3E **21**
Swale Cl. TQ2: Torq 4F **21**
Swallowfield Ri. TQ2: Torq........................5B **20**
Swallowfields TQ9: Tot 2E **35**
SWALLOWFIELDS...2E **35**
Swallows Acre EX7: Daw 3E **5**
Swanborough Rd. TQ12: New A.................4C **16**

Swan Ct. TQ6: Dartm 4B **34**
....(off Victoria Rd.)
Swannaton Rd. TQ6: Dartm......................6B **34**
Swan St. TQ2: Torq...................................5C **24**
....(off Fleet St.)
Swedwell La. TQ2: Torq............................3F **21**
Swedwell Rd. TQ2: Torq............................3F **21**
Sweethriar Cl. EX7: Holc 1G **13**
Sweetbriar La. EX7: Holc...........................1G **13**
Swift Ind. Est. TQ12: Kingst 5C **10**
Swim Torquay 2C **24**
Swincombe Dr. TQ3: Paig 5C **26**
Sycamore Cl. TQ4: Broads........................6G **29**
Sycamore Way TQ5: Brixh.........................5B **32**
Symons Cl. TQ13: Bov T............................1E **7**
Symons Pas. TQ9: Tot...............................4G **35**

T

Tacket Ct. TQ7: Kingsb..............................4B **38**
Tacketwood TQ7: Kingsb 4C **38**
Talbot Ct. TQ14: Teignm...........................4C **12**
....(off Bitton Pk. Rd.)
Tallow Wood Cl. TQ3: Paig........................5B **26**
Tamar Av. TQ2: Torq.................................2E **23**
Tamworth Cl. TQ12: E Ogw.......................5E **15**
Tamwyn Cl. TQ3: Pres...............................3F **27**
Tanners Rd. TQ4: Good.............................1F **29**
Tansy Cl. TQ12: New A..............................6E **9**
Tapley Gdns. TQ14: Bi'ton 5H **13**
Tarraway Rd. TQ3: Pres............................2G **27**
Tarr's Av. TQ12: Kingst.............................4D **10**
Tarrs End TQ12: Kingst.............................4D **10**
Tarr's La. TQ12: Kingst 4D **10**
Taunton Ct. TQ9: Tot................................4G **35**
....(off New Wlk.)
Tavis Rd. TQ3: Paig 3C **26**
Tavistock Pl. TQ4: Good............................5E **29**
Tavy Av. TQ2: Torq 1E **23**
Tayberry Av. TQ4: Paig 3A **28**
Taylor Cl. EX7: Daw 5C **4**
Taylors Newtake TQ12: Live 1A **8**
Teal Cl. TQ2: Torq.....................................5B **20**
Teignbridge Bus. Cen. TQ12: H'fld............4E **7**
Teign Cl. TQ14: Bi'ton...............................5F **13**
Teign Corinthian Yacht Club 4F **13**
Teign Cl. TQ14: Bi'ton...............................5H **13**
Teignfield Cvn. Site TQ14: Shal 6A **12**
Teign Fort Dr. TQ12: Kingst 5E **11**
TEIGNGRACE..3G **9**
Teigngrace Rd. TQ12: New A 4H **9**
TEIGNMOUTH..5E **13**
Teignmouth Golf Course...........................1A **12**
Teignmouth Hill EX7: Daw........................5E **5**
Teignmouth Lido......................................4E **13**
Teignmouth Rd. EX7: Daw........................1G **13**
Teignmouth Rd. EX7: Holc........................1G **13**
Teignmouth Rd. TQ1: Maid 2A **24**
Teignmouth Rd. TQ1: Torq.......................2A **24**
Teignmouth Rd. TQ12: Kingst 4E **11**
Teignmouth Rd. TQ14: Bi'ton....................6H **13**
Teignmouth Rd. TQ14: Teignm..................2F **13**
Teignmouth Station (Rail) 4E **13**
Teign Rd. TQ12: New A.............................2A **16**
Teign St. TQ14: Teignm.............................5D **12**
Teign Vw. TQ13: Chud K............................1H **7**
Teign Vw. Pl. TQ14: Teignm 5D **12**
Tembani Cl. TQ3: Pres 4F **27**
Temperance Pl. TQ5: Brixh........................2E **33**
Temperance St. TQ2: Torq........................4B **24**
Templar Ter. TQ13: Bov T..........................5C **6**
Templer Pl. TQ13: Bov T............................6C **6**
Templer Rd. TQ3: Pres..............................6D **22**
Templer's Rd. TQ12: New A.......................1A **16**
Templer's Way TQ12: Kingst......................2C **10**
Templer Way TQ12: New A 1B **16**
....(not continuous)
Templer Way TQ12: Teigng........................1G **9**
Teneriffe TQ1: Torq..................................4D **24**
....(off Middle Warberry Rd.)
Tennyson Cl. TQ1: Torq.............................1B **24**
Terrace, The TQ1: Torq..............................5C **24**

Terrace Wlk. TQ13: Ashb...........................3E **37**
Thatcher Av. TQ1: Torq.............................6G **25**
Thatcher Dr. TQ14: Teignm 1E **13**
Thatcher Hgts. TQ1: Torq..........................6G **25**
Third Av. EX7: Daw 5D **4**
Third Av. TQ1: Torq 1B **24**
Third Av. TQ14: Teignm.............................4C **12**
Third Dr. TQ14: Teignm.............................4D **12**
Thistle Cl. TQ2: Torq.................................6E **9**
Thomas Newcomen Ct. TQ6: Dartm..........4A **34**
....(off Ivatt Rd.)
Thompson Cl. EX7: Daw.............................3F **5**
Thorncliff Cl. TQ1: Torq.............................4F **25**
Thorn Cl. TQ12: New A..............................1D **14**
Thorn Cross TQ12: New A..........................5B **6**
Thorne Pk. Rd. TQ2: Torq..........................4G **23**
Thorning St. TQ8: Salc..............................2H **39**
Thornley Dr. TQ14: Teignm 4C **12**
Thorn Orchard TQ12: Ipp..........................5C **18**
Three Corners TQ12: Kingst 3E **11**
Throgmorton Ho. TQ9: Tot 4G **35**
Thrushel Cl. TQ5: Brixh.............................5B **32**
Thurlestone Ct. TQ6: Dartm......................4B **34**
....(off Victoria Rd.)
Thurlestone Gdns. TQ6: Dartm..................4B **34**
Thurlestone Rd. TQ12: New A....................1G **15**
Thurlow Hill TQ1: Torq..............................3B **24**
Thurlow Pk. TQ1: Torq...............................3B **24**
Thurlow Rd. TQ1: Torq 3B **24**
Ticklemore St. TQ9: Tot 4G **35**
Timbers Cl. TQ11: B'leigh..........................6A **36**
Timbers Ct. TQ11: B'leigh..........................6A **36**
Timber Ter. TQ12: Kingsk...........................3G **19**
Times M. TQ9: Tot 4F **35**
Tintagel Cl. TQ2: Torq...............................1A **24**
Titchfield Gdns. TQ3: Paig 4C **26**
Tollit Gdns. TQ9: Tot.................................4G **35**
....(off Weston Rd.)
Topcliff Rd. TQ14: Shal.............................6B **12**
....(not continuous)
TORBAY...3F **27**
Torbay Bus. Pk. TQ4: Paig.........................4B **28**
Torbay Ct. TQ5: Brixh................................2F **33**
Torbay Golf Cen. Driving Range................3E **29**
Torbay Holiday Chalets TQ5: Brixh.............1C **32**
TORBAY HOSPITAL..1G **23**
TORBAY HOSPITAL (ANNEXE)........................6C **20**
Torbay Leisure Cen. 2E **29**
Torbay Olympic Gymnastic Club...............6E **21**
Torbay Rd. TQ2: Torq...............................2G **23**
Torbay Rd. TQ4: Paig................................5F **27**
Torbay Trad. Est. TQ5: Brixh.....................3D **32**
Tor Chu. Rd. TQ2: Torq.............................4A **24**
Tor Cl. TQ4: Broads...................................6E **29**
Tor Dale TQ1: Torq...................................3B **24**
Tor Gdns. TQ12: E Ogw............................4C **14**
Tor Haven TQ2: Torq.................................5C **24**
....(off Abbey Rd.)
Tor Hill Rd. TQ2: Torq 4B **24**
Tor Pk. Rd. TQ2: Torq................................3A **24**
Tor Pk. Rd. TQ4: Paig................................2A **28**
TORQUAY...4B **24**
Torquay Coach Station..............................3B **24**
Torquay Crematorium...............................6D **20**
Torquay Golf Course.................................6H **21**
Torquay Holiday Pk. TQ2: Torq 4D **20**
Torquay Mus. 5D **24**
Torquay Rd. TQ12: Kingsk.........................2H **15**
Torquay Rd. TQ12: Kingsk.........................3H **19**
Torquay Rd. TQ12: New A..........................2H **15**
Torquay Rd. TQ14: Shal............................6C **12**
Torquay Rd. TQ2: Torq 5H **19**
Torquay Rd. TQ3: Paig..............................5E **27**
Torquay Rd. TQ3: Pres..............................5E **27**
Torquay Station (Rail)................................6A **24**
Torquay United FC 2C **24**
TORRE..4A **24**
Torre Abbey..5A **24**
Torre Station (Rail)....................................3H **23**
Torridge Av. TQ2: Torq..............................2E **23**
Tors, The TQ12: Kingsk..............................3G **19**
Tor Sands TQ4: Paig 6F **27**
....(off Sands Rd.)

Tor Sq. Ho. TQ2: Torq 3A **24**
....*(off South St.)*
Tor Va. TQ1: Torq...................................3A **24**
Tor Vw. TQ11: B'leigh 5A **36**
Tor Vw. Av. TQ12: New A 3C **16**
Tor Vw. Gdns. TQ3: Paig..........................5D **26**
Torwood Cl. TQ1: Torq 6D **24**
Torwood Ct. TQ1: Torq 5E **25**
Torwood Gdns. Rd. TQ1: Torq..................6D **24**
Torwood Mt. TQ1: Torq 5D **24**
Torwood St. TQ1: Torq 5D **24**
Tothill Ct. TQ14: Shal................................6C **12**
TOTNES **4F 35**
Totnes Castle 3E **35**
Totnes Cinema 4F **35**
TOTNES COMMUNITY HOSPITAL.............3F **35**
Totnes Down Hill TQ9: Tot 5F **35**
Totnes Elizabethan House Mus................4F **35**
Totnes Fashion & Textiles Mus................4F **35**
Totnes Image Bank & Rural Archive.........4G **35**
....*(within Tourist Info. Cen.)*
Totnes Ind. Est. TQ9: Tot.........................3F **35**
Totnes Pavilion Leisure Cen.....................3F **35**
Totnes Rare Breeds Farm 1F **35**
Totnes Riverside Station South Devon Railway
....2F **35**
Totnes Rd. TQ11: B'leigh 4D **36**
Totnes Rd. TQ12: A'well 6B **18**
Totnes Rd. TQ12: Ipp 6B **18**
Totnes Rd. TQ12: New A..........................6B **18**
Totnes Rd. TQ12: Two O..........................6B **18**
Totnes Rd. TQ2: Torq...............................6D **22**
Totnes Rd. TQ3: Paig 6C **26**
Totnes Station (Rail).................................3F **35**
Totnes Town Mill 4G **35**
....*(within Tourist Info. Cen.)*
Tower Rd. TQ3: Paig.................................5E **27**
Town Cl. TQ6: Dartm 1A **34** (4B **34**)
Town Cotts. TQ12: A'well 1C **18**
Town Hall Pl. TQ13: Bov T 2C **6**
Town Pk. TQ7: W Alv 4A **38**
Town Quay TQ9: Tot 4G **35**
....*(off The Plains)*
Townsend Hill TQ12: Ipp 5A **18**
Townsend Rd. TQ7: W Alv 4A **38**
TOWNSTAL **4A 34**
Townstal Cres. TQ6: Dartm 4A **34**
Townstal Hill TQ6: Dartm 1A **34** (4B **34**)
Townstal Pathfields TQ6: Dartm...............4A **34**
Townstal Rd. TQ6: Dartm 4A **34**
Town Tree Hill EX7: Daw...........................4D **4**
Tracey Va. TQ13: Bov T 4B **6**
Trafalgar Cl. TQ12: New A........................6A **10**
Trafalgar Ter. TQ5: Brixh 1D **32**
.............................*(off Higher Furzeham Rd.)*
Trago Mills 2B **8**
Tramways TQ1: Torq 2C **24**
Treacle Hill TQ12: Kingst 4D **10**
....*(off Fore St.)*
Trebblepark Rd. TQ7: Kingsb 2B **38**
Trebblepark Wlk. TQ7: Kingsb 2B **38**
Treefields TQ5: Brixh 3C **32**
Treesdale Cl. TQ3: Paig...........................5C **26**
Trelissick Cl. TQ3: Paig 4A **26**
Trelissick Rd. TQ3: Paig 4A **26**
Trematon Av. TQ1: Torq 4B **24**
Tremlett Gro. TQ12: Ipp 5B **18**
Trentham Cl. TQ3: Paig 3B **26**
Treston Cl. EX7: Daw................................3E **5**
Trevanna Rd. TQ7: Kingsb 4B **38**
Trevenn Dr. TQ12: Kingst 4H **19**
Triangle, The TQ14: Teignm 5E **13**
Triangle Pl. TQ14: Teignm 5E **13**
Tricorn Cl. TQ3: Paig 6B **20**
Trinity Cl. TQ14: Teignm 3D **12**
Trinity Hill TQ1: Torq 6D **24**
Trinity Ho. TQ1: Torq 4H **21**
Trinity Ho. M. TQ1: Torq 4H **21**
Trinity M. TQ14: Teignm 2D **12**
....*(off Maudlin Dr.)*
Triumph Pl. TQ14: Teignm 2E **13**
Trojan Ind. Pk. TQ4: Paig 1B **28**
Trough La. TQ13: Bov T 2C **6**

Trumans Pl. EX7: Daw..............................4E **5**
....*(off High St.)*
Trumlands Rd. TQ1: Torq 6F **21**
Truro Av. TQ2: Torq 6F **21**
Tudor Cl. TQ12: New A 2G **15**
Tudor Cl. TQ4: Paig..................................3D **28**
Tudor Ct. TQ13: Ashb 4F **37**
....*(off North St.)*
Tudor Rd. TQ12: New A 2G **15**
Tumbly Hill TQ7: Kingsb 4C **38**
Tuplins TQ12: Kingst 3D **10**
Tweenaways TQ11: B'leigh 5A **36**
TWEENAWAYS **6B 26**
Tweenways TQ12: Kingst 4C **10**
Twelve Oaks Farm Cvn. Pk. TQ12: Teigng....3H **9**
Twickenham Rd. TQ12: New A 3C **16**
Two Acre Cl. TQ3: Paig.............................5B **26**
TWO MILE OAK **2A 18**

U

Undercliffe TQ6: Dartm.................. 1B **34** (3C **34**)
....*(off Broadstone)*
Underhay Cl. EX7: Daw..............................2F **5**
Underheath TQ1: Torq 4E **25**
..................................*(off Middle Warberry Rd.)*
Underhill Rd. TQ2: Torq 6H **23**
Underidge Cl. TQ3: Paig 5B **26**
Underidge Dr. TQ3: Paig............................5B **26**
Underidge La. TQ3: Paig............................5B **26**
Underidge Rd. TQ3: Paig...........................5B **26**
Under Way TQ12: Coff 1H **19**
Underwood Cl. EX7: Daw...........................6D **4**
Union La. TQ5: Brixh 2D **32**
Union St. TQ1: Torq 4B **24**
Union St. TQ12: New A 2G **15**
Union St. TQ2: Torq 3A **24**
Union St. TQ6: Dartm 1A **34** (4C **34**)
....*(off Market Sq.)*
Union St. TQ8: Salc 2H **39**
Uplands Rd. TQ3: Pres 1D **26**
Upper Braddons Hill Rd. TQ1: Torq............5D **24**
Upper Cockington La. TQ2: Torq................3F **23**
Upper Headland Pk. Rd. TQ3: Pres 2F **27**
Upper Hermosa Rd. TQ14: Teignm 4D **12**
Upper Longlands EX7: Daw........................3C **4**
Upper Manor Rd. TQ3: Pres 3E **27**
Upper Morin Rd. TQ3: Pres 4F **27**
Upper Penns Rd. TQ3: Pres 2F **27**
UPTON **3B 24**
Upton Hill TQ1: Torq 3B **24**
Upton Hill Rd. TQ5: Brixh 5D **32**
Upton Mnr. Pk. TQ5: Brixh 5D **32**
Upton Mnr. Rd. TQ5: Brixh 5C **32**
Upton Rd. TQ1: Torq 3A **24**

V

Vale Cl. TQ5: Galm 2E **31**
Valenia Ter. TQ13: Ashb 4F **37**
Valerian Pl. TQ12: New A 6E **9**
Vale Rd. TQ12: Kingsk 2H **19**
Vale Rd. TQ12: New A................................4A **16**
Valiant Soldier Mus. & Heritage Cen., The....4C **36**
Valletort Pk. TQ5: Brixh 3B **32**
Valley Cl. TQ14: Teignm 2B **12**
Valley Path TQ12: New A 1D **14**
Valley Vw. Cl. TQ1: Torq 2A **24**
Vane Hill Rd. TQ1: Torq 6D **24**
Vansittart Rd. TQ2: Torq 3A **24**
Varian Ct. TQ9: Tot 4H **35**
Vaughan Pde. TQ2: Torq 6C **24**
Vaughan Rd. TQ2: Torq 6C **24**
Vavasours Slip TQ6: Dartm 3C **34**
Veales Rd. TQ7: Kingsb 4B **38**
Veille La. TQ2: Torq 1F **23**
....*(not continuous)*
Velland Av. TQ2: Torq................................3E **21**
Venford Cl. TQ4: Good 5E **29**
Venn Orchard TQ12: Kingst 4C **10**
Venture Ct. TQ12: New A............................2F **15**
Verbena Ter. TQ14: Shal............................6B **12**
Vernon Cl. TQ1: Torq 6D **24**

Veryan Cl. EX7: Daw..................................1E **5**
Vetch Pl. TQ12: New A................................6E **9**
Vicarage Cl. TQ5: Brixh 2D **32**
Vicarage Cl. TQ9: Sto G 6A **28**
Vicarage Gdns. EX7: Daw...........................4C **4**
Vicarage Gro. TQ9: Sto G 5A **28**
Vicarage Hill TQ3: Marl Church Hill 5A **22**
Vicarage Hill TQ3: Marl Nether Mdw. 6A **22**
Vicarage Hill TQ12: Kingst.........................4D **10**
Vicarage Hill TQ2: Torq 5F **23**
Vicarage Hill TQ5: Brixh 2D **32**
Vicarage Hill TQ6: Dartm.............. 1A **34** (4B **34**)
Vicarage Rd. TQ12: A'well 1C **18**
Vicarage Rd. TQ2: Torq 5G **23**
Vicarage Rd. TQ3: Marl 1B **26**
Vicarage Rd. TQ5: Brixh 4D **32**
Vicarage Rd. TQ9: Sto G 5A **28**
Vicary Cl. TQ12: New A 2F **15**
Victoria Ct. TQ1: Torq 4C **24**
....*(off Victoria Rd.)*
Victoria Ct. TQ9: Tot 4F **35**
Victoria Hgts. TQ6: Dartm 4B **34**
Victoria Pde. TQ1: Torq 6C **24**
Victoria Pk. Rd. TQ1: Torq 2C **24**
Victoria Pl. TQ12: New A 2H **15**
Victoria Pl. TQ5: Brixh 1D **32**
.............................*(off Higher Furzeham Rd.)*
Victoria Pl. TQ6: Dartm 1A **34** (4C **34**)
Victoria Pl. TQ8: Salc 2H **39**
Victoria Quay TQ8: Salc 2H **39**
Victoria Rd. TQ1: Torq 3C **24**
Victoria Rd. TQ5: Brixh 1G **33**
Victoria Rd. TQ6: Dartm 1A **34** (4A **34**)
Victoria Sq. TQ4: Paig 5F **27**
....*(off Parkside Rd.)*
Victoria St. TQ4: Paig.................................5E **27**
Victoria St. TQ9: Tot 4F **35**
Victoria Ter. TQ12: Kingst 4D **10**
....*(off Oakford)*
Victoria Ter. TQ13: Bov T 2C **6**
....*(off Mary St.)*
Victoria Ter. TQ14: Shal.............................6C **12**
....*(off Bridge Rd.)*
Victoria Ter. TQ5: Brixh 3D **32**
....*(off Mt. Pleasant Rd.)*
Victory Cl. TQ12: New A 6A **10**
Victory Ho. TQ6: Dartm............... 2A **34** (4C **34**)
....*(off Higher St.)*
Victory Rd. TQ6: Dartm 4A **34**
Vigilance Av. TQ5: Brixh 2G **33**
Village Rd. TQ3: Marl..................................6A **22**
Villas, The TQ12: Kingst 1C **10**
Villiers Av. TQ12: New A 3C **16**
Vincents Rd. TQ7: Kingsb 3C **38**
Vine Rd. TQ2: Torq 3A **24**
Vinery, The TQ1: Torq 5C **24**
....*(off Montpellier Rd.)*
Vine Ter. TQ7: Kingsb 2B **38**
Violet Dr. TQ12: New A...............................6D **8**
Virginia Lodge TQ1: Torq 5E **25**
....*(off Lwr. Erith Rd.)*
Vittery Cl. TQ5: Brixh 2C **32**
Vomero TQ1: Torq 5D **24**
Vue Cinema Paignton 5F **27**

W

WADDETON **1B 31**
Waddeton Cl. TQ4: Paig.............................4C **28**
Waddeton Cotts. TQ5: Wadd 1B **30**
Waddeton Dr. TQ4: Paig.............................4C **28**
Waddeton Rd. TQ4: Paig 4C **28**
....*(not continuous)*
Waddeton Rd. TQ5: Wadd 1B **30**
Waddeton Rd. TQ9: Sto G 5B **28**
Wain La. TQ12: New A 1F **15**
......................................*(not continuous)*
Walcot Pl. TQ5: Brixh 2D **32**
.............................*(off Higher Furzeham Rd.)*
Waldon Ct. TQ2: Torq 5C **24**
....*(off St Luke's Rd. Sth.)*
Waldon Ho. TQ2: Torq 5C **24**
....*(off St Luke's Rd. Sth.)*

Waldon Point – Wilson Ter.

Waldon Point TQ2: Torq 5C **24**
(off St Luke's Rd. Sth.)
Walkham Ri. TQ2: Torq 1E **23**
Wallace Av. EX7: Daw 3E **5**
Wallace Av. TQ2: Torq 1F **23**
Wallfield Rd. TQ13: Bov T 5A **6**
Wallingford Rd. TQ7: Kingsb 2C **38**
Wallis Gro. TQ14: Bi'ton 5H **13**
Wall Pk. Cl. TQ5: Brixh 2F **33**
Wall Pk. Rd. TQ5: Brixh 2F **33**
Walls Hill Rd. TQ1: Torq 2E **25**
Walnut Cl. TQ9: Tot 3E **35**
Walnut Ct. TQ5: Brixh 3E **33**
(off Higher Ranscombe Rd.)
Walnut La. TQ2: Torq 5H **23**
Walnut Rd. TQ2: Torq 5H **23**
Waltham Rd. TQ12: New A 2F **15**
Warberry Rd. W. TQ1: Torq 4C **24**
Warberry Va. TQ1: Torq 3C **24**
Warborough Rd. TQ5: Chur F 1F **31**
Warbro Ct. TQ1: Torq 2C **24**
(off St Marychurch Rd.)
Warbro Rd. TQ1: Torq 2C **24**
Ware Barton Cvn. Site TQ12: Kingst 5F **11**
Ware Cl. TQ12: Kingst 4E **11**
Warecroft Rd. TQ12: Kingst 4E **11**
Ware Cross TQ12: Kingst 4E **11**
Ware Cross Gdns. TQ12: Kingst 4E **11**
Warefield Rd. TQ3: Paig 4F **27**
WARFLEET 6D **34**
Warfleet Creek Rd. TQ6: Dartm 6D **34**
Warfleet Rd. TQ6: Dartm 5D **34**
Warland TQ9: Tot 4F **35**
Warren, The TQ12: New A 2E **15**
Warren Hill TQ2: Torq 5C **24**
Warren Rd. EX7: Daw 2G **5**
Warren Rd. TQ2: Torq 5B **24**
Warren Rd. TQ7: Kingsb 5D **38**
Warwick Cl. TQ1: Torq 2F **25**
Washabrook La. TQ7: Kingsb 2D **38**
Washabrook Way TQ7: Kingsb 3D **38**
Washbourne Cl. TQ5: Brixh 2F **33**
Washington Cl. TQ3: Pres 2E **27**
WATCOMBE 4G **21**
Watcombe Beach Rd. TQ1: Torq 4H **21**
Watcombe Hgts. Rd. TQ1: Torq 3G **21**
Waterdale Mobile Home Pk. TQ12: Kingsk 3H **19**
(off Waterdale Pk.)
Waterdale Pk. TQ12: Kingsk 3H **19**
Water La. TQ12: Kingsk 3H **19**
Water La. TQ12: New A 1E **15**
Water La. TQ2: Torq 1F **23**
Waterleat Av. TQ3: Paig 6B **26**
Waterleat Cl. TQ3: Paig 6C **26**
Waterleat Ct. TQ3: Paig 6C **26**
Waterleat Dr. TQ3: Paig 6C **26**
Waterleat Rd. TQ3: Paig 6B **26**
Waterloo Rd. TQ1: Torq 3C **24**
Waterloo Rd. TQ7: Kingsb 2C **38**
Waterloo St. TQ14: Teignm 5E **13**
Water Mdws. TQ2: Torq 6H **23**
(off Underhill Rd.)
Water Mdw. Wlk. TQ9: Darti 2E **35**
Watermill Ct. TQ5: Brixh 3D **32**
(off Bolton St.)
Waterpool Rd. TQ6: Dartm 2A **34** (5A **34**)
Waterside TQ13: Bov T 3C **6**
Waterside TQ7: Kingsb 4C **38**
Waterside TQ9: Tot 4G **35**
Waterside Holiday Pk. TQ4: Broads 4F **29**
Waterside Ho. TQ9: Tot 4G **35**
(off The Plains)
Waterside Rd. TQ4: Broads 4F **29**
Waterside Vw. TQ4: Broads 4F **29**
Waterwell La. TQ12: Hacc 5E **17**
Watkins Way TQ3: Paig 4A **26**
Waverley Rd. TQ12: New A 1G **15**
Waverley Rd. TQ7: Kingsb 4B **38**
Waves Leisure Pool 5A **24**
Wayside TQ5: Brixh 3B **32**
Wayside Cl. TQ5: Brixh 3B **32**
Wear Farm Cvn. & Camping Pk. TQ14: Bi'ton 5H **11**
Weaver Ct. TQ2: Torq 1E **23**
Weavers Way TQ12: Kingsk 3G **19**
Webber Cl. TQ12: E Ogw 5E **15**
Webster Cl. TQ12: New A 2H **15**
Wedgwood Ct. TQ14: Teignm 5D **12**
(off Somerset Pl.)
Wedlake M. EX7: Daw 4D **4**
(off Brook St.)
Weech Cl. EX7: Daw 4C **4**
Weech Rd. EX7: Daw 4C **4**
Weekaborough Dr. TQ3: Marl 1A **26**
Week La. EX7: Daw 1F **5**
Week La. EX7: Daw W 1F **5**
Weeksland Rd. TQ2: Torq 3F **23**
Weirfields TQ9: Tot 3F **35**
Well Cl. TQ12: Kingst 4D **10**
Welle Ho. Gdns. TQ7: Kingsb 2C **38**
Wellesley Rd. TQ1: Torq 3C **24**
Wellington Pl. TQ1: Torq 3C **24**
Wellington Rd. TQ1: Torq 4C **24**
Wellington St. TQ14: Teignm 5E **13**
Well St. TQ3: Paig 5D **26**
WELLSWOOD 4E **25**
Wellswood Av. TQ1: Torq 4E **25**
(not continuous)
Wellswood Gdns. TQ1: Torq 4F **25**
Wellswood Mnr. TQ1: Torq 4E **25**
Wellswood Pk. TQ1: Torq 4E **25**
Wellswood Path TQ1: Torq 4E **25**
Welsury Rd. TQ2: Torq 5B **20**
Wembury Dr. TQ2: Torq 5G **21**
Wentworth Rd. TQ12: H'fld 5E **7**
Wesley Cl. TQ2: Torq 4F **21**
Wesley Ct. TQ2: Torq 4F **21**
Wesley Ct. TQ6: Dartm 1A **34** (4C **34**)
(off Market Sq.)
Wesley M. TQ2: Torq 5F **21**
(off Starpitten La. W.)
Wesley Vw. TQ12: Ipp 5B **18**
(off Croft Rd.)
Westabrook Av. TQ13: Ashb 3E **37**
Westabrook Cl. TQ13: Ashb 3E **37**
Westabrook Dr. TQ13: Ashb 3E **37**
WEST ALVINGTON 4A **38**
West Alvington Hill TQ7: Kingsb 4A **38**
Westbourne Rd. TQ1: Torq 2B **24**
Westbrook Av. TQ14: Teignm 4C **12**
West Buckeridge TQ14: Teignm 3D **12**
West Cliff EX7: Daw 4E **5**
(off The Mews)
Westcliff TQ14: Teignm 5D **12**
(off Mulberry St.)
West Cliff Cl. EX7: Daw 5D **4**
Westcliffe Ter. TQ5: Brixh 2E **33**
(off Nth. Furzeham Rd.)
West Cliff Pk. Dr. EX7: Daw 5D **4**
West Cliff Rd. EX7: Daw 4C **4**
Westcombe Pk. TQ12: Kingsk 1H **19**
West End Rd. TQ11: B'leigh 5A **36**
West End Ter. TQ13: Ashb 5E **37**
Westerland La. TQ3: Marl 1A **26**
Western Backway TQ7: Kingsb 3B **38**
(off Fore St.)
Western Bus. Pk. TQ4: Paig 3C **28**
Western By-Pass TQ9: Tot 5E **35**
Western Dr. TQ12: New A 1E **15**
Western Rd. TQ1: Torq 6G **21**
Western Rd. TQ12: New A 3H **15**
Western Rd. TQ13: Ashb 5E **37**
Western Ter. TQ9: Tot 4E **35**
(off Lwr. Collins Rd.)
Western Vs. TQ9: Tot 4E **35**
(off Lwr. Collins Rd.)
Westfield Bus. Pk. TQ4: Paig 4A **28**
Westfield Cl. TQ5: Brixh 4C **32**
West Golds Rd. TQ12: New A 6A **10**
West Golds Way TQ12: New A 6A **10**
Westhill Av. TQ1: Torq 1C **24**
Westhill Av. Cl. TQ1: Torq 2C **24**
Westhill Cres. TQ3: Paig 4E **27**
Westhill Rd. TQ1: Torq 1B **24**
Westhill Rd. TQ3: Paig 4D **26**
Westhill Ter. TQ12: Kingsk 3H **19**
Westholme TQ1: Torq 4D **24**
(off Middle Warberry Rd.)
Westlands La. TQ1: Torq 2C **24**
West La. TQ3: Marl 4A **22**
Westleat Av. TQ3: Paig 5B **26**
West Mt. TQ12: New A 4A **16**
Weston Cl. TQ5: Brixh 4D **32**
Westonfields TQ9: Tot 4H **35**
Weston La. TQ9: Tot 4H **35**
Weston Rd. TQ9: Tot 4G **35**
Westover Cl. TQ5: Brixh 3E **33**
West Pafford Av. TQ2: Torq 5F **21**
West St. TQ13: Ashb 4E **37**
West St. TQ14: Bi'ton 5G **13**
West Town TQ14: Bi'ton 5F **13**
West Town Mdw. TQ14: Bi'ton 5F **13**
West Vw. Cl. TQ12: E Ogw 4E **15**
West Vw. Rd. TQ3: Marl 6A **22**
West Vw. Ter. TQ8: Salc 3F **39**
Westville Hill TQ7: Kingsb 4B **38**
(off Frogmore Ter.)
Westward Cl. TQ9: Tot 4F **35**
Westward Vw. TQ12: New A 3D **16**
Westwood Cleave TQ12: E Ogw 5E **15**
Westwood Rd. TQ12: E Ogw 5F **15**
Wharf Rd. TQ12: New A 1A **16**
Wheatlands Rd. TQ4: Good 1D **28**
Wheatridge La. TQ2: Torq 1H **27**
Whickham Lodge EX7: Daw 3E **5**
Whidborne Av. TQ1: Torq 5G **25**
Whidborne Cl. TQ1: Torq 5G **25**
Whiddon Rd. TQ12: A'well 2A **18**
Whiddon Rd. TQ12: Two O 2A **18**
Whilborough Rd. TQ12: Kingst 6E **19**
Whilborough Rd. TQ12: N Whil 6E **19**
Whistley Hill TQ13: Ashb 4F **37**
Whitear Cl. TQ14: Teignm 2B **12**
Whitears Way TQ12: Kingst 4D **10**
Whitebeam Cl. TQ3: Paig 4B **26**
White Cl. TQ3: Pres 1E **27**
White Gables TQ2: Torq 5H **23**
White Heather Ter. TQ13: Bov T 2C **6**
Whitehill Cl. TQ12: New A 6A **10**
Whitehill Cotts. TQ12: New A 6G **9**
Whitehill Rd. TQ12: New A 6G **9**
Whitelake Pl. TQ12: New A 6A **10**
White Rock Cl. TQ4: Good 4C **28**
White Rock Ct. TQ4: Good 5C **28**
White Rock Rd. TQ4: Good 5C **28**
White Rock Sports Cen. 4B **28**
White Rock Way TQ4: Paig 4C **28**
Whiteway Rd. TQ12: Kingst 4C **10**
Whitley Rd. TQ4: Paig 1D **28**
WHITSTONE 1B **6**
Whitstone La. TQ13: Bov T 1B **6**
Whitstone Rd. TQ4: Paig 6E **27**
Widdicombe Farm Touring Pk. TQ3: Marl 4B **22**
Widemoor La. TQ5: Chur F 3F **31**
Wilbarn Rd. TQ3: Paig 4F **27**
Wilbraham Ct. TQ14: Teignm 2E **13**
(off Higher Woodway Rd.)
Wilbury Way EX7: Daw 3E **5**
Wildwoods Cres. TQ12: New A 1C **16**
Wilkins Dr. TQ4: Paig 3B **28**
Willake Rd. TQ12: Kingsk 2H **19**
Willhays Cl. TQ12: Kingst 2D **10**
William of Orange Statue 2E **33**
Williams Cl. EX7: Daw 5C **4**
Williams Ct. TQ11: B'leigh 4B **36**
Willicombe Rd. TQ3: Paig 6D **26**
Willis Ct. TQ1: Torq 2B **24**
Willoughby Rd. TQ1: Torq 3D **24**
Willow Av. TQ2: Torq 4F **21**
Willow Cl. TQ12: New A 5C **16**
Willowfield Rd. TQ2: Torq 5E **21**
Willowpark La. TQ12: Coff 2B **20**
Willows, The TQ2: Torq 5C **20**
Willow St. TQ14: Teignm 4D **12**
Wills Av. TQ3: Pres 2F **27**
Wills Rd. TQ9: Tot 3G **35**
Wilnecote Lodge TQ1: Torq 3B **24**
(off Furzehill Rd.)
Wilson Ter. TQ1: Torq 3A **24**

Wilton Cl. TQ12: A'well 1C **18**
Wilton Rd. TQ3: Pres 1E **27**
Wilton Way TQ12: A'well 1B **18**
Winchester Av. TQ2: Torq 6E **21**
Windeatt Sq. TQ9: Tot 4G **35**
....(off Warland)
Windermere Rd. TQ1: Torq.......................3D **24**
Winding Wlk. TQ6: Dartm..........................3C **34**
Windmill Av. TQ3: Pres..............................2D **26**
Windmill Cl. TQ5: Brixh 3E **33**
Windmill Ct. TQ5: Brixh 3E **33**
Windmill Gdns. TQ3: Pres 2D **26**
Windmill Hill TQ5: Brixh 3D **32**
Windmill La. TQ12: N Whil..........................6E **19**
Windmill La. TQ3: Pres...............................2C **26**
Windmill Rd. TQ3: Pres 2D **26**
Windmill Rd. TQ5: Brixh 3E **33**
Windsor Av. TQ12: New A 2C **16**
Windsor Cl. TQ1: Torq 3C **24**
Windsor Cl. TQ12: New A 3H **15**
Windsor Ct. TQ7: Kingsb............................3C **38**
Windsor Rd. TQ1: Torq 3C **24**
Windsor Rd. TQ6: Dartm.............................4A **34**
Windsor Rd. TQ7: Kingsb............................3C **38**
Windward La. EX7: Holc..............................1H **13**
Windward Ri. EX7: Holc...............................1H **13**
Windward Rd. TQ2: Torq.............................4D **20**
Winner Hill Rd. TQ3: Paig 5D **26**
Winners 2000 Fitness Ltd.......................6D **10**
Winner St. TQ3: Paig 5D **26**
Winner St. (Rear) TQ3: Paig 5D **26**
....(off Winner St.)
Winnings Way TQ1: Torq.............................2E **25**
....(off Princes St.)
Winsford Rd. TQ2: Torq..............................6F **23**
Winston Cl. TQ12: Kingst............................4D **10**
Winston Ct. TQ14: Teignm..........................3E **13**
Winstone Av. TQ2: Torq..............................6F **21**
Winsu Av. TQ3: Pres 3D **26**
Winterbourne Rd. TQ14: Teignm.................4D **12**
Wishings Rd. TQ5: Brixh.............................4E **33**
Wisteria Cl. TQ7: Kingsb............................3C **38**
....(off Windsor Rd.)
Wizz-Kidz 2C **32**
Woburn Cl. TQ3: Paig 4A **26**
WOLBOROUGH 4E **15**

Wolborough Chu. Path TQ12: New A..........3F **15**
Wolborough Cl. TQ12: New A......................3H **15**
Wolborough Gdns. TQ12: New A................3H **15**
Wolborough Gdns. TQ5: Brixh....................1F **33**
Wolborough Ga. TQ12: New A....................3H **15**
....(off Wolborough Cl.)
Wolborough St. TQ12: New A......................3F **15**
Wolston Cl. TQ5: Brixh...............................1C **32**
Wolverton Dr. TQ12: Kingst........................4C **10**
Woodbrook Rd. TQ9: Tot............................4H **35**
Woodend Rd. TQ1: Torq.............................5E **25**
Woodfield Ct. TQ1: Torq.............................6E **25**
Woodhayes Cl. EX7: Daw..........................2F **5**
Woodhouse Cl. TQ7: Kingsb.......................4B **38**
Woodland Av. TQ12: Kingsk.......................2G **19**
Woodland Av. TQ14: Teignm.......................2F **13**
Woodland Bus. Pk. TQ2: Torq....................1H **23**
Woodland Cl. TQ2: Torq.............................1H **23**
Woodland Gdns. TQ14: Teignm..................4E **13**
....(off Lwr. Brimley Rd.)
Woodland Pk. TQ3: Paig.............................4E **27**
Woodland Rd. TQ13: Ashb..........................4F **37**
Woodland Rd. TQ2: Torq.............................1H **23**
Woodlands Cl. TQ14: Teignm......................4E **13**
Woodlands Gdns. TQ12: New A 3C **16**
Woodlands Rd. TQ12: New A......................3C **16**
Woodlands Wlk. TQ13: Bov T......................6B **6**
Woodland Ter. TQ6: Kingsw........................4D **34**
Wood La. TQ12: A'well................................1B **18**
Wood La. TQ12: Two O..............................1B **18**
Wood La. TQ6: Kingsw...............................4D **34**
Woodleigh Pk. TQ14: Shal..........................6D **12**
Woodleigh Rd. TQ12: New A.......................2E **15**
Woodleys Mdw. TQ2: Torq.........................1H **27**
Woodmere Way TQ12: Kingst.....................5D **10**
Woodpark La. TQ3: Marl 1B **22**
Woods, The TQ1: Torq................................5F **25**
Woodside Dr. TQ1: Torq.............................5D **24**
Woodvale Ct. TQ12: New A.........................2G **15**
....(off East St.)
Wood Vw. TQ12: New A..............................2F **15**
Woodville Rd. TQ1: Torq.............................3C **24**
Woodway Cl. TQ14: Teignm........................2E **13**
Woodway Dr. TQ14: Teignm........................3E **13**
Woodway Rd. TQ14: Teignm.......................2E **13**
Wordsworth Cl. TQ2: Torq..........................3H **23**
Wren Cl. TQ5: Brixh...................................3D **32**

Wren Hill TQ5: Brixh 3D **32**
Wren Pk. 5C **20**
Wright's La. TQ1: Torq................................2B **24**
Wrigwell La. TQ12: Ipp...............................6C **18**
Wroxall Grange TQ1: Torq..........................5D **24**
....(off Grafton Rd.)
Wyatt Cl. TQ13: Bov T................................1E **7**
Wychwood Cl. EX7: Daw............................3E **5**
Wymering Ct. TQ14: Teignm.......................2E **13**
Wyre Cl. TQ4: Paig.....................................3D **28**

Y

Yalberton Ind. Est. TQ4: Paig.....................2A **28**
....(not continuous)
Yalberton Rd. TQ4: Paig.............................2A **28**
Yalberton Tor Ind. Est. TQ4: Paig................2A **28**
Yannon Dr. TQ14: Teignm 3C **12**
Yannon La. TQ12: Kingsk............................2F **19**
....(not continuous)
Yannons, The TQ14: Teignm.......................3D **12**
Yannons Rd. TQ4: Paig...............................3B **28**
Yannon Ter. TQ14: Teignm..........................3D **12**
Yards La. TQ5: Brixh...................................6C **32**
Yealm Gro. TQ2: Torq.................................2F **23**
Yeolands, The TQ9: Sto G..........................5A **28**
Yew Cl. TQ5: Brixh......................................5A **32**
Yew Tree Dr. TQ12: Kingst..........................5D **10**
Yolhey La. TQ12: A'well..............................2D **18**
Yonder Mdw. TQ9: Sto G............................5A **28**
Yon St. TQ12: Kingsk..................................3G **19**
York Cres. TQ1: Torq..................................1D **24**
Yorke Rd. TQ6: Dartm................................5A **34**
York Gdns. TQ4: Paig 1E **29**
York Rd. TQ1: Torq.....................................1D **24**
York Rd. TQ4: Paig.....................................1D **28**
York Vs. TQ1: Torq.....................................1D **24**
....(off Babbacombe Rd.)
Young's Pk. La. TQ4: Good.........................1F **29**
Young's Pk. Rd. TQ4: Good 1F **29**

Z

Zion Pl. TQ6: Dartm 1A **34** (3C **34**)
Zion Rd. TQ2: Torq.....................................4A **24**

Published by Geographers' A-Z Map Company Limited
An imprint of HarperCollins Publishers
Westerhill Road
Bishopbriggs
Glasgow
G64 2QT

www.az.co.uk
a-z.maps@harpercollins.co.uk

HarperCollinsPublishers
Macken House, 39/40 Mayor Street Upper, Dublin 1, D01 C9W8, Ireland

7th edition 2023

© Collins Bartholomew Ltd 2023

This product uses map data licenced from Ordnance Survey
© Crown copyright and database rights 2022 OS AC0000808974

AZ, A-Z and AtoZ are registered trademarks of Geographers' A-Z Map Company Limited

A catalogue record for this book is available from the British Library.

ISBN 978-0-00-856046-1

10 9 8 7 6 5 4 3 2

Printed in India

MIX
Paper | Supporting
responsible forestry
FSC™ C007454

This book is produced from independently certified FSC™ paper
to ensure responsible forest management.

For more information visit: www.harpercollins.co.uk/green